JFK'S FORGOTTEN CRISIS

JFK'S FORGOTTEN CRISIS

TIBET, THE CIA, AND SINO-INDIAN WAR

BRUCE RIEDEL

BROOKINGS INSTITUTION PRESS
WASHINGTON, D.C.

The Brookings Institution is a private nonprofit organization devoted to research, education, and publication on important issues of domestic and foreign policy. Its principal purpose is to bring the highest quality independent research and analysis to bear on current and emerging policy problems. Interpretations or conclusions in Brookings publications should be understood to be solely those of the authors.

The map on page xv is reproduced courtesy of the Heritage Foundation.

Library of Congress Cataloging-in-Publication data

Riedel, Bruce O.
   JFK's forgotten crisis : Tibet, the CIA, and Sino-Indian War / Bruce Riedel. — 1st Edition.
      pages cm
   Includes bibliographical references.
   ISBN 978-0-8157-2699-9 (hardcover : alk. paper) — ISBN 978-0-8157-2700-2 (epub) — ISBN 978-0-8157-2701-9 (pdf)
   1. United States—Foreign relations—India.   2. India—Foreign relations—United States.   3. United States—Foreign relations—1961–1963.   4. Kennedy, John F. (John Fitzgerald), 1917–1963.   5. Sino-Indian Border Dispute, 1957– I. Title. II. Title: John Fitzgerald Kennedy's forgotten crisis.
   E183.8.I4R54 2015
   327.73054'09046—dc23   2015019160

9 8 7 6 5 4 3 2 1

Typeset in Sabon

Composition by Westchester Publishing Services

TO ELIZABETH

CONTENTS

AT MOUNT VERNON

The magic of the Kennedy White House, Camelot, had settled in at Mount Vernon. It was a dazzling evening, a warm July night, but a cool breeze came off the Potomac River and kept the temperature comfortable. It was Tuesday, July 11, 1961, and the occasion was a state dinner for Pakistan's visiting president, General Ayub Khan, the only time in our nation's history that George Washington's home has served as the venue for a state dinner. President John F. Kennedy had been in office for less than six months, but his administration had already been tarnished by the failed CIA invasion of Cuba at the Bay of Pigs and a disastrous summit with Soviet leader Nikita Khrushchev in Vienna, Austria. Ayub Khan wrote later that the president was "under great stress."[1] The Kennedy administration was off to a rocky start: It needed to show some competence.

The idea of hosting Ayub Khan at Mount Vernon came from Kennedy's wife, Jacqueline Bouvier Kennedy, who was inspired by a dinner during the Vienna summit held a month earlier at the Schönbrunn Palace, the rococo-style former imperial palace of the Hapsburg monarchy built in the seventeenth century. Mrs. Kennedy was impressed by the opulence and history displayed at Schönbrunn and at a similar dinner held on the same presidential trip at the French royal palace of Versailles. America had no royal palaces, of course, but it did have the first president's mansion just a few miles away from the White House on a bluff overlooking the Potomac River. The history of the mansion and the fabulous view of the river in the evening would provide a very special atmosphere for the event.

On June 26, 1961, the First Lady visited Mount Vernon privately and broached the idea with the director of the Mount Vernon Ladies' Association, which manages the estate. It was a challenging proposal. The old mansion was too small to host an indoor dinner so the event would have to take place on the lawn. The mansion had very little electricity in 1961 and was a colonial antique, without a modern kitchen or refrigeration, so that the food would have to be prepared at the White House and brought to the estate and served by White House staff. But the arrangements were made, with the Secret Service and Marine Corps providing security, and the U.S. Army's Third Infantry Regiment from Fort Myer providing the colonial fife and drum corps for official presentation of the colors. The National Symphony Orchestra offered the after-dinner entertainment. Tiffany and Company, the high-end jewelry company, provided the flowers and decorated the candlelit pavilion in which the guests dined.

The guests arrived by boat in a small fleet of yachts led by the presidential yacht, *Honey Fitz*, and the secretary of the navy's yacht, *Sequoia*. They departed from the Navy Yard in Washington and sailed the fifteen miles down river to Mount Vernon past National Airport and Alexandria, Virginia; the trip took an hour and fifteen minutes. On arrival the most vigorous guests, such as the president's younger brother, Attorney General Robert Kennedy, climbed the hill to the mansion on foot, but most took advantage of the limousines the White House provided.

The guest list was led by President Ayub Khan and his daughter, Begum Nasir Akhtar Aurangzeb, and included the Pakistani foreign minister and finance minister, as well as Pakistan's ambassador to the United States, Aziz Ahmed, and various attaches from the embassy in Washington. Initially the ambassador was upset that the dinner would not be in the White House, fearing it would be seen as a snub. The State Department convinced Ahmed that having it at Mount Vernon was actually a benefit and would generate more publicity and distinction.[2]

The Americans invited to the dinner were the elite of the new administration. In addition to the president, attorney general, and vice president and their wives, Secretary of State Dean Rusk, Secretary of Defense Robert McNamara, Secretary of the Navy John Connally, Chairman of the Joint Chiefs of Staff Lyman Lemnitzer, and their wives joined the party. Six senators including J. W. Fulbright, Stuart Symington, Everett Dirksen, and Mike Mansfield were joined by the Speaker of the House and ten congressmen, including a future president, Gerald Ford, and their wives. The U.S. ambassador to Pakistan, William Roundtree; the chief of the United States Air Force, General Curtis Lemay; Assistant Secretary of State Phillips Talbot; Peace Corps Director Sargent Shriver; and the president's military assistant, Maxwell Taylor, were also in attendance. Walter Hoving, chairman of Tiffany, and Mrs. Hoving, and a half-dozen prominent Pakistani and American journalists, such as NBC correspondent Sander Vanocur, attended from outside the government. In total more than 130 guests were seated at sixteen tables.

Perhaps the guest most invested in the evening, however, was the director of the Central Intelligence Agency, Allen W. Dulles. The Kennedys had long been friends of Allen Dulles. A few years before the dinner Mrs. Kennedy had given him a copy of Ian Fleming's James Bond novel, *From Russia, with Love*, and Dulles, like JFK, became a big fan of 007.[3] Dulles was also a holdover from the previous Republican administration. He had been in charge of the planning and execution of the Bay of Pigs fiasco that had tarnished the opening days of the Kennedy administration, but Dulles still had the president's ear on sensitive covert intelligence operations, including several critical clandestine operations run out of Pakistan with the approval of Field Marshal Ayub Khan.

Before sitting down for dinner just after eight o'clock, the guests toured the first president's home and enjoyed bourbon mint juleps or orange juice. Both dressed in formal attire for the occasion, Kennedy took Ayub Khan for a walk in the garden alone. At that time, the CIA was running two very important clandestine operations in Pakistan. One had already made the news a year earlier when a U-2 spy plane had been shot down over the Soviet Union by Russian surface-to-air missiles; this plane had started its top-secret mission, called Operation Grand Slam, from a Pakistani Air Force air base in Peshawar, Pakistan. The U-2 shootdown had wrecked a summit meeting between Khrushchev and President Eisenhower in Paris in 1960 when Ike refused to apologize for the mission. The CIA had stopped flying over the Soviet Union, but still used the base near Peshawar for less dangerous U-2 operations over China.

The second clandestine operation also dated from the Eisenhower administration, but was still very much top secret. The CIA was supporting a rebellion in Communist China's Tibet province from another Pakistani Air Force air base near Dacca in East Pakistan (what is today Bangladesh). Tibetan rebels trained by the CIA in Colorado were parachuted into Tibet from CIA transport planes that flew from that Pakistani air base, as were supplies and weapons.[4] U-2 aircraft also landed in East Pakistan after flying over China to conduct photo reconnaissance missions of the communist state.

Ayub Khan had suspended the Tibet operation earlier that summer. The Pakistani president was upset by Kennedy's decision to provide more than a billion dollars in economic aid to India. Pakistan believed it should be America's preferred ally in South Asia, not India, and shutting down the CIA base for air drops to Tibet was a quiet way to signal displeasure at Washington without causing a public breakdown in the U.S.-Pakistan relationship. Ayub Khan wanted to make clear to Kennedy that an American tilt toward India at Pakistan's expense would have its costs. In his memoirs, Khan later wrote that he sought to press Kennedy not to "appease India."[5]

Before the Mount Vernon dinner, Allen Dulles had asked Kennedy to meet alone with Ayub Khan, thinking that perhaps a little Kennedy charm and the magic of the evening would change his mind. The combination worked; the Pakistani dictator told Kennedy he would allow the CIA missions over Tibet to resume from the Pakistani Air Force base at Kurmitula outside of Dacca.[6] Ayub Khan did get a quid pro quo for this decision later in his visit: Kennedy promised that, even if China attacked India, he would not sell arms to India without first consulting with Pakistan.[7] However, when China did invade India the following year, Kennedy ignored this promise and provided critical aid to India, including arms, without consulting Ayub Khan, who was deeply disappointed.

The main course for dinner was poulet chasseur served with rice and accompanied by Moet and Chandon Imperial Brut champagne (at least for the Americans), followed by raspberries in cream for dessert. President Kennedy hosted a table at which sat Begum Aurangzeb, who wore a white silk sari. Khan enjoyed the beauty of a Virginia summer evening with America's thirty-one-year-old First Lady; he sat next to Jackie, who wore an Oleg Cassini sleeveless white organza and lace evening gown sashed at the waist in chartreuse silk. In his toast the Pakistani leader warned that "any country that faltered in Asia, even for only a year or two, would find itself subjugated to communism." In turn Kennedy hailed Ayub Khan as the George Washington of Pakistan. After midnight the guests were driven back to Washington down the George Washington Parkway.[8]

The CIA operation in Tibet had its detractors in the Kennedy White House, including Kennedy's handpicked ambassador to India, John Kenneth Galbraith, who called it "a particularly insane enterprise" involving "dissident and deeply unhygienic tribesmen" that risked an unpredictable Chinese response.[9] However, the operation did produce substantial critical intelligence on the Chinese communist regime from captured documents seized by the Tibetans at a time when Washington had virtually no idea what was going on inside Red China. The U-2 flights from Dacca were even more important to the CIA's understanding of China's nuclear weapon development at its Lop Nur nuclear test facility.[10]

But Galbraith was in the end correct to be skeptical. The operation did have an unpredicted outcome: The CIA operation helped persuade Chinese leader Mao Zedong to invade India in October 1962, an invasion that led the United States and China to the brink of war and began a Sino-India rivalry that continues today. It also created a Pakistani-Chinese alliance that still continues. The contours of modern Asian grand politics thus were drawn in 1962.

The dinner at Mount Vernon was a spectacular social success for the Kennedys, although they received some predictable criticism from conservative newspapers over its cost. It was also a political success for both Kennedy and the CIA, keeping the Tibet operation alive. As an outstanding example of presidential leadership in managing and executing covert operations at the highest level of government, it is an auspicious place to begin an examination of JFK's forgotten crisis.

India, China Disputed Borders

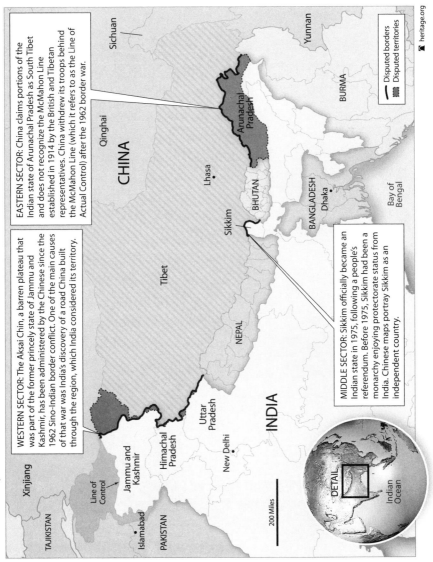

WESTERN SECTOR: The Aksai Chin, a barren plateau that was part of the former princely state of Jammu and Kashmir, has been administered by the Chinese since the 1962 Sino-Indian border conflict. One of the main causes of that war was India's discovery of a road China built through the region, which India considered its territory.

EASTERN SECTOR: China claims portions of the Indian state of Arunachal Pradesh as South Tibet and does not recognize the McMahon Line established in 1914 by the British and Tibetan representatives. China withdrew its troops behind the McMahon Line (which it refers to as the Line of Actual Control) after the 1962 border war.

MIDDLE SECTOR: Sikkim officially became an Indian state in 1975, following a people's referendum. Before 1975, Sikkim had been a monarchy enjoying protectorate status from India. Chinese maps portray Sikkim as an independent country.

Disputed borders
Disputed territories

heritage.org

TAJIKISTAN
Xinjiang
Islamabad
PAKISTAN
Line of Control
Jammu and Kashmir
Himachal Pradesh
Uttar Pradesh
New Delhi
INDIA
200 Miles
DETAIL
Indian Ocean

CHINA
Qinghai
Tibet
Lhasa
NEPAL
Sichuan
Yunnan
BHUTAN
Sikkim
Arunachal Pradesh
BURMA
BANGLADESH
Dhaka
Bay of Bengal

JFK'S FORGOTTEN CRISIS

INTRODUCTION

In the fall of 1962 President John Fitzgerald Kennedy faced two great international crises. In Cuba, the Soviet Union was secretly deploying nuclear weapons, ballistic missiles, and bombers capable of targeting Washington and much of the southeastern United States. In Asia, the People's Republic of China was planning an invasion of its neighbor India intended to result in a humiliating defeat. The president faced a combustible international environment that threatened to put America at war simultaneously with the two largest countries in the world on opposite sides of the globe.

Kennedy "wondered aloud which crisis would be the more significant in the long run," according to his close aide, Ted Sorenson, who was at his side during them.[1] The Cuban crisis risked escalating to a U.S. invasion of Cuba and a nuclear exchange with Russia that would be catastrophic. The Chinese invasion risked dismembering and crippling India and forcing the United States to start bombing advancing Chinese forces. Kennedy feared the India crisis would lead to an "all-out war between the two most populous nations on earth that might rival the confrontation in the Caribbean in long run implications."[2]

The president explained to another close aide, historian Arthur Schlesinger, that he associated the Cuban missile crisis with the Chinese attack on India. Together they formed "a climactic period," the president argued, which was "bound to have its effects, even though they can't be fully perceived now."[3]

The Chinese attack on India that began in October 1962 inflicted major casualties on the poorly equipped and badly led Indian army and resulted in China's occupation of 14,500 square miles of territory claimed by India in Kashmir called Aksai Chin or the desert of white stones. So grave was the defeat that Prime Minister Jawaharlal Nehru was compelled to ask Kennedy for "immediate American military aid to India, including an airlift of infantry weapons and light equipment for troops fighting on the border, and even American piloted transportation planes, and he had authorized a formal request to Washington for consideration of a joint air defense, involving American air cover for Indian cities to free India's air force for tactical raids against the Chinese. Hundreds of U.S. military advisers and air force personnel descended on New Delhi," as one eminent American historian of modern India has written.[4]

In large part thanks to the decisions Kennedy made in those tense autumn days, neither crisis escalated out of control. The Soviet decision to withdraw its missiles from Cuba was made possible by a quiet assurance that U.S. missiles would later be withdrawn from Turkey. In India Kennedy swiftly assured Nehru of American support and warned China against "forcing the hand of the President of the United States." One Indian general, who was captured by the Chinese in the war, later wrote, "President Kennedy assumed the role of 'big brother' and true friend of India. Significantly the Chinese withdrew two days after his warning."[5] The president's diplomacy also kept Pakistan on the sidelines of the war, preventing it from becoming a larger conflict.

John Kennedy's role in the Cuban missile crisis is well known today. If he had made the wrong choices in Cuba the result could have been the apocalypse for humankind, so it rightly deserves the attention and coverage given it. Kennedy's closest advisers, including Sorenson, Schlesinger, and his brother Robert, wrote extensively on the Cuban crisis, and historians, filmmakers, and many ordinary citizens have since studied the Cuban crisis.

In contrast, Americans have largely forgotten the simultaneous crisis in India. Only Kennedy's ambassador in New Delhi, John Kenneth Galbraith, wrote about India. In his memoirs, he recalled, "In the same week, on almost the same day that the two great western powers confronted each other over Cuba, the two great Asian countries went to war in the Himalayas."[6]

Kennedy's critical role in the Sino-Indian War of 1962 has also been largely ignored. This book seeks to fill that lacuna. It is important to study Kennedy's forgotten crisis not only to gain a better appreciation of his presidency but also because of the inherent importance of the two great Asian countries, India and China, then at war. Together they account for more than one-third of the world's population. Their border dispute still remains unresolved, more than a half-century after JFK's assassination: It is the longest disputed border in the world today. No wonder that when President Xi Jinping met with Prime Minister Narendra Modi on July 14, 2014, Xi said, "When India and China meet, the whole world watches."[7]

Embedded within the story of JFK's forgotten crisis in India in 1962 is another almost forgotten episode in American espionage. The United States from 1957 until the early 1970s clandestinely supported the Tibetan people in their resistance to Chinese occupation. It was an extraordinary covert action project in which "Tibetan youth were exfiltrated via East Pakistan (now Bangladesh), sent first to Saipan and then to Colorado for training and then parachuted by CIA aircraft back into Tibet after taking off from East Pakistan."[8] There they fought the People's Liberation Army, the largest army in the world. Kennedy was deeply involved in the effort even though his ambassador in India, Galbraith, thought it a crazy idea. Thus before 1962 the United States was engaged in a highly provocative effort to destabilize Tibet at a time when Nehru was trying for the most part to avoid war with China. Then after the 1962 war the project expanded into a joint Indo-American effort to help the Tibetans against China.[9]

There is one more special aspect to this story: the role played by Jacqueline Bouvier Kennedy (JBK), the First Lady. JBK was the hostess for several key visits by Nehru and his Pakistani counterpart Ayub Khan to the United States, and she traveled to both countries in 1962 for a very successful visit. She also came up with the idea to hold a state dinner at Mount Vernon, which is where the prologue starts the saga of Kennedy's forgotten crisis.

The 1962 crisis has deep reverberations today. More than fifty years after the war there are still cross-border incursions; fortunately very few produce casualties. The alliance system that dominates Asian politics—pitting China and Pakistan as allies against India, with the United States tilting toward India—was created in the 1962 crisis. Although the alliance structure has gone through many pertubations since, it is essentially the same as in 1962 and will likely remain so.

All of the territory that China acquired in the Sino-Indian War in 1962 was a part of Kashmir. The largely uninhabited area called Aksai Chin lies along a crucial land link between Tibet and Xinjiang. This adds another layer of complexity to the already difficult and unresolved question of Kashmir's future, still divided three ways between India, Pakistan, and China. The Kashmir imbroglio has fostered three Indo-Pakistani wars since 1947 and remains a source of tension today.

The forgotten crisis also initiated a continuing arms race in South Asia. In response to China's invasion India embarked on a military buildup that led several decades later to its developing nuclear weapons. When India tested the bomb in 1999, it cited the 1962 invasion by China as justification for acquiring its own bomb. After 1962 China and Pakistan began secretly engaging in military cooperation, including the development of nuclear weapons, another factor cited by India in 1999. This triangular arms race today is the most dynamic and expensive in the world.

The Tibetan people's anguish continues today as well, and Tibet remains a serious sticking point between India and China. The Dalai Lama still lives in exile in India, and India maintains a large force of Tibetan exiles under the operational control of the Indian army, the Special Frontier Force, which was created immediately after the 1962 war with the help of the CIA.[10] Thus in many ways Kennedy's forgotten crisis is still influencing the world more than a half-century later.

This book is also a study in leadership. Kennedy faced an existential crisis in the Caribbean and a conflict in the Himalayas that threatened to engulf all of Asia. He listened to the advice of many, but did not let the "experts" decide. In India he had two key partners: John Kenneth Galbraith and Jawaharlal Nehru. In London Kennedy had another key partner, British prime minister Harold Macmillan, who joined in the airlift to supply India during the war and in the postwar diplomacy with India and Pakistan. How Kennedy managed two crises on opposite sides of the globe holds lessons for decisionmakers today.

The Kennedys' lives and JFK's administration have sparked a massive literature. Every aspect of the president's life, including his medical condition and his sexual escapades, has been studied and written about in detail. A sizable literature has also explored every facet of JBK's life and style. As mentioned, the Cuban missile crisis is one of the most-studied episodes in American foreign and national security policy. The Kennedy Library in Boston in 2002 published a reading list about the crisis that ran to thirteen pages and listed more than 220 books or manuscripts. Yet this is the first book to address Kennedy's role in the Tibet project and the Sino-Indian War of 1962.

CHAPTER ONE

IKE AND INDIA, 1950–60

Gettysburg, Pennsylvania, is hallowed ground in America. In July 1863 it was the scene of a major battle in America's Civil War. The decisive moment in that epic battle came on its third day when the Confederate Army of Northern Virginia launched a massive assault on the center of the Union Army of the Potomac. This assault, known as Pickett's Charge, failed disastrously: half the attacking force were wounded or killed, and the rebel army never again invaded the North.

On December 17, 1956, President Dwight David Eisenhower, who owned a farm in Gettysburg, took his houseguest, Indian prime minister Jawaharlal Nehru, to visit the spot from which Pickett's Charge was launched. Then as now a large monument topped with an equestrian statute of Confederate commander Robert E. Lee marks the spot. The two men spent the better part of an hour looking at the site of Pickett's Charge as the president explained the significance of the Civil War to American history, culture, and politics.

Then they returned to Eisenhower's farm just a mile away. In fact, Eisenhower had bought the farm in 1950 because it was close to the battlefield. The original farmhouse had served as a temporary hospital for wounded Confederate soldiers during the battle. Ike, as he was called, had first visited Gettysburg in 1915 as a West Point military academy cadet. From his living room he could see the ridge where Lee's statue stood in the distance.

Nehru was spending the night at the farm so the two leaders could spend time together in a relaxed private venue.[1] It was a challenging visit; the two men were world-famous leaders, but worlds apart in their thinking. Eisenhower had led the D-Day invasion of Europe in 1944 that defeated Nazi Germany and believed he was engaged in another life-and-death struggle with the communist world in the 1950s. Nehru had been jailed for thirteen years in British prisons in India for fighting for independence from Great Britain. He had led the "Quit India" movement during World War II, seeking to sabotage the British war effort and colonial government, which ultimately helped to bring independence for his country. In the 1950s Nehru was the leader of the nonaligned movement that sought to unite the newly independent countries of Asia and Africa in a neutral bloc during the cold war. At that time the Indian press portrayed America as a hot-tempered imperialist power; the U.S. press portrayed India as soft on communism and weak willed.

Yet as the leaders of the two largest democracies in the world, both Ike and Nehru knew they needed to work together despite their differences, and the trip to Gettysburg was intended to allow time for a quiet and candid exchange of views free from the glare of the press. The president prepared carefully for the event; he had the White House and State Department ascertain Nehru's food and drink preferences, for example. It turned out that the leader of the world's largest Hindu country liked filet mignon and enjoyed an occasional Scotch as long as it was all in private. Nehru's daughter, Indira, accompanied him to the farm and reportedly shared his food preferences.[2]

By his own admission, Eisenhower was fascinated with India, although in 1956 he had not yet visited the country. He was also fascinated by Nehru, whom he regarded like most Americans at the time as "a somewhat inexplicable and occasionally exasperating personality" because he often seemed to condemn American and British actions more vigorously than he condemned Soviet behavior.[3] In the fall of 1956, for example, Nehru had strongly condemned the British-French-Israeli invasion of Egypt while more mildly criticizing the Soviet invasion of Hungary.

Just before his visit to the United States, Nehru had met with two key visitors in New Delhi in November. First he met with Tibet's new young monarch, the Dalai Lama, who had left his palace in Lhasa to visit India and was considering whether to seek political asylum to escape China's invasion of his homeland. He asked Nehru to raise the issue of China's takeover of Tibet in his subsequent visit with Eisenhower. Nehru's second visitor was the prime minister of China, Zhou Enlai, who urged Nehru to tell the Dalai Lama to return to his palace and pressed India not to interfere in what he called China's internal affairs. The Dalai Lama did return to Tibet in March 1957.[4]

The two leaders spent fourteen hours talking in Gettysburg, and Eisenhower wrote down fourteen pages of notes on the talks when he got back to the White House. In private he found Nehru much more critical of Soviet behavior in Hungary than he had been in public. Nehru was "horrified" at the Soviet invasion and predicted that it "spelled the eventual death knell of international communism, because 'nationalism is stronger than communism.' "[5] But Nehru, Eisenhower concluded, would always be tougher on European and American actions, which reminded him of British imperialism, than on Russian and Chinese activities, which were often undertaken in support of anti-imperialist nationalist movements in the developing world.

China was a major topic of their discussions. Nehru pressed Eisenhower to support giving Communist China the seat in the United Nations Security Council that Nationalist China had been given in 1945 at the end of World War II, making it one of the five permanent members of the Council with the right to veto any resolution it did not approve. It was "only logical that any government controlling six hundred million people will sooner or later have to be brought into the council of nations," Nehru argued. The prime minister dismissed any possibility that China would attack India, given the "fortunate location of the Himalayan mountain chain" on their 1,800 miles of common border. India could not afford the cost of building a defense along this long border: Taking part in an arms race would jeopardize its hopes of development. Better, Nehru concluded, that India stay neutral in the cold war and seek to build friendly ties with China.[6] Eisenhower, with China's role in the Korean War still fresh in his memory, refused to budge on China and the UN seat. There is no record in the Eisenhower notes of Nehru's raising the Dalai Lama's request for help against China's occupation of Tibet.

Nehru was critical of U.S. arms sales to Pakistan, but he was confident that the two South Asian states could ultimately resolve their differences, including the dispute over Kashmir. He was more critical of Portugal, which still was holding onto its small colony in India at Goa. Because Portugal was a NATO member and an American ally, Nehru pressed Ike to get Lisbon to let go of its vestiges of empire.

The two did not come to agreement on all issues or even on most, but Eisenhower concluded that he "liked Prime Minister Nehru; Pandit Jawaharlal Nehru was not easy to understand: few people are, but his was a personality of unusual contradictions."[7] The two leaders left the farm with a much better appreciation of each other's point of view and were more inclined to understand each other's position than before. Nehru's preeminent biographer, Stanley Wolpert, later wrote that the "two days of top secret talks helped defuse the world conflagration in late 1956 and turned the tide of Indian-U.S. relations."[8] That may be a bit of an exaggeration. The two democracies remained estranged for decades to come, but the summit did at least clear the air between the two leaders.

KOREA

Ike owed his presidency to the Korean War. After twenty years of Democrats in the White House, the war hero Eisenhower was elected on the promise that he would go to Korea to end an unpopular war that Americans were desperate to conclude. The war was the backdrop for U.S. policy and intelligence in Asia in the second half of the twentieth century and is an important place to start in understanding the CIA's role in India and Tibet that shaped Kennedy's forgotten crisis in 1962.

The American intelligence community's experience with the People's Republic of China and North Korea began with a disaster, a catastrophic intelligence failure in 1950 that cost the lives of thousands of Americans. Worse, it was a self-imposed disaster—the result of terrible intelligence management, not the poor collection or analysis of information. To add insult to injury the government of India had warned the United States that disaster loomed, but was ignored.

Mao Zedong formally announced the creation of the People's Republic of China (PRC) in October 1949. After decades of civil war and struggle against Japan, Mao restored the unity of China and made himself the unquestioned dictator of the world's most populous nation. It was an amazing triumph both for Mao and the Chinese Communist Party, which had been forced only fifteen years before to abandon most of Chinese territory to its domestic and foreign enemies and to retreat in the famous Long March across 6,000 miles in 370 days to the remote northern province of Yenan in 1934.

A year after the creation of the PRC, Mao made two historic decisions. On October 7, 1950, he sent Chinese troops across the border into Tibet, the remote Himalayan kingdom between China and India that had achieved something close to de facto independence during China's long decline in the nineteenth century. At first the invasion was limited to border areas, but gradually China exerted more and more control over Tibet, as described later.

At the same time Mao made another historic decision: China would enter the Korean War and fight the United States and its United Nations allies for control of the Korean peninsula. The war in Korea had begun on June 25, 1950, when communist North Korea invaded the South. Two days later the UN Security Council agreed to send troops to defend the South; Russia, which at that time was boycotting the Security Council, thus failed to veto the troop deployment. More than twenty nations ultimately contributed troops to the UN fighting force. Mao had not been party to North Korea's plans and was only told of the invasion after the fact. Russia, however, was North Korea's closest partner at the start of the war, and Kim Il Sung, North Korea's communist dictator, did obtain Russian permission to attack. Joseph Stalin, not Mao, was thus the decider.

Within days of crossing the border, the North Koreans routed the southern army and captured the South's capital at Seoul. President Harry Truman decided to send American troops to prevent the complete defeat of the Republic of Korea, ordering his commander in Japan, General Douglas MacArthur, to send U.S. troops then stationed in Japan to defend the South. In September MacArthur, a hero of World War II, stopped the North Korean advance and then launched an amphibious attack behind enemy lines at Inchon, which recaptured Seoul and led to the rout of the North Korean army. MacArthur's troops fought with the UN force.

The United States was uncertain about how to proceed after recapturing Seoul. MacArthur wanted to pursue the defeated North Koreans back across the 38th parallel, the prewar border, and march all the way to the Yalu River, Korea's historic border with China. The South Korean government was even more eager to move northward and reunite the country. However, many in Washington and other Western capitals, including London, were more cautious and worried that moving into the North would provoke the

Chinese. MacArthur, in control of the troops on the scene, prevailed, taking them on the march to the Yalu.

Mao decided in early October to send his army south across the Yalu River and fight MacArthur's forces. On October 8, 1950, Mao told Kim Il Sung that Chinese troops were on their way and that he had ordered them to cross the Yalu to "repel the invasion launched by the American imperialists and their running dogs."[9] The Chinese Communist Forces (or CCF as they were referred to in the war) were commanded by one of Mao's comrades from the Long March, Peng Dehuai, and they secretly moved into North Korea in mid-October. By late November Peng had 400,000 CCF troops in more than thirty divisions in North Korea.[10]

The American army in Korea and Japan, the Eighth Army, was poorly prepared for the war. The occupation troops in Japan who were rushed to the Korean front were not combat ready; many of the officers were too old for frontline battlefield conditions. Training was "slipshod and routine."[11] The relatively easy victory over North Korea at Inchon had reinforced a sense of complacency among the commanders and GIs that the war was all but over. MacArthur promised that the troops would be home by Christmas 1950.

Faulty Intelligence

MacArthur had always understood that if you "control intelligence, you control decision making."[12] He had built an intelligence community in his area of command that listened attentively to what he wanted and gave him intelligence that reinforced his already held views. MacArthur wanted total control of the war and its execution, not second-guessing by his subordinates or outside interference by Washington, especially by the White House and the Pentagon. If his Tokyo command headquarters were solely responsible for collecting and assessing intelligence on the enemy, then MacArthur alone could decide how big the enemy threat was and thus what to do about it.

MacArthur's authority put America's relatively new civilian intelligence agency, the Central Intelligence Agency, in an awkward position. It was not permitted to have a representative in Tokyo or participate in preparing intelligence estimates for the Eighth Army. During World War II, MacArthur had done the same thing, excluding the CIA's predecessor, the Office of Strategic Services (OSS), from his South West Pacific command. MacArthur, who never spent a single night in Korea during the war, preferring to sleep in his headquarters in Japan, wanted no outside intelligence challenger. As one historian of the war wrote later, "Only after the great and catastrophic failure on the whereabouts and intentions of China's armies would the CIA finally be allowed into the region."[13]

MacArthur's intelligence chief, or G2, was General Charles Willoughby, who had been with his commander since serving in the Philippines in 1939, before World War II. A self-styled admirer of the general, Willoughby later wrote a sycophantic biography of MacArthur that was more than a thousand pages long. He was born in Germany as Karl Weidenbach and styled himself a Prussian, a most unusual role model for an American officer in the wake of two wars against Germany, but one he relished, even occasionally wearing a monocle.[14] He was also an admirer of Spain's fascist military dictator Francisco Franco. One prominent CIA officer in the early 1950s, Frank Wisner, said Willoughby was "all ideology and almost never any facts."[15]

In June 1950 Willoughby assured MacArthur that North Korea would not invade the South, despite alarms raised by then-CIA director Admiral Roscoe Hillenkoetter.[16] In the fall of that year Willoughby's office refused to believe or confirm reports that thousands of CCF troops were in North Korea. Even when Chinese prisoners were captured, Willoughby dismissed them as a few experts or advisers, not as a group of soldiers. The G2 in Tokyo recognized that some Chinese divisions had entered the North, but argued that they were not full-strength combat units. Willoughby "doctored the intelligence in order to permit MacArthur's forces to go where they wanted to go militarily, to the banks of the Yalu," with no contrary or dissenting voices heard in Tokyo or Washington.[17] The Tokyo estimate of the number of CCF forces in Korea was less than one-tenth the reality.

On October 15, 1950, MacArthur had met with President Truman on Wake Island in the mid-Pacific. The general told the president that the war would be over by Thanksgiving and most troops would be home by Christmas. When Truman asked, "What will be the attitude of Commie China?" MacArthur said it would not intervene. Even if China tried, it could not get more than 50,000 troops across the Yalu River, MacArthur promised, citing his G2's intelligence estimate. In fact, by October 19, 260,000 CCF soldiers had already crossed into Korea.[18]

Even the first encounters with Chinese forces on the battlefield did not shake the faulty intelligence estimate. In late October the Eighth Army fought a bitter and costly battle with CCF forces at Unsan in the North. The Americans were routed, but then the Chinese pulled back. They wanted to entice the Eighth Army northward to trap it far from its supply lines and to isolate it near the Chinese frontier. Willoughby dismissed the Unsan battle as unimportant and continued to claim that the Chinese would not intervene in force. So did MacArthur. The Chinese decision to trap an American unit in Unsan, then stop and regroup, would be unerringly similar to the Chinese invasion of India twelve years later in which they used the same tactic—attack, halt, and then attack again—to defeat the Indian army.

MacArthur made one of his lightning-quick trips to Korea from Tokyo on November 24, 1950, telling the U.S. ambassador in Seoul there were only 25,000 Chinese troops in Korea. Then he had his return flight to Tokyo fly along the Yalu River, making possible a personal reconnaissance intended to impress the media. His report to Washington dismissed the danger of Chinese intervention. Three days later Peng's armies struck the American forces as they were driving to the Yalu River.[19]

The result was a disaster. The Eighth Army was routed again and its South Korean allies destroyed. Thousands of allied troops died and were wounded. As the British military historian Max Hastings described later, the total disintegration "resembled the collapse of the French in 1940 to the Nazis and the British at Singapore in 1942 to the Japanese."[20] By December 31, 1950, the Americans had been driven 120 miles south back to the 38th parallel and were still retreating. Seoul would fall to Peng's armies in early 1951. It was by far the worst military debacle the U.S. armed forces suffered in the entire twentieth century. A new American commander, General Matthew Ridgway, took over from MacArthur in Korea. One of his first acts was to bring the CIA into theater to provide an alternative intelligence viewpoint from that given by Willoughby's Tokyo headquarters.

India's Role in the Korean Conflict

As mentioned earlier, India had tried to warn America that Chinese forces would enter the Korean War and was proven correct. From the start of the war India tried to broker a truce. As early as July 1950 Nehru's government had suggested to the allies that China might press North Korea to accept a cease-fire in Korea along the 38th parallel, thereby restoring the status quo ante, if the Americans allowed Communist China to take control of China's seat in the UN Security Council still controlled by the Nationalist Chinese government now exiled on the island of Taiwan. Washington did not take the proposal seriously.[21]

India refused to send combat troops to join the UN forces in Korea. Although it did send a medical unit, the 60th Parachute Field Ambulance Regiment, to help the allies, it tried to remain neutral in the conflict.[22] Moreover, India was one of a small number of noncommunist governments that had formally recognized the PRC and had an ambassador in Beijing. India's ambassador was an experienced diplomat named K. M. Panikkar, who had also written several books on the struggle against Western imperialism in Asia. The ambassador knew his account very well; he had been India's first and only ambassador to the Nationalist government led by Chiang Kai-shek after Indian independence in 1947 and then was appointed India's first ambassador to the communist government in 1949. He also had Tibet experience, having traveled there in 1949 on Nehru's behalf to sound out the Tibetans on whether they would resist a Chinese takeover.[23] Panikkar enjoyed very good contacts in China. He had regular access to the top leadership of the People's Republic, including Chairman Mao and Prime Minister Zhou Enlai. His memoirs make clear he admired his hosts for ending the chaos that had enveloped their country during the preceding century.[24] Meanwhile U.S. leaders considered Panikkar and Nehru to be "soft" on communism and too neutral in the global struggle with Stalin and Mao.

In September 1950 Panikkar's military contacts in Beijing began to warn him that the PRC would not sit still and allow the UN forces including the Eighth Army to march to the Yalu. Chinese military officials told him that Mao was prepared to risk nuclear war to stop those forces from advancing. The Indian embassy in Beijing reported that trainloads of CCF troops were moving to the border region, and the Indian government passed these reports on to Washington and London.

On October 2, 1950, Panikkar was summoned at midnight to meet the Chinese prime minister, Zhou Enlai, Mao's closest confidant. After being driven through the deserted streets of Beijing, Panikkar was received by the prime minister, who also served as foreign minister, at thirty minutes past midnight. As Panikkar described the meeting, despite the late hour and the seriousness of the issue—the "peace of the world"—Zhou was as "courteous and charming as ever and did not give the least impression of worry or nervousness or indeed of being in any particular hurry." It was only after tea was served that Zhou got to the point. He told Panikkar that if American troops crossed the 38th parallel China would intervene.[25] At 1:30 a.m. Panikkar cabled the warning to Nehru, who had it sent to the UN allies.[26]

The British were particularly alarmed by the Indian message. The United Kingdom and its Commonwealth allies had the second-largest contingent of troops—two brigades—in the UN force in Korea. The British were also worried that provoking China in Korea could lead to a Chinese attack on their colony in Hong Kong. The stakes were high for London.

The British Joint Chiefs of Staff were led by the commander of the British forces in India and Burma during World War II, Field Marshal Sir William Slim, who knew a great deal about China. Slim had been worried since July that moving north of the 38th parallel would provoke Chinese intervention. When Panikkar's message arrived in London it considerably reinforced the joint chiefs' anxieties. The British intelligence community, led by the Joint Intelligence Committee (JIC), which prepared synthesized estimates for the prime minister, was more cautious and thought that Chinese intervention was still unlikely but possible. It dismissed Zhou's warning as not being specific enough.[27] As the JIC noted in late 1951, the British intelligence community in 1950 did not yet understand that Mao was the only real decisionmaker in Beijing and that he was making his decisions based not on Western thinking about global politics but on his own view of China's interests.[28] The JIC's watered-down warning did not reassure the British joint chiefs, who kept sounding the alarm in London.

In Tokyo MacArthur and Willoughby completely dismissed the Indian warning as merely communist propaganda delivered by an untrustworthy source. The CIA analysts in Washington were more inclined to accept Panikkar's warning as genuine, but being heavily influenced by the view from Eighth Army headquarters they also thought the Chinese would not intervene in force. The CIA did prepare a National Intelligence Estimate, the collective opinion of the entire intelligence community in Washington, on November 6, 1950, titled "Chinese Communist Intervention in Korea"; however, it assessed that there were only 30,000 Chinese troops south of the Yalu. An update on November 24 put the number at 70,000 in just four divisions, an estimate still wildly off the mark.[29]

In any case, the CIA, assuming that the communist world was a monolith in which Stalin dictated all the moves, believed that the decision to intervene in Korea would be made in Moscow by the Soviet leader. What the agency did not know was that Stalin was encouraging the Chinese to fight, while promising only very limited Soviet aid and assistance—not troops—for the war.[30] Stalin did not even promise to provide any air cover. Mao was angered that Stalin would not send Russians to fight, but decided to strike anyway. The dispute over Korea added fuel to Mao's distrust of Stalin and exacerbated the emerging Sino-Soviet rivalry for control of the communist movement worldwide, but that was still a secret to outsiders.

In Washington the secretary of state, Dean Acheson, was one of the smartest men in the Truman administration on most matters, but he too was convinced the Chinese would not intervene. It would be "sheer madness" for Mao to take on America, Acheson said, and the Indian warning was the "mere vaporings of a panicky Panikkar."[31]

Frustrated, Panikkar wrote in his diary later in 1950 that "America has knowingly elected for war, with Britain following. The Chinese armies now concentrated on the Yalu will intervene decisively in the fight. Probably some of the Americans want that. They probably feel that this is an opportunity to have a show down with China. In any case MacArthur's dream has come true. I only hope it does not turn into a nightmare."[32]

Future of the U.S.-China Relationship

The catastrophe on the Yalu would have a lasting impact on American thinking about China. Coming after the communists' victory in the Chinese civil war, the Korean debacle fueled a domestic political debate over "who lost China" that pitted the handful of China experts in Washington against a powerful lobby that argued the China hands were either soft on communism or, worse, were communist agents serving foreign interests. Led by Senator Joe McCarthy and Congressman Richard Nixon, the right wing of the Republican Party fought any effort to rethink American policy toward China, to give the PRC the UN Security Council seat, or even to talk with China for the next two decades. Ironically it would be Nixon who finally implemented all of these changes in 1971.

The Korean War was crucial to framing American impressions that China was a crazy communist state that was even more dangerous than the Soviet Union and much more inscrutable. The Chinese communists were perceived as reckless and ready for nuclear war. Talking to them was considered a waste of time and possibly immoral. Mao came to be seen as an irrational but cunning leader.

The intelligence disaster would also frame how Americans later viewed the Chinese invasion of India in 1962. Americans had vivid memories of how China had surprised them in 1950, defeating an American war hero and almost driving UN forces out of Korea. When China attacked India in 1962, JFK and other Americans assumed the worst: China would be unstoppable.

The war also galvanized the CIA to look for ways to strike back at China, both to weaken the communists' hold on power and to divert the country's attention internally to domestic unrest. The CIA wanted to demonstrate to the new U.S. president, Ike, that it could do better than the Tokyo intelligence operation had done in 1950, not only by analyzing Chinese behavior and intentions more accurately but also by actually running covert operations inside the PRC to weaken it.

The Korean War came to an end in 1953, with the Indians playing an important role in arranging the cease-fire between the PRC and the UN. India helped with the repatriation of captured prisoners to each side, a very delicate issue because thousands of North Korean and Chinese prisoners wanted to be free to stay in the South and not go home. The Indians supervised a careful process that ensured they were able to defect, but without too much humiliation for the communist regimes.

TIBET

Ambassador Panikkar was also at the center of the other crisis Mao created in October 1950 when he decided to invade Tibet. At that time Tibet was an almost medieval impoverished theocracy run by Buddhist monks. It was a remote, landlocked country that had little access to the outside world. Almost 500,000 square miles in size, the equivalent of Western Europe, Tibet is bounded by tall mountains on three sides. Only to the east on the border with China does the terrain permit relatively easy access. To the south the Himalayas make transportation very difficult, and two other mountain chains block easy passage from the west and north.[33]

Tibet was formally a protectorate of China since 1720. However, since the two Anglo-Chinese Opium Wars in the mid-nineteenth century, Chinese control over this far western province had become increasingly weakened; after the 1911 Chinese revolution, Tibet's political connections with China became even more attenuated. Beset by internal civil wars and external aggression from Japan, the weak Nationalist government held little sway in Lhasa, Tibet's capital. Meanwhile Britain's interest in Tibet increased. The British Empire in India preferred a weak Tibet as a useful buffer on the Raj's northern border and treated Tibet as an all but independent country while acknowledging ultimate Chinese sovereignty. In 1914 the British signed a treaty with Tibet at Simla in India that gave the British the India-Tibet border lines that London wanted. The Chinese were invited to sign the treaty as well, but refused.[34]

No Chinese government would accept that Tibet was an independent country, and certainly not one that had just won a civil war and was determined to reunite all of historic China under its authority. Nor did India claim to have any sovereignty over Tibet. It was the British in 1914 who drew the boundary between Tibet and India to the Raj's advantage. In the west of India this boundary was known as the Johnson Line, which divided Kashmir from China; in the east the border was known as the McMahon Line dividing eastern India, Assam, from China—both lines being named after the British diplomats who drew them. When the communists won the Chinese civil war in 1949, they accepted neither the semi-independence of Tibet nor the boundary lines drawn by British imperialism between Tibet and India.

In early October 1950, just as he was dealing with Zhou's warning that China would invade Korea, Panikkar received reports that 20,000 Chinese forces had crossed into Tibet and seized control of a strip of land along the frontier dividing Tibet from China. On October 25, China announced that it had begun "the process of 'Liberating Tibet' and the fat was in the fire," in the ambassador's words.[35] Nehru instructed Panikkar to issue a strong démarche to the Chinese government protesting China's use of force. Zhou replied with an equally strong message claiming that China only wanted to restore its control of Tibet and would seek to do so, if possible, by peaceful means. India made clear in its subsequent diplomatic messages that it recognized China's sovereignty over Tibet and did not intend to intervene in internal Chinese affairs, but was only protesting its use of military force.

Nehru faced pressure at home and abroad to do more. The Indian press was full of stories about Chinese atrocities in Tibet and the potential for China to use Tibet to threaten India. His own intelligence chief, B. N. Mullik, head of the Intelligence Bureau (IB) from 1950 until after Nehru died, warned Nehru that China's move into Tibet was "sinister" and would threaten India's interests. Mullik also thought Panikkar was too soft on China.[36] In the United Nations, which had already deployed forces to fight the Chinese in Korea, there was pressure to label the PRC as an aggressor and to condemn the invasion. Nehru worked quietly both to calm down his agitated domestic constituency and to keep the Tibet issue out of the UN.

Chinese forces did not occupy all of Tibet in 1950; rather China's strategy was to seize the border area and then negotiate full control over the kingdom with the weak theocratic government in Lhasa, which was powerless to resist the People's Liberation Army (PLA). The "stiffness" in Chinese-Indian relations caused by the invasion, as Panikkar described it, proved to be short-lived. Nehru had neither the capability nor the intention of fighting for control of Tibet, and Mao was not eager to overplay his very strong hand. Instead, Mao was content to gradually absorb Tibet and welcomed Nehru's behind-the-scenes help in the UN. After all China had enough on its agenda with a full-scale war with the United States and the UN underway in Korea.

In Tibet the Chinese incursion understandably created panic. The post of Dalai Lama, Tibet's divinely chosen head of state, was hastily filled with the accession of a fifteen-year-old young man on November 17, 1950. He had been named heir at the age of four, but was still studying for the role when the invasion occurred. The new Dalai Lama fled the capital and moved to a Buddhist monastery close to the Indian border. The U.S. ambassador in New Delhi, Loy Henderson, secretly urged the young man to leave Tibet and seek asylum outside the country, thereby keeping alive a Tibetan government in exile.[37] The American consulate in Calcutta, the closest U.S. diplomatic post to Tibet, opened a communications channel to the Tibetan leadership remaining in Tibet. The Dalai Lama's older brother (aged twenty-nine), Thubten Norbu, traveled to the United States as a guest of a San Francisco-based group, the Committee for a Free Asia, which was financed by the CIA.[38]

Washington was very eager to get the Tibetans to engage in armed resistance against China, thereby opening another front against Mao. The assistant secretary of state for Far Eastern affairs was Dean Rusk, a hawk on China. Rusk and Henderson, however, were constrained by the United States' continued support for

Nationalist China whose leaders, like Mao, claimed that Tibet was a part of China. They were also constrained by Nehru's reluctance to support military operations in Tibet where China had every military advantage.[39]

Even before the Chinese invaded, the Tibetans, in light of their isolation and weakness, had initiated talks with China. The Tibetan leaders reluctantly signed a seventeen-point agreement in Beijing that acknowledged China's authority in Tibet, but preserved the institution of the Dalai Lama. In September 1951 the Tibetan government formally accepted the Chinese takeover of Tibet. The PLA entered Lhasa, and the young Dalai Lama returned to the capital to preside over a puppet regime. Nehru endorsed the deal; Rusk and Henderson were outflanked.

Earlier that year, on January 26, the Indian Embassy in Beijing had celebrated the first anniversary of the creation of the Indian Republic. To the surprise of everyone, Mao himself attended the dinner event at the Peking Hotel along with his wife, an unprecedented symbol of friendship both for India and its ambassador. In his toast Mao praised the "thousands of years of friendship between the people of India and China."[40] Mao's gesture indicated that the Tibet crisis of 1950 had ended.

Zhou and Panikkar were able to resolve many of the outstanding bilateral Sino-Indian issues concerning Tibet. The Indian diplomatic mission in Lhasa, inherited from the British, was turned into a consulate under the authority of the embassy in Beijing. In turn China opened a consulate in Bombay to keep symmetry in the relationship. China accepted that India had legitimate trade relations with Tibet, and New Delhi fully acknowledged Chinese political sovereignty in Tibet.[41] Only the issue of the border between India and Chinese Tibet was unresolved. It remains so today.

In 1954 India and China formalized their areas of agreement in a treaty concerning Tibet. It began with a statement of five principles of coexistence, or Panch Sheela as they are called in Hindi: Indo-Chinese relations based on mutual respect for each other's territorial integrity and sovereignty, mutual nonaggression, mutual non-interference in each other's internal affairs, equality, and peaceful coexistence. The Panch Sheela principles seemed to place India and China on a long-term path of peaceful relations.

However, Nehru's intelligence chief, B. N. Mullik, felt that the treaty was a bad bargain, ceding Indian interests in Tibet in return for vague promises of good behavior and goodwill. He wrote that a "weak and friendly Tibet" was being replaced by a "strong and belligerent China" on India's northern border. But Mullik agreed with Nehru that India did not have the military capability to aid the Tibetans or stop Chinese advances in Tibet, because the military balance was so lopsided in Mao's favor.[42]

For Nehru, in contrast, the treaty was a significant accomplishment. China and India had never quarreled in their long history as Asia's great civilizations, and Nehru was convinced that they would become great nations again. Both had been the victims of imperialism, especially British imperialism. With the end of the age of imperialism, China and India could lead the newly independent countries of Asia and Africa as an alternative to the two superpowers, then engaged in the cold war.[43]

After signing the treaty, Nehru visited China for the first time as prime minister in October 1954. The visit highlighted the two countries' friendly relationship and shared anti-imperialist ideology. Nehru felt comfortable enough to raise the border issue, noting China's issuance of maps that showed large parts of India along both the Johnson and McMahon Lines as belonging to China. Zhou told Nehru that these were old maps from the Nationalist period and that the PRC had yet to print new ones. Nehru found this answer unsatisfactory, but it did not change his desire to emphasize the positive in Indo-Chinese relations.[44]

Tibet stayed on the back burner of world diplomacy in the 1950s as China gradually tightened its grip on the region, following a stage-by-stage plan for incorporating Tibet into the PRC. First, it built a network of modern roads and airports to link the remote area more and more closely to China's infrastructure, thereby facilitating its military control. One such road was built on territory that India claimed as part of Kashmir, in the region called Aksai Chin. More Chinese troops arrived in Lhasa to control the capital, preparing the way for the second stage: replacing indirect rule by the Dalai Lama with direct military rule. In the third stage—the "Sinoization of Tibet" as one author described it—significant numbers of ethnic Han Chinese began to settle in the region, threatening to make the ethnic Tibetans a minority in their own country. Yet the unique Tibetan sociopolitical system based on the rule of the Buddhist priestly caste and the Dalai Lama was kept superficially intact until the Dalai Lama made his trip to New Delhi in late 1956.[45]

Zhou Enlai visited New Delhi three times during the several months that the Dalai Lama was in India, urging Nehru to send him home and promising respect for Tibetan rights. Both Nehru and the Dalai Lama decided to take Zhou's promises seriously. But after the return of the "god king" in March 1957, the situation in Tibet deteriorated. China's determination to reduce the kingdom to a province of the communist dictatorship became increasingly obvious, and Tibetan resistance grew more serious. An insurrection began in parts of the province, and the PLA deployed more and more soldiers to crush it. Clearly China was no longer abiding by the terms of the 1954 treaty with India.

In 1965 the CIA did a top-secret postmortem of the Sino-Indian War that was later declassified. In assessing the early years of the dispute between Nehru and Mao over Tibet, the CIA concluded correctly that China "played on Nehru's Asian, anti-imperialist mental attitude; his proclivity to temporize, and his sincere desire for an amicable Sino-Indian relationship." China's "strategy was to avoid making explicit, in conversations and communications with Nehru, any Chinese border claims, while avoiding any retraction of those claims which would require changing Chinese maps."

The CIA postmortem concluded it "was a masterpiece of guile executed by Chou en Lai."[46]

PAKISTAN

The Eisenhower administration took office in January 1953. At the top of its foreign policy team were two brothers: The older one, John Foster Dulles, became secretary of state, and the younger brother, Allen Dulles, became the director of the Central Intelligence Agency. Their grandfather had lived in India as a Presbyterian missionary for five years in the 1850s and later wrote a book titled *Life in India* that extolled the British imperial regime as a model of beneficent white people bringing civilization to non-Christian brown peoples. John Foster Dulles inherited many of his grandfather's strict moral views. By the 1950s these views had hardened into a black-and-white vision of the world, in which America was fighting a holy crusade against godless communism and neutrality was immoral. India under Nehru, with its ties to "Red" China and its refusal to join America's anticommunist bloc of alliances, was on the wrong side of the elder Dulles's view of good and evil.

The younger Dulles was just as committed to the prosecution of the cold war as his brother, but his manner was a bit less judgmental. Many in Washington saw him as a true professional intelligence officer, not a partisan. Kennedy's aide Arthur Schlesinger, for example, wrote later about Allen Dulles that he was "urbane, courtly and honorable, almost wholly devoid of the intellectual rigidity and personal self righteousness of his brother" and his "coolness and proficiency" were admirable.[47]

Allen was a boy wonder. At the age of eight he published his first article, a critique of British imperialism in the Boer War. After graduating with honors from Princeton he received a grant to teach in India at Ewing Christian College. In 1914 as World War I began, he traveled via Paris to India. On the long steamship voyage Allen read Rudyard Kipling's famous novel *Kim* about the great game in South Asia, the espionage war between the Russians and the British at the turn of the twentieth century, and he became entranced with spycraft. He never parted with his copy of *Kim*; it was on his bedside table when he passed away. In India Dulles met Jawaharlal Nehru, who had just completed his education in Cambridge. A year later, in 1915, Dulles returned to the United States and joined the Foreign Service; his first posting was in Vienna, capital of the Austro-Hungarian Empire, which was losing the Great War.[48]

During World War II Allen Dulles served with the OSS, America's first civilian spy organization; he ran its office in Bern, Switzerland, a key neutral country in the heart of Europe. Allen relished the job and was good at it. He was involved in the July 1944 secret plot to assassinate Adolf Hitler, which was immortalized in the movie *Valkyrie*, and helped orchestrate the surrender of German forces in Italy in 1945. He joined the CIA, OSS's successor, in January 1951 as deputy director for plans, heading its covert action side. At that time the American intelligence community was still reeling from the fiasco in Korea. In August 1951 Dulles was promoted to deputy director of the CIA, and in January 1953 Eisenhower made him director of central intelligence (DCI).

At the same time Eisenhower appointed Allen's older brother as secretary of state. On assuming that office John Foster Dulles embarked on a global campaign to build an alliance network of countries that would surround the Union of Soviet Socialist Republics (USSR) and the People's Republic of China (PRC); the goal was to extend the North Atlantic Treaty Organization (NATO) alliance that protected Europe from the USSR into a worldwide bloc fighting on America's side in the cold war.

Nehru wanted no part of a bipolar world war against communism, but India's neighbor Pakistan saw opportunity in the Dulles scheme. One-fourth the size of its neighbor and acutely worried about Indian ambitions, Pakistan was eager to find a foreign protector; in turn America was eager to protect Pakistan. Pakistan joined not just one alliance with America but two—becoming a founding member of the Central Treaty Organization (CENTO) in the Middle East and the Southeast Asia Treaty Organization (SEATO) in Southeast Asia. By the mid-1950s, Pakistanis could claim to be America's most allied ally. Large amounts of military and economic aid followed. Pakistan's motives, of course, were to find allies and resources to confront India, not the USSR and PRC. The first Pakistani commander of the Pakistani Army, field marshal (and later president) Mohammad Ayub Khan, wrote later that "the crux of the problem for Pakistan was Indian hostility," and that is why Pakistan joined CENTO and SEATO.[49]

While John Foster Dulles built alliances in public, Allen was building secret alliances between the CIA and friendly intelligence services. In Pakistan that meant the ISI—the Inter Services Intelligence Directorate—which had been created by an Australian officer seconded to the Pakistani army in early 1948. Major General Walter Joseph Cawthorne was born in Melbourne and served in World War I with the Australia New Zealand Army Corps (ANZAC) at Gallipoli against the Turks and in Flanders against the Germans. After the war he joined the British Indian Army and served in the North West Frontier Province, policing the Pashtun tribes along the Afghanistan border. During World War II he was the first head of intelligence for British forces in the Middle East (1939–41) and then director of intelligence for the India Command and deputy director of intelligence for the South East Asia Command.

After the partition of India, Cawthorne chose to serve in the new Pakistani army, which was initially commanded by a British officer, General Douglas Gracey. Cawthorne was given the job of creating a professional military intelligence service for the Pakistani military. In 1951 he was promoted to deputy chief of staff of the new Pakistani army before returning to Australia to be director of the Joint Intelligence Bureau in the Australian Ministry of Defense.

In 1954 he became the first Australian High Commissioner (ambassador) in Karachi. He also served as Australia's ambassador to Canada in the late 1950s. Cawthorne died in 1970.

The ISI created by Cawthorne was focused on military intelligence and had no role in domestic spying. It was modeled on the British secret intelligence service, MI6, from which it received training and assistance. From its inception it was responsible for serving as a liaison with foreign intelligence services, and so the ISI was the CIA's natural partner.

As mentioned, Pakistan's first Pakistani military commander in chief was Ayub Khan, who took over from Gracey in January 1951. Khan was a graduate of the British military academy Sandhurst and in World War II fought in Burma with the British Fourteenth Army against the Japanese. After Pakistan achieved independence he was commander of Pakistani forces in East Pakistan before becoming chief of the army. He met often with Allen Dulles during his visits to the United States in the 1950s. In 1958 Ayub Khan became Pakistan's first military dictator in a bloodless coup.

During the cold war, Dulles advocated for covert action as a low-profile and inexpensive alternative to military action to advance American interests around the world. His first big success came in Iran in 1953, when Operation Ajax, a joint mission with the British, overthrew a nationalist government in Tehran led by Mohammad Mossadegh. In his place the Shah of Iran was restored to full authority as the dictator of Persia. In one stroke, Allen Dulles had moved Iran from being a wobbly neutral in the cold war to one of America's closest allies in the Muslim world and a firm bulwark of containment of the USSR on its southern border. No American lives had been lost, and the American role was plausibly deniable. Ike was very pleased; the president "marveled that the operation had been carried out with the loss of just a few hundred lives, none of them American. Allen had shown that he could crush foreign leaders secretly, cheaply, and almost bloodlessly."[50]

In Central America the CIA succeeded in overthrowing a leftist government in Guatemala. Other missions were less successful. Efforts to stir up anticommunist resistance in Poland, Albania, and inside the USSR itself failed. In Indochina a long and costly battle with communism began in the early 1950s to try to salvage the French colonial empire there; it evolved into the Vietnam War. Yet the Iran operation outshone the failures.

By the mid-1950s the CIA had become a global organization, having grown sixfold since its founding in 1947. Dulles commanded 15,000 employees in fifty countries with a budget in the hundreds of millions of dollars. Working with his brother the secretary of state and an enthusiastic president, Allen Dulles was a player at the most senior decisionmaking table of American national security.[51]

In 1957 Dulles turned to Pakistan for help with launching a CIA operation in Tibet. This required cooperation between two divisions of his covert Directorate of Plans: the Far East (FE) Division and the Near East (NE) Division. FE had responsibility for China operations, and NE for Pakistan and India operations. FE was enthusiastic about operations in China, whereas NE was more reluctant to involve its clients in adventures inside that country. This bureaucratic division of labor would have its consequences over time, but at the start the two cooperated.

The Tibet resistance leaders identified a small group of six Tibetans to be sent for CIA training in insurgency tactics and clandestine operations. The Dalai Lama's older brother, who was then living in the United States and was already in contact with the CIA, helped select the six trainees. With Pakistani assistance they were exfiltrated out of Tibet into East Pakistan in mid-1957. The ISI arranged for them to stay briefly at an abandoned World War II air base named Kurmitula about ten miles north of Dacca, then the capital of East Pakistan. Built by the Royal Air Force in the war, the base was relatively primitive with a landing strip 1,000 meters long.[52]

A CIA plane flew the first batch of recruits from Kurmitula to a CIA training facility on the island of Saipan that had been used previously for training fighters from other countries. By October 1957 the first team of Tibetans was ready to go home and use their newly developed skills to help the rebellion. The plan was to use an unmarked CIA-owned B-17 bomber to fly them to Kurmitula and, after refueling, to fly over Indian territory into Tibet where the recruits would parachute to the ground and join the insurgents. Polish anticommunist émigrés piloted the plane so that no American would be in risk of capture if anything went wrong. The mission was a success, and a second flight from East Pakistan followed in November 1957. By the end of the year, the CIA was in close contact with the Tibetan resistance and supporting their fight to free their country. Dulles was ecstatic.[53]

The operation became more regular in 1958 when the ferrying of resistance fighters was accompanied by periodic paradrops of arms, communications radios, and other equipment flown out of Pakistan; 18,000 pounds were dropped by the end of the year. More Tibetans fled their country and contacted the CIA for training. Some were trained at the CIA's Virginia facility known as the Farm, but most were sent to an abandoned prisoner of war camp in Colorado—Camp Hale—that had been used to hold Germans captured from the famous Afrika Korps in World War II. Colorado had a topography and climate somewhat similar to the Himalayas, which enhanced the training regime.

The Chinese were aware of some elements of the CIA activity: They had captured Tibetans who were knowledgeable about the operation, and some of the equipment dropped in Tibet had fallen into the PLA's hands. In July 1958 China officially protested to India, its southern neighbor, that "subversive and disruptive activities against China's Tibet region were being carried out by the United States with fugitive reactionaries from Tibet." This protest suggests that the Chinese assumed some degree of Indian complicity in the CIA operation. The Chinese apparently were not aware of the Pakistani role because they did not lodge a protest in Karachi.[54]

As the rebellion expanded, the Dalai Lama regretted his 1957 decision to return to Lhasa and live under Chinese occupation. Concluding that Zhou Enlai had lied to him and Nehru about China's peaceful intentions in Tibet, the Dalai Lama decided it was time to flee the country and set up an opposition in exile to rally international support against the Chinese. By this point three divisions of the PLA were occupying Lhasa, and clashes had broken out between the Dalai Lama's supporters and the Chinese army.[55] The royal palace even came under fire from the PLA, and some 4,000 Tibetans were killed in the attack on the city. By 1958 up to 200,000 PLA troops were deployed across Tibet, occupying the country and suppressing the insurgency.[56]

On March 17, 1959, the Dalai Lama secretly left his palace in Lhasa and fled with his entourage and guards to India. According to Harry Rositzke, the Dalai Lama "was accompanied on his flight by a CIA trained radio operator who was able to keep Washington posted on his often hazardous progress."[57] On March 27, Allen Dulles told the president that his operatives were escorting the Dalai Lama to freedom and political asylum in India. It was another coup for the DCI.

The director was also an enthusiastic proponent of new technology in the fight against communism. Dulles backed a project to develop a reconnaissance aircraft, the U-2, which could fly at the edge of space for hundreds of miles while taking photographs of the earth below. When the imagery was recovered at the end of the mission, CIA photo interpreters could look inside the USSR and PRC and see what the communist regimes were secretly building at their factories, airfields, nuclear facilities, and other hidden locations. For the first time in human history an intelligence service could look down from the sky and see inside its enemies' most top-secret facilities.

The U-2 project was led by one of Dulles's protégés, Richard Bissell who, like the director, was widely admired in Washington. Schlesinger wrote years later that he was "a man of character and remarkable intellectual gifts" whose U-2 project was the "greatest intelligence coup since the war."[58]

With the development of the U-2, which went from concept to implementation in less than eighteen months, Dulles had given Eisenhower another intelligence victory.[59] Its first operational missions took place over East Germany and Czechoslovakia in June 1956, but the top-priority targets for the U-2 were the Soviet Union and the People's Republic of China. Pakistan's location made it a critical partner for flight operations over both countries. Dulles persuaded Ayub Khan to allow the aircraft to deploy and operate from an air base near Lahore in Pakistan; from there the planes would fly across Europe to the USSR. Operation Soft Touch began on August 5, 1957, with the first flight over the USSR. On August 21, 1957 another first occurred: A U-2 mission flew from Lahore over Tibet to peer into the forbidden province of Red China.

The president personally approved every U-2 mission in advance, given the high stakes in operating piloted aircraft so deep behind the iron curtain and over China.[60] Bissell would brief him in the White House on each plane's flight route, targets for intelligence collection, and the anticipated risk from communist air defenses. Bissell by all accounts was a terrific briefer who always had done his homework.

CIA-ISI cooperation increased after Ayub Khan's "revolution," as he called his 1958 coup. In West Pakistan a more permanent facility was set up at a base near Peshawar for U-2 operations, and flights began from there in 1959. On May 13, when a U-2 landed in East Pakistan after flying across the PRC from the Philippines, it was the first time a Pakistani Air Force base outside Dacca was used for top-secret surveillance of China; another mission soon followed.[61] In addition, not just Americans but also Royal Air Force (RAF) pilots flew U-2 missions. The first RAF pilot, Wing Commander Robbie Robinson, flew a U-2 mission from Peshawar over the USSR on December 6, 1959. Other missions followed.[62]

Ayub Khan also agreed to permit the establishment of an intelligence collection facility near Peshawar in 1959. To seal the arrangements, on March 5, 1959, the United States and Pakistan signed a bilateral security agreement supplementing the CENTO and SEATO security treaties. Ayub demanded a price for his cooperation: He wanted state-of-the-art American jet fighters, allegedly to prevent overflights of his intelligence bases.[63] After some delay American military aid expanded to include delivery of the F-104 jet fighter, then the top-of-the-line American fighter plane. Pakistan had become America's crucial intelligence partner in South Asia with facilities in both wings of the country, East and West Pakistan, providing critical support to Allen Dulles's CIA. In his autobiography Khan cryptically thanks the younger Dulles for all his help he provided to Pakistan.[64]

EISENHOWER GOES TO SOUTH ASIA

In December 1959 President Eisenhower became the first American president in office to travel to South Asia. Only one American president had even traveled to South Asia before: After the end of his second term in office Ulysses S. Grant and his wife had made an historic round-the-world trip beginning in England in May 1877. After a grand tour of Europe and the Holy Land, the Grants visited Aden and Bombay. They were hosted by the governor general in Bombay and then went by train to the Taj Mahal and the holy city of Benares on the Ganges. After leaving Calcutta, Grant went to Burma, Singapore, Thailand, Hong Kong, Beijing, and Tokyo. The world travelers returned to San Francisco in December 1879. No American president before or since has traveled so long and so far abroad.[65]

Ike's three-week tour to Italy, Tunisia, Turkey, Pakistan, Afghanistan, India, Iran, Greece, France, Spain, and Morocco set its own record: No American president in office had ever visited so many countries in a single trip. Due to poor health, the president's wife Mamie did not accompany her husband. It was also the maiden voyage for Air Force One, the president's Boeing 707 that would become a symbol of American technology and power for decades after.[66]

The president arrived in Karachi on December 7, 1959 (the anniversary of the Pearl Harbor attack in 1941), where he was met by a crowd of 750,000 cheering Pakistanis. Eisenhower and Ayub Khan reviewed their cooperation on intelligence issues, which formed by now the heart of the bilateral relationship. Khan pressed the president to push India to negotiate a solution to the Kashmir dispute, an unresolved issue from the partition of the subcontinent in 1947. The Hindu maharajah of Kashmir had chosen to join India then, despite the fact that the majority of his subjects were Muslims who probably wanted to be part of Pakistan. India and Pakistan fought a war to control the province and ended up splitting it between them when a cease-fire was arranged in 1948. Nehru, whose family roots were in Kashmir, had consistently refused to negotiate a peace agreement on any basis other than the status quo, leaving Pakistan with an irredentist demand for control of the Indian-held part of the province. Eisenhower made no promises to Khan, knowing that Nehru would not budge.

Ike also took in some tourist sites in Karachi, including watching a cricket match between Pakistan and Australia. Ayub Khan hated Karachi, the capital chosen by Pakistan's founder Muhammad Jinnah in 1947, because he thought it ugly and too rowdy. He disliked its crowded streets and feared his political opponents could easily mobilize a mob there.[67] Ayub Khan therefore decided to build a new capital city to be named Islamabad close to the general headquarters of the Pakistani army in Rawalpindi and his birthplace near Abbottabad in the Punjab. But in 1959 Islamabad was a dream, not a reality, so the government seat was still in Karachi.[68]

After three days in Pakistan, Air Force One took the president for a brief visit to Afghanistan. He toured Kabul and had discussions with Prime Minister Mohammad Daoud who told the president that Pakistan, not the Soviet Union, was the greatest threat to his country. Later that day Air Force One flew to New Delhi.

Eisenhower later wrote that the whole trip across three continents was planned so he could fulfill his desire to visit India, a desire that had been sparked by his conversations with Nehru in Gettysburg three years before. The crowds in New Delhi were even larger than those in Karachi: Millions came out to cheer the American president. Ike spent four days in India, including a trip to visit the Taj Mahal in Agra.

As at Gettysburg, China was at the center of the president's dialogue with Nehru. China was still printing maps showing its claim to territory that India believed was its own. Yet much had changed since 1956. The Indian Intelligence Bureau had discovered that the Chinese had built a major highway across the Aksai Chin region, territory that India claimed was part of Kashmir and thus under Indian sovereignty. The area was uninhabited, but was critical to facilitate transportation and communication for the Chinese occupation of Tibet. The road linked Tibet to the other Chinese central Asian province of Sinkiang or Xinjiang.[69]

When the Indian press reported the construction of the strategic road, there was an outcry. Nehru demanded that China withdraw from the disputed territory. Zhou Enlai refused, suggesting in a letter instead that China take Aksai Chin in return for giving up its claim to Indian territory at the other end of the Chinese-Indian border in the North East Frontier. Nehru would not accept the exchange, and by 1959 Chinese relations with India had deteriorated. The 1965 CIA postmortem concluded that the Tibet uprising had gravely compromised Nehru's ability to keep Indian relations with China friendly. The crisis between the two countries was now in the open, with the Indian press pushing Nehru not to give Mao any concessions.[70]

In November 1959 Zhou had invited Nehru to a summit meeting in Beijing to defuse tensions over the border issue. In advance of the meeting, the Chinese had again suggested a de facto trade: China would give up its claims to northeast India, accepting the McMahon Line, and in turn India would accept Chinese control of Aksai Chin. The Indian press summarized the deal as China would take what it had already stolen and promise not to steal more. Nehru did not accept the invitation and refused to negotiate further.[71]

The Dalai Lama's presence in India was another major point of friction between India and China. Nehru had granted the monarch political asylum in March 1959 when he fled the PLA. The Dalai Lama was given a home in Dharamsala, a hill station town built by the British, where he received visitors, including from the media, and decried the Chinese occupation of his homeland. Nehru sought to navigate a difficult balance—providing humanitarian help to the Tibetan leader without alienating China—by allowing him to set up an informal government in exile in India. However, China saw the Dalai Lama as a mortal enemy trying to subvert its control of Tibet.

Nehru undoubtedly had some knowledge of the CIA's connections with the Tibetans and the Dalai Lama, but he was probably unaware of the Pakistani role in the covert operation in Tibet.[72] The Dalai Lama asked the U.S. Embassy in New Delhi to arrange a meeting with Eisenhower while he was in India, but Nehru refused to allow it. He told U.S. ambassador Ellsworth Bunker that an American-Tibetan summit meeting would antagonize China too much and that he still hoped to find an accommodation with Mao.[73]

In contrast with Nehru, IB director B. N. Mullik saw China as India's main threat, along with Pakistan. Starting from scratch with no intelligence capability in 1948, India had greatly increased its intelligence infrastructure along the northern border in response to the Chinese occupation of Tibet. The first IB post on the northern border was set up in 1950; by 1952 thirty IB posts were collecting information along the disputed frontier, and by 1960 the number of posts had more than doubled to sixty-nine. By 1962 the IB had seventy-seven such posts along the border manned by almost 1,600 personnel. Many were in remote areas difficult to reach by land and so required support from the Indian Air Force. These patrols often clashed with PLA forces. This improved intelligence collection provided Nehru an increasingly bleak picture of Chinese intentions and capabilities.[74] It also gave him a good picture of what the Dalai Lama was doing in his home in exile in India.

In their final dinner with just the two of them, Ike and Nehru discussed China, with Eisenhower mostly listening to Nehru's description of the border and Tibet issues. Nehru explained his constraints and the limits of his support for the Tibetans. The earlier American outrage about Indian neutrality was now gone (John Foster Dulles had also passed away) and was replaced by a "cordial sympathy, verging at times on a suitor's ardor" for India.[75] Nehru urged Eisenhower to use American influence with Pakistan to get Ayub Khan to agree to a "no war" pledge with India, in which the two countries would pledge publicly to resolve all their differences peacefully and to commit to nonbelligerency. Ike promised to use his influence and to have his ambassador raise the idea with the field marshal, but Ayub Khan refused to make that pledge.[76]

Yet the president's trip was a great personal success for Eisenhower. He was greeted as a hero both in Pakistan and India. "I like Ike," his campaign motto, seemed to be true in South Asia as much as it was true back home.

Meanwhile, as the backdrop to Ike's visit, the CIA's covert war in Tibet was intensifying. After the Dalai Lama's defection to India, Allen Dulles had asked for presidential authorization to step up aid to the insurgents, and on April 1, 1959, Ike gave the go-ahead. More Tibetan recruits were flown from Kurmitola for training and then dropped by parachute back into Tibet.[77] To help facilitate the missions and collect intelligence on Chinese forces, Ike also authorized U-2 flights over Tibet to provide aerial imagery of the battlefield.[78] As mentioned earlier, two U-2 missions flew across China from the Philippines to the Kurmitola airstrip in mid-May 1959, in flights covering more than 4,000 miles. Three more U-2 missions crossed Tibet in September 1959.[79]

THE U-2 CRISIS

Then disaster struck Dulles's prized project. Pakistan's crucial role in American spy missions was exposed to the entire world on May 1, 1960, when the Soviets shot down Operation Grand Slam, a U-2 aircraft flying from the Peshawar base over Soviet Union airspace to an airfield in northern Norway, in the town of Bodo. The plane's pilot, Francis Gary Powers, survived the missile strike that destroyed the aircraft, parachuted safely, and was taken prisoner by the Soviets.[80]

Eisenhower had agonized over the decision to approve Grand Slam, the most ambitious U-2 mission yet flown and the first to ever completely cross the USSR. He knew the Soviet air defenses were improving and also how catastrophic a shootdown of a CIA U-2 plane could be for U.S.-Soviet relations. However, Ike planned to attend a four-power summit in Paris beginning on May 16, 1960, that he hoped would mark a period of détente between the West and the USSR and result in a cooling of the temperature of the cold war and perhaps modest cooperation between the United States, France, Britain, and the Soviet Union on nuclear arms control and the status of Berlin. In advance of the summit, Eisenhower needed intelligence on the USSR's deployment of intercontinental ballistic missiles (ICBMs), then in its inception. Only the U-2 could accurately report how many ICBMs the USSR was deploying.[81]

Allen Dulles and Richard Bissell pressed Ike to approve Grand Slam. They also told the president that the odds of a pilot surviving a missile strike on a U-2 were "one in a million." And even if the pilot did survive the crash, he had a poison pin available to commit suicide. Although the CIA did not order the pilots to use the pin if shot down, the agency clearly presented it as an option.[82] So Eisenhower reluctantly gave the go-ahead to Grand Slam.

When the Soviets initially announced they had shot down an American plane deep inside Russia, they did not say they had captured the pilot. In response, the United States sought to minimize the affair and claimed that a weather plane had gone off course accidentally. Then Soviet leader Nikita Khrushchev announced triumphantly that the U.S. government was lying, that the pilot had been captured along with his poison pin. Powers also had seven gold women's rings with him for use in buying help from those who found him if he did survive a crash. Khrushchev mocked the rings, suggesting "perhaps he was supposed to have flown still higher, to Mars and seduced Martian ladies."[83] Eisenhower was at his Gettysburg farm when Khrushchev delivered his news to the world press. Ike refused to apologize for the overflights, although he ordered Dulles to stop U-2 missions over Russia because they were too dangerous.

The Paris summit, held just days after, was a disaster. Khrushchev demanded an apology for the U-2 mission and then stormed out of the first session of the talks, leaving to return to Moscow by way of East Berlin. Any hope of détente in the final year of the Eisenhower presidency was gone. U-2 planes would still fly over China and many other countries, but their days of collecting intelligence over Russia were over.

Eisenhower did not fire Dulles or Bissell, nor did he curb the CIA's covert operations around the world. The president had known the risks of each U-2 flight and had approved the decision to fly Grand Slam. He still welcomed the intelligence the CIA provided. The Tibet project continued with Pakistan's help. Despite the embarrassment of the discovery that he was hosting a U-2 airbase, Ayub Khan and the ISI continued to work closely with the Americans.

However, Dulles and Bissell increasingly focused on two new operations. In the Congo, a recently independent Belgian colony, the CIA was involved in an operation to prevent a leftist politician named Patrice Lumumba from taking power. Lumumba was suspected of being pro-Soviet and was to die shortly at the hands of his Congolese enemies and Belgian mercenaries.[84]

Much closer to home, Fidel Castro had taken power in Cuba. Like Lumumba he was suspected of leaning toward Moscow and being pro-communist. Dulles, Bissell, and Eisenhower set in motion a plot to overthrow Castro. That plan would be the first major challenge to Ike's successor, John F. Kennedy.

CHAPTER TWO

GALBRAITH AND INDIA, 1961

Harvard University played a key role in John F. Kennedy's life and presidency. He graduated from Harvard College, America's oldest institution of higher education founded in 1636. His senior thesis at Harvard was published in 1941 as *While England Slept*, an indictment of England's appeasement of Hitler. His father Joseph P. Kennedy played a key role in its publication, which was deeply ironic because he had been a strong supporter of appeasement while serving as U.S. ambassador to the United Kingdom from 1938 to 1940. JFK's father and brothers were also Harvard graduates.

Many of the top members of Kennedy's national security team, including his national security adviser McGeorge Bundy, also had connections to Harvard. Although a graduate of Yale, Bundy had become a professor of government at Harvard despite lacking a doctorate. Then at the age of thirty-four, Bundy became the youngest ever dean of the Faculty of Arts and Sciences at Harvard and embarked on a sweeping program of reform in the university. Secretary of Defense Robert McNamara had been the youngest ever professor at Harvard Business School. Kennedy's biographer and aide Arthur Schlesinger was a professor of history at Harvard. The

South Asia specialist at the National Security Council, Robert Komer, was another Harvard graduate who had joined the CIA in 1947 as an analyst. There were so many Harvard men in Kennedy's administration that he joked he needed a Harvard quota to limit their number.

Most importantly for this story, John Kenneth Galbraith, Kennedy's choice for ambassador to India and the central American player in the 1962 Sino-Indian crisis, came into government service from Harvard. Born in Ontario, Canada, on October 15, 1908, Galbraith spent a half-century at Harvard as a professor of economics. He graduated from Ontario Agricultural College with a major in animal husbandry before earning his Ph.D. from the University of California, Berkeley in 1934. Then he received a untenured position at Harvard teaching economics, becoming an American citizen in 1937; he later served during World War II in the Office of Price Administration. He joined the Harvard faculty permanently in 1949 and moved to Cambridge, Massachusetts.[1]

Ken, as he preferred to be called, was a tall man, six foot eight inches, with strong opinions and a brilliant mind. By the late 1950s he had established himself as one of the leading economists in the world and had written a series of much-read books. Written to appeal to the general reader as well as economists, Galbraith's books, including *The Great Crash, 1929* and *The Affluent Society*, were liberal in political orientation, which helped him secure his position as adviser to the Democratic Party and to Kennedy.

Galbraith had a high opinion both of his work and himself, which often grated on those around him, although he could make fun of himself. He was also scathingly critical of others. After Kennedy appointed him ambassador to India, the *New York Times* published an otherwise very favorable profile of him that called him arrogant. When Ken complained to Kennedy about the *Times* characterizing him that way, the president responded, "Why not? Everybody else does."[2]

Kennedy had gotten to know Ken more than twenty years earlier; when he and his older brother Joseph attended Harvard College in the late 1930s, they lived in Winthrop House, where Galbraith was one of the tutors. After the war Galbraith became increasingly active in Democratic Party politics just as Kennedy was starting his political career. After Kennedy decided to run for president he began seeking Galbraith's advice on many foreign and domestic issues. They dined together frequently in Cambridge, and Kennedy recalled later that Galbraith always ordered lobster stew. Galbraith was a senior adviser in the 1960 campaign and one of JFK's floor managers at the Democratic National Convention in Los Angeles responsible for the West Coast states.[3]

Galbraith and his wife Kitty first visited India in February 1956, after Ken delivered several lectures at the American University of Beirut on the way. The purpose of this trip, which lasted several months, was for Galbraith to study Indian economics in Calcutta. Once the capital of the British Empire in India, by the 1950s Calcutta was an enormous but run-down city with huge slums characterized by abject poverty. Both Ken and Kitty found India fascinating. They visited New Delhi, Bombay, Benares, Darjeeling, and Kashmir and began collecting Mughal-era miniatures. During his visit Galbraith met with Prime Minister Nehru to discuss economic theory.

Before leaving India the Galbraiths also had lunch with the U.S. ambassador, John Sherman Cooper, at the embassy in New Delhi. Afterward Galbraith told his wife, "When the Democrats get back in power, I think I will get myself made ambassador to India."[4] Three years later in May 1959 the couple returned to India for another visit, also stopping in Sri Lanka. Again Galbraith met with Nehru. After returning to Cambridge by way of Soviet Central Asia and Moscow, Galbraith gave Kennedy a thorough briefing on his trip.[5]

Kennedy only visited India once in his life. After being lauded as a war hero fighting the Japanese in the south Pacific, Kennedy in 1946 was elected to Congress from the eleventh congressional district that included Cambridge and the North End of Boston. Five years later, in the midst of the Korean War he embarked on a fact-finding trip to Asia, along with his younger brother Robert, known popularly as Bobby.[6] Israel, French Indochina, Japan, and India were among the stops.

When Kennedy was visiting India, the U.S. embassy in New Delhi convinced Prime Minister Nehru to give him an audience. As Jackie Kennedy later recalled, the embassy staff told Kennedy that "whenever Nehru gets bored with you, he taps his fingertips together and looks up at the ceiling." After only ten minutes with Kennedy, she said, "Nehru started to look up at the ceiling" and began tapping his fingertips. It was in inauspicious start to their relationship.[7] According to another account, Nehru was much more interested in Pat Kennedy, JFK's attractive twenty-seven-year-old sister, than in either Jack or Bobby.[8]

Later in the trip Kennedy became very ill and had to be hospitalized in Okinawa where he nearly died. The Kennedy family credited his brother Bobby with saving his life by recognizing quickly how dangerous the situation was and rushing him to the hospital. In fact JFK was a very ill man his whole life, suffering from Addison's disease (a potentially fatal malfunctioning of the adrenal gland), chronic back pain that resulted in several major unsuccessful surgeries, spastic colitis that triggered diarrhea, prostatitis, urethritis, and allergies. Kennedy was injured severely in World War II when his small torpedo boat, the PT-109, was rammed and sunk by a Japanese destroyer in 1942. He took many prescription medications every day, wore a back brace, and was often in considerable pain. He tried to ease the pain by frequent baths and swims. But he kept his health problems a carefully guarded secret from everyone but his closest family members. During the 1960 campaign there were two mysterious break-ins at his doctors' offices that may have been efforts by the Nixon campaign team to uncover his medical records.[9]

The 1951 trip forged a very tight bond between JFK and Bobby for the first time in their lives. It also helped Kennedy establish his foreign policy credentials, and the next year he won the U.S. Senate seat from Massachusetts. On September 12, 1953, he married Jacqueline Lee Bouvier in Newport, Rhode Island. Three years later he decided to run for vice president, but lost the nomination at the 1956 Democratic Party convention; the very next year he resolved to run for president in 1960. His father's wealth, his own war record, his years on Capitol Hill, and his photogenic young family made him a very attractive candidate to a nation grown tired of the elderly Eisenhower. Only his Catholic religion seemed to hold him back, for no Catholic had ever been elected president.

THE CAMPAIGN

To establish his credentials as a statesman and world leader Kennedy made foreign policy a major part of his 1960 campaign for the presidency. Although John Foster Dulles had died in 1959, his moralistic black-and-white approach to foreign policy was very much part of Kennedy's opponent Richard Nixon's record as vice president. Indeed, Nixon's foreign policy epitomized the Eisenhower-Dulles approach to South Asia. An outspoken supporter of Pakistan and a sharp critic of Nehru and India, Nixon was a firm believer in the notion that neutrality and nonalignment in the cold war were immoral. The vice president was an impassioned supporter of Ayub Khan and for providing more military and economic assistance to Pakistan, especially after Ayub Khan's 1958 coup. After a visit to South Asia as vice president, Nixon said that Pakistan "is a country I would do anything for. They have less complexes than the Indians."[10]

Kennedy proposed a different approach to the cold war, one that sought to build friends and partners among the newly independent nations in Asia and Africa that were resisting engaging in treaty alliances, especially with their former colonial masters. Kennedy felt that the Nixon approach was out of step with the changes sweeping the world, particularly the independence granted to countries newly freed from European imperialism. Those countries needed to be courted, not alienated by America. Kennedy was a strong cold warrior, but he wanted to fight a smarter cold war that recognized the age of European empires was at an end. He first made public his argument in the case of Algeria.

On July 3, 1957, the day before America's own Independence Day celebrations, Kennedy gave a speech in the U.S. Senate introducing a resolution calling for the United States to support independence for the French colony of Algeria. The Algerians had begun an armed rebellion against France several years before; a million Algerians would die before their eight-year war for independence ended. When their rebellion began, the Eisenhower administration termed it a purely internal French affair and refused to call for Algerian independence. Since World War II, successive governments in Paris had stated that Algeria was an integral part of France, not a foreign colony, although Algerians had no voice in the French political process. France had joined the North Atlantic Treaty Organization in 1949 with a specific guarantee that Algeria, alone among European colonies in Africa and Asia, would be regarded as a part of France and thus an integral part of NATO.

In his Senate speech titled "Imperialism—The Enemy of Freedom," Kennedy sharply criticized the Eisenhower administration, especially Nixon and Dulles, for trying to prop up a French colonial empire that was visibly failing, despite the deployment of 400,000 French troops to fight the rebels. He called Algeria the most difficult challenge facing American foreign policy in 1957 and one "we have refused to even recognize is our problem at all." The Soviets and Chinese were exploiting the war to gain favor with nationalists across Asia and Africa, whereas "the record of the United States in this case is a retreat from the principles of independence and anticolonialism" for which America had stood since 1776.

Kennedy used the Algerian example as a basis for his broader message advocating support for nationalist governments in Asia, Africa, and Latin America instead of "abandoning them to Soviet agents." The senator noted that France was not alone, that American allies such as Belgium and Portugal were also still trying to hold onto colonies despite their demands for freedom. Kennedy even noted that nationalist and neutral India, which "often assumed to be spokesman for nationalism for nationalism's sake," had a more reasonable and responsible approach to Algeria than did the United States.

The July 1957 Algeria speech defined Kennedy as a critic of Eisenhower and Dulles who was not soft on communism or a defeatist, but rather was a progressive who realized that the world was changing and America needed to change with it. He was suggesting a nuanced cold war strategy to undermine "Soviet imperialism." He did not want to betray our "oldest and first ally," France, but to help it end a war that was draining its manpower, resources, and spirit.[11] This speech was a breakthrough moment for Kennedy, as one scholar noted: "No speech on foreign affairs by Senator Kennedy attracted more attention at home or abroad, and under pressure United States official policy on Algeria began to shift."[12]

In May 1959 Kennedy gave another major foreign policy speech, this time on India and China. Galbraith had helped draft it before leaving on his second visit to India. Kennedy began by saying that "no struggle in the world today deserves more of our time and attention than that which now grips the attention of all Asia. That is the struggle between India and China for leadership of the East, for the respect of all Asia, for the opportunity to demonstrate which way of life is the better."[13]

The senator painted a picture of a "subtle" but "very real battle" between a democratic India that supports "human dignity and individual freedom" against "Red China which represents ruthless denial of human rights, with considerable aid from the USSR." Thanks to lots of Soviet help, Kennedy argued, China was developing three times as quickly as India. In the race to prove which system of government worked best in the newly independent states, Kennedy said that Red China was winning, and this victory would have global consequences. He drew a comparison to 1949 when the United States was supporting the rebuilding of Western Europe with the Marshall Plan and also thereby countering the influence of Soviet Russia, saying that in 1959 "we must take measure of a new power— China, whose mounting strength is the cardinal political development of this area."

To help India win its race with Red China, Kennedy proposed that the NATO allies and Japan put together a comprehensive package of loans to strengthen the Indian economy and work to secure an annual foreign direct investment in India of $1 billion per year. These loans and investment would boost Indian economic growth, enabling it to outmatch population growth, and set the country on a path to sustainable long-term prosperity. It was the duty of the "free world" to help India outshine "Red China."

Kennedy's rhetoric was extraordinary. He was placing India at the center of the cold war at a time when many Americans had long regarded it as, if not an enemy, an unwitting accomplice of communism. He did exaggerate the amount of help that the USSR was giving China; in fact the alliance between the two was on the verge of breaking down and most Russian advisers would soon leave China. But his analysis of China's economic gains and its outperforming India was correct.

At the start of his speech JFK did mention "the unhappy tide of events in Tibet" "where the world is being shown once again that man's eternal desire to be free can never be suppressed." However, he made no recommendations about how the United States should respond to the Chinese occupation of Tibet. He did not refer at all to Pakistan, an omission the Pakistani government was sure to notice. The contrast between the ardently pro-Pakistan Eisenhower, Dulles, and Nixon, on the one hand, and JFK on the other, wooing India, was striking.

In the 1960 presidential election Kennedy won a very narrow victory: Only 112,827 votes of 69,000,000 cast separated Kennedy from Nixon, a winning margin of 0.17 percent. Because the vote was so close Kennedy could not claim a clear mandate, and he needed to be much more sensitive to Republican concerns from the start of his administration than if he had won with a clear majority.

BAY OF PIGS

Although Allen Dulles was a Republican, JFK asked him to stay on as director of the CIA after the election to show his willingness to include Republicans in his foreign policy team.[14] It was one of Kennedy's first appointments. Just three weeks after the inauguration Dulles hosted a dinner for a dozen of the president's top advisers and a dozen CIA senior officers at a private club in Washington so they could all get to know each other informally. At the dinner, the head of operations at the CIA, Richard Bissell, introduced himself as "I'm your man-eating shark."[15]

Kennedy soon discovered that the CIA was much less bureaucratic and top heavy in its management than the more established parts of the national security bureaucracy, such as the State Department and the Department of Defense. He told Bundy, "If I need some material fast or an idea fast, CIA is the place I have to go."[16] The CIA indeed had a plan for Kennedy.

Soon after Kennedy took office, Dulles and Bissell briefed him and his top advisers on the various covert action operations the CIA was running around the world, including the Tibet project. At the top of the list was a project to overthrow Fidel Castro in Cuba. Just ninety miles from Florida, Cuba had been an American protectorate from 1898 to 1958. The United States had seized the island from Spain in the Spanish-American War and had controlled it since through a series of dictators, with occasional military interventions by the U.S. Marines. In the 1903 Cuban-American Treaty, a major harbor, Guantanamo Bay, was ceded to the U.S. Navy in perpetuity.

The ascension to power of Fidel Castro threatened U.S. control. Although not a communist himself when he took power, Castro was determined to free the island from American domination. His brother Raul was a communist, and many of Fidel's top aides were communists, who naturally looked to the Soviet Union for assistance. Khrushchev was attracted to Fidel as a revolutionary and to Cuba as an outpost for communism in America's backyard. Soviet arms began to be shipped to Cuba in 1960 in increasing amounts.

In response Eisenhower instructed Dulles to come up with a plan to overthrow Castro. The plan that Kennedy inherited was anything but covert. The CIA had recruited 1,400 Cuban dissidents in exile in Guatemala to build a small army, navy, and air force. The plan was for the exiles to invade Cuba after airstrikes destroyed Castro's air force. In support of the Cuban brigade the CIA had more than 500 officers and staff working on the plan, with 160 in Miami alone. To resist the invasion, Castro had an army and militia with 230,000 men who were increasingly armed with Soviet weapons.

By the time of Kennedy's inauguration in January 1961 the press had already reported the existence of the Cuban exile force in Guatemala and the CIA's role in recruiting, training, and arming its members.[17] The president was thus boxed in. If Kennedy abandoned the operation and dismissed the exiles, he would be labeled soft on communism and unwilling to defend the Western Hemisphere from Soviet aggression. Kennedy had little choice but to accept the plan he was offered.

The CIA plan was not a small operation to infiltrate Cuba and instigate an insurrection against Castro: Instead it was an invasion, which Arthur Schlesinger, Kennedy's adviser, likened to the invasion of Italy at Anzio in 1943. Bissell was the guiding force behind the plan; Schlesinger later recalled, "All of us—Kennedy and Bundy and the rest were hypnotized by Dick Bissell to a degree, and assumed that he knew what he was doing." Kennedy asked the Joint Chiefs of Staff (JCS) to review the plan, and they concurred with the CIA's recommendation.[18] Both the intelligence experts and the military promised the new president that the planned invasion would topple Castro.

However, Kennedy questioned elements of the plan and wanted to reduce American involvement, so that it would be seen as a Cuban, not a CIA, operation. He did not want a prolonged U.S. air attack before the invasion, which would give away its American connection too quickly. These changes reduced the odds of success, but Bissell insisted the plan would work despite the reduction in air support. The CIA and the JCS assumed that if the exile brigade got into trouble Kennedy would send in U.S. forces to salvage the operation and invade Cuba.

But Kennedy made clear from his first briefing on the plan that he would not send in the Marines and the Navy if things went wrong. Schlesinger said later that "few believed it—the CIA did not believe it—when Kennedy said that whatever happens, there will be no American military involvement. He meant it."[19] Thus there was a complete policy disconnect between the White House and the CIA on the plan: Kennedy thought he was supporting an operation that was plausibly deniable if it went wrong, whereas Dulles was convinced his plan would be backed up by the U.S. military if anything went amiss. This fundamental difference between the policymaker and the covert operator doomed the mission.

Brigade 2506 landed on the beach at the Bay of Pigs shortly after midnight on April 17, 1961. Almost immediately the invasion began to go wrong. The limited airstrikes failed to destroy the Cuban air force, which, along with the Cuban army, attacked the landing beach. The brigade was completely destroyed: 124 Cubans were killed and 1,189 became Castro's prisoners.[20] Years later it was revealed that four American pilots from the Alabama National Guard working for the CIA died in the fighting as well; despite Kennedy's orders to keep Americans out of the fight, the CIA had dispatched them at the last minute to try to reverse the tide of the battle.[21]

Within forty-eight hours Kennedy faced a disaster. The president convened his top national security aides after midnight on April 19 after attending a fancy reception for Congress held in the White House earlier that evening. Dressed in white-tie formal attire, Kennedy was informed by Bissell that the Cuban exiles were being defeated and needed immediate help from the U.S. military. The Navy proposed to intervene decisively to turn the tide against Castro. The discussion went on until almost three in the morning, but JFK refused to send in American combat forces. Kennedy had been in office less than a hundred days. He was faced with a public relations disaster, a failed covert operation, and a communist victory. His wife Jackie found him weeping the morning after the midnight meeting; he told her he had sent the Cubans off "with all their hopes high (only) to be shot down like dogs."[22] He took complete responsibility for the disaster in a press conference a few days later. He promised himself never to trust either the CIA's or Joint Chiefs' advice again. He told Ted Sorenson, "All my life I've known better than to depend on experts. How could I have been so stupid to let them go ahead?"[23] Kennedy briefly considered replacing Dulles immediately with his brother Robert as the head of the CIA and told Schlesinger that keeping Dulles as DCI had been a "mistake."[24] Dulles resigned in November 1961.

The agency's own postmortem on the operation was devastating. It criticized the CIA for not accurately assessing Castro's level of vulnerability and how much popular support he enjoyed. The Cuban Task Force planning the operation had spent too much time listening to exiles in Miami and not using on-the-ground intelligence in Cuba. Written by CIA Inspector General Lyman Kirkpatrick, the postmortem was so critical that Dulles ordered it suppressed.[25]

For Kennedy the Bay of Pigs was a crucial learning experience. He learned not to rely on expert advice from the military or the intelligence community, but instead on his own instincts and his own handpicked advisers. He learned he had to take charge and accept the responsibility for mistakes, as he did in assuming sole responsibility for the defeat in a press conference held shortly after the failed invasion. The Bay of Pigs was a serious setback, but Kennedy learned much from the experience.

As mentioned earlier, Kennedy did not fire Dulles immediately, but continued to rely on Dulles's expertise for dealing with the Tibet operation, among other activities. Despite the tragedy and disaster at the Bay of Pigs, the Kennedy White House continued to support CIA covert operations around the world to fight communist governments. Just three months after the Cuban fiasco, Dulles was with Kennedy at Mount Vernon, entertaining General Ayub at the candlelit dinner described in the Prologue.

TIBET OPERATIONS

One visible manifestation of Kennedy's continued reliance on the CIA was found inside the West Wing of the White House itself. The president had been frustrated during the Cuban invasion by his inadequate access to timely top-secret information from his own government. During World War II, Franklin Roosevelt had set up a "Map Room" inside the mansion, loosely modeled on Winston Churchill's Cabinet Rooms in London, to follow the course of the war, but it had been dismantled after 1945. After the Bay of Pigs Kennedy, using the Map Room as a model, had a situation room built in the basement of the West Wing manned by CIA watch officers round the clock to monitor all the message traffic, press reports, and intelligence flowing into the U.S. government from around the world; this White House Situation Room (WHSR) had formerly been a bowling alley.[26] The president also moved the office of his national security adviser, McGeorge Bundy, from the Old Executive Office Building next door to the White House to the first floor of the mansion's West Wing, just upstairs from the WHSR, so that Bundy would be close at hand to both it and the Oval Office.[27]

The WHSR became the venue for CIA briefings for its future covert operations. The planning of the Bay of Pigs operation had dominated the operational activity of the agency in the early weeks of the Kennedy administration. But within two months the administration was brought up to date on conflict situations around the world.

The situation along the Sino-Indian border had changed significantly in the two years since the Tibetan uprising, which began on March 10, 1959, in Lhasa. The CIA had prepared a National Intelligence Estimate (NIE) in 1960 titled "Sino-Indian Relations" that noted that the "outbreak of the Tibetan revolt in early 1959 caused China to take rapid and ruthless action to put it down. Peiping was suspicious that the revolt was supported by India, and gave little thought to Indian sensibilities." The NIE claimed that it was still possible for China and India to settle their border dispute, but it was very unlikely that they would return to the warm relations of the early 1950s. The CIA also projected that China would "maintain—and probably increase—its military superiority over India."[28]

The NIE argued that the border dispute had "resulted in a sharp upsurge of anti-Chinese sentiment in India," and the "failure of Nehru's policy of befriending Communist China caused a noticeable decline in his prestige." It claimed that because of this policy Nehru would be "unlikely again to enjoy the virtually unquestioned power to direct India's foreign policy" that he had in the 1950s.[29] The dispute had "tended to create among Indian leaders a more sympathetic view of US opposition to Communist China," although "Nehru has no intention of altering India's basic policy of nonalignment." It also suggested that India was likely to look to the Soviet Union for help with China; Moscow had taken a neutral posture toward the border quarrel, even though the NIE noted that "the USSR has been perturbed by the crudeness, if not the substance of China's actions."[30]

On the basis of this NIE, Dulles had planned to brief the president-elect on the Tibet covert action project as early as November 18, 1960, very soon after the election, but the meeting was completely dominated by Cuba. Not until mid-February 1961 was the president briefed about the Tibet air drops and the covert use of Pakistani territory to support the Tibetan resistance. On Valentine's Day, February 14, 1961, at a briefing with the president's interagency "Special Group" made up of senior representatives of the CIA, State, Defense, and the National Security Council that oversaw covert action, Kennedy approved continuation of the mission.[31]

There is no record of that Valentine's Day CIA briefing. But we can surmise the outline of it from the memoirs of one of the CIA officers involved in the Tibet project, John Kenneth Knaus, who wrote a 1999 book, *Orphans of the Cold War*, about the operation. According to Knaus, by 1961 the CIA had conducted more than thirty air drops to the Tibetan rebels and delivered more than 250 tons of "equipment, arms, ammunition, radios, medical supplies and other military gear from 1957 to 1961." After the initial B-17 missions, the CIA had used C-118 aircraft, but by 1961 it was using larger C-130 planes.[32]

But the Tibet operation was in trouble by then. The Chinese forces had eliminated most of the teams the CIA had parachuted into Tibet: only twelve of forty-nine trained operatives dropped into Tibet survived. Dulles informed the outgoing Eisenhower team of advisers that "the resistance boys had been badly trapped,"[33] and the PLA was winning the war against the rebellion. A new team had not been parachuted in since before the 1960 U.S. presidential election because the CIA leadership was waiting to see if Ike's successor wanted to continue the program. As soon as Kennedy's Special Group authorized continuation of the missions, the CIA sent a new team of Tibetans from the Colorado training camp into Tibet in March 1961. Within a few weeks its members were killed by Chinese communist troops.[34]

During the rest of 1961, the focal point of the operation therefore changed from dropping resistance fighters and equipment inside Tibet to supporting a Tibetan resistance enclave inside Nepal near its border with China. Mustang, as this small territorial enclave was known, occupies a few hundred square miles that juts into Tibet. Even by the standards of Tibet and Nepal, Mustang is a remote area isolated by mountains and canyons. In 1960 the king of Nepal exercised virtually no authority over the area; instead a local Buddhist monarch of Tibetan origin ruled Mustang.

By late 1960, several hundred Tibetan resistance fighters had flocked to Mustang to escape the Chinese forces in their homeland. The CIA wanted the Kennedy administration to approve continued air drops not only of fighters inside Tibet but also of supplies to those currently in the Mustang enclave, with whom it already had connections.[35]

In making this request, the CIA did not claim that the resistance force would be able to defeat the PLA; even from the start of the uprising in 1959 it was obvious that the Tibetan resistance was no match for the PLA in numbers, training, or weapons. But the Tibetans intended to fight with or without outside support, and Dulles believed it was in America's interest to help them, even if they were only a nuisance to China. Kennedy's decision to continue the operation in February 1961 shows that he agreed with Dulles. The program also enjoyed strong bipartisan backing in Congress, including from influential Democratic senators such as Hubert Humphrey and William Fulbright.[36]

The CIA also knew the limits of its capabilities in Tibet. As the head of the CIA's Tibet Task Force recalled, "In the fifties neither the CIA nor the State or Defense Department had any depth of knowledge about the Tibetan people or the topography of their country. Almost none of the officers involved in these operations had ever been to Tibet." Even communicating with the Tibetans who were being trained in Colorado was challenging because they spoke no English and all communication was through translators. There was a certain amount of "operational hubris in an exciting effort to mount and sustain paramilitary operations that stretched from the reflecting pool in Washington, to the Colorado Rockies, Okinawa and airfields in Southeast Asia, all the way to the Roof of the World to support Tibetans in their fight for freedom."[37]

In March 1961 Galbraith entered the picture. Harvard had granted him a two-year leave from teaching, but he would lose his tenured position if he stayed away from the university longer. Kennedy nominated Ken to be ambassador to India in February and the Senate confirmed his nomination in March 1961. Before leaving for New Delhi Galbraith visited the CIA headquarters on March 29, 1961, for a comprehensive briefing on CIA operations in India and South Asia. Richard Bissell led the briefing, joined by James Critchfield, chief of the Near East (NE) Division, and Desmond FitzGerald, Far East (FE) Division chief, both of the Directorate of Plans.[38] Both men were veterans of World War II: Critchfield had been a tank commander with General Patton's Third Army in France, and FitzGerald had fought in Burma against the Japanese. FitzGerald in particular was very enthusiastic about recruiting clandestine armies in Asia to fight communism and had an almost romantic attachment to his "mountain warriors."[39]

The briefing did not go well. Bissell briefed Galbraith on how the CIA was training Tibetans in Colorado, parachuting them into Tibet from the air base in East Pakistan, and trying to assist the Tibetan insurgency with air drops of arms and equipment. The CIA wanted to increase its ability to help the Tibetans by expanding the operation into India's Himalayan neighbor Nepal. He thus laid out a new plan to use Mustang, the remote part of Nepal, to provide more proximate support to the rebels.

Galbraith thought the whole Tibet covert operation was too dangerous, recklessly provoking the Chinese while having little chance of thwarting their takeover of Tibet. Worse, he feared that the operation would damage American relations with India. Overflying Indian territory without New Delhi's permission while working closely with Pakistan to do so seemed like a recipe for disaster. Using Nepal to provide support for the rebels was even more dangerous. Ken stormed about a foolish mission, saying, "This sounds like the Rover Boys at loose ends."[40] He called the planned use of Mustang a "particularly insane enterprise" with "planes dropping weapons, ammunition and other supplies for dissident and deeply unhygienic tribesmen who now relieve their boredom with raids back into the territory from which they had been extruded" by the Chinese army.[41] Bissell was "flabbergasted" by Ken's views: He was not used to being told he was wrong.[42]

In Galbraith's private diary he presented his reaction as more restrained. He wrote that he had a briefing on March 29 "by the CIA on various spooky activities, some of which I do not like. I shall stop them."[43] In his memoirs, which were published twenty years later, he was more candid. While expressing much admiration for Bissell ("a man of quietly courteous manner with a deeply intelligent face who involved himself in enterprises far below his worth"), he wrote that the Tibet enterprise "both appalled and depressed me." Galbraith did succeed in having covert programs engaging in propaganda activities against the Indian Communist Party canceled by appealing to Kennedy in May 1961. In his memoir he expressed great pride in ending these propaganda operations, which he characterized as "perhaps my single most useful service that spring."[44] But he was unsuccessful in having the Tibet operation shelved.

Even within the CIA, not everyone was convinced about the wisdom of the Tibet operations. The FE Division, which was China focused, was very enthusiastic. After all the operation was taking the cold war into China by supporting the Tibetans. The chief of the FE Division in the late 1950s and early 1960s, Desmond Fitz-Gerald, saw it as "his program."[45] Combined with the U-2 missions from Pakistan, the operation was providing intelligence on the

People's Republic of China's most remote areas near Tibet and the neighboring Xinjiang province.

The NE Division was less enthusiastic and much more worried about the Tibetan operation's effect on U.S.-India relations, which it knew was a high priority for the Kennedy administration. One NE official, Harry Rositzke, another OSS veteran who had graduated from Harvard, was particularly critical. As he saw it, the "Far East Division got all the kudos but the Near East Division risked the potential embarrassment."[46] He and Galbraith became allies in their efforts to stop the Tibetan program. Galbraith wrote fondly of Rositzke in his memoirs.

Richard Helms, one of Bissell's deputies, had discussed the Tibetan operation in vague terms with Nehru's Intelligence Bureau chief B. N. Mullik in Hawaii earlier in 1960. Exactly how much Mullik was told is unclear; likely the Pakistan role was not emphasized. However, he had access to other sources of information about the CIA's involvement: Mullik was in contact with many of the Tibetan resistance leaders, and the IB had sources in the Tibetan community in India. Clearly he did understand that the CIA was covertly helping the Tibetans and overflying Indian airspace to do so. He had a very close relationship with Nehru, whom he undoubtedly kept informed about the CIA's operation.[47] As the leading anti-China hawk in Nehru's inner circle, Mullik did not object to the project,[48] though he did warn the Americans that if one of the CIA's covert aircraft crashed in Indian territory it would be a very damaging blow to U.S.-India relations.

Over Galbraith's objections and despite the Bay of Pigs debacle, the Kennedy administration decided to side with Allen Dulles and go forward with the Tibet covert operations.[49] The CIA began planning a large air drop of 29,000 pounds of equipment—enough arms and ammunition for 400 rebels—to the new Tibetan base in Nepal at Mustang. In addition, it would drop several graduates from the Colorado base into Mustang. The drop was conducted successfully in April 1961.[50]

Then Ayub Khan pulled the plug on the operation, at least temporarily. By April 1961, led by Galbraith in New Delhi, the new administration was moving forward on one of Kennedy's priorities, an improvement in U.S.-India relations. That month, the Kennedy White House promised one billion dollars in economic aid to India for its next five-year development plan. Rumors circulated that Washington might sell tanks to the Indian army at a low cost. The Pakistanis' worst nightmare was coming true. The most allied ally of America saw Washington helping India build its economy and maybe its military. Ayub Khan felt betrayed.

Before Ayub Khan's visit to Washington in the summer of 1961, Kennedy asked the CIA for an assessment of Pakistan. The Special National Intelligence Estimate delivered to the White House on July 5, 1962, concluded that Ayub Khan was firmly in power, but that there was a grave risk the U.S. relationship with Pakistan "would seriously erode" because of his obsession with India and Kashmir. The estimate also forecast that Pakistan would engage in "more comprehensive negotiations with Communist China on Himalayan border questions" and other measures to improve ties with Mao. It anticipated that Ayub Khan would deliver a strong message to Kennedy that Pakistan was unhappy with the administration's overtures to India.[51]

The CIA's assessment was correct: To demonstrate his anger and unhappiness, Khan cut off use of the East Pakistan airfield for operations to assist the Tibetans, putting the whole operation in limbo. However, he did not prohibit use of the U-2 base in West Pakistan, demonstrating that his actions were carefully calibrated not to antagonize the Americans too much. By shutting down only one CIA operation Ayub Khan communicated his unhappiness, but did not close the door on relations with the new president.[52]

As we saw in the Prologue, Kennedy was able to reverse Ayub Khan's decision at their dinner meeting at Mount Vernon on July 11, 1961. The Pakistani dictator probably concluded he had made his point and did not need to further disturb his relationship with Kennedy, so he agreed to allow use of the East Pakistan airfield for infiltrating more Tibetan resistance fighters into Nepal for operations inside Tibet. In return Ayub Khan got the important commitment from Kennedy that the United States would not provide arms to India, even if attacked by China, without first consulting with Pakistan. The president gave the field marshal an engraved custom-built Winchester shotgun as a gift after the Mount Vernon dinner, an oddly appropriate reflection of a bilateral relationship that revolved around American guns for Pakistan.[53]

In October 1961 one of the CIA-trained Tibetan teams scored a significant intelligence coup: It ambushed a PLA jeep inside Tibet and captured a leather satchel filled with documents. The documents were highly classified reports about a variety of sensitive issues, including the Sino-Soviet relationship, food shortages in China, and the strength and morale of the Chinese military. When the documents were brought back to Langley they proved to be a major intelligence windfall for the CIA. The material was so abundant that the CIA had to ask Stanford University to help with the translation.[54]

The dramatic intelligence windfall saved the Tibet and Mustang operations. Dulles brought the blood-stained leather satchel to a meeting of the Special Group in the White House Situation Room to prove that the Tibet operation was producing quality information. Despite another attempt by Galbraith to end the mission in November 1961, the president decided to keep the CIA in the game.[55]

However, it was too late to save Dulles's and Bissell's jobs: Kennedy told Dulles he had to go. Dulles, who had selected the site for and helped design the CIA's new headquarters building in Langley, Virginia, was allowed to stay, as a mark of respect for his years of service to his country, until its formal dedication. On November 28, 1961, Kennedy presented Dulles with a medal at the dedication ceremony, saying, "Your successes are unheralded, your failures trumpeted," and then adding, "I sometimes have that feeling myself." The curtain was then pulled back in the building's large marble entrance to reveal a biblical verse carved in the marble: "And ye shall know the truth, and the truth shall make you free."[56]

Dulles was replaced by another Republican, John McCone. He was the scion of a wealthy Catholic California family, was educated at the University of California at Berkeley in mechanical engineering, and had worked in the family iron foundry business. The company made a fortune in World War II building ships. Eisenhower appointed him head of the Atomic Energy Commission (AEC) in 1958. He was still in that position in 1960 when the intelligence community discovered Israel's secret nuclear reactor in Dimona; McCone's tough response impressed Kennedy.[57]

Bobby Kennedy had persuaded his brother to appoint McCone as DCI "as a firewall against Republican criticism of the administration's failed Cuban policy." McCone, however, would soon become an irritant to Kennedy because he predicted earlier than anyone else that Khrushchev would place nuclear weapons and missiles in Cuba.[58] Even during his honeymoon in southern France in the summer of 1962, McCone sent ever more alarming warnings to the White House about Soviet intentions in Cuba and requested that more U-2 flights be approved to fly over the island. The famous "honeymoon cables" would prove to be all too correct.[59]

Bissell did not last much longer than Dulles; in February 1962 Richard Helms succeeded him as the deputy director for plans. As chief of operations Helms was much more skeptical about the wisdom of covert actions than his predecessor, believing they almost always carried far more downsides and risks than gains. After his retirement from government service in the 1970s (he had later become DCI and then ambassador to Iran) Helms spoke to me often about the danger of covert operations. In her recently published memoir his wife wrote that Helms had deliberately refused to attend a single planning meeting for the Bay of Pigs because "he heartily opposed it from the start. He harbored a residual resistance to covert action because so many things could go wrong in a secret mission that often became not so secret."[60]

Fellow Harvard graduate David Blee was charged by Helms with increasing the NE Division's control of the Tibet operation at the expense of the FE Division. The bureaucratic change signaled that enthusiasm for the operation was waning in Langley.[61] Galbraith's opposition to the covert operations now had top-level support inside the CIA.

The White House remained supportive of covert action, however. Both JFK and Bobby wanted much more done, especially to try to get rid of Castro, after the Bay of Pigs debacle. Bobby was put in charge of covert action in Cuba as head of an interagency team, tasked with finding a way to oust Castro and the communists in a plan called Operation Mongoose. McCone had 400 CIA officers working on the project in Langley and Miami. Bobby asked him, "Why can't you get things cooking like 007?"[62]

The White House also wanted more done on Tibet, both covertly and overtly. On December 20, 1961, the United States, led by the State Department, persuaded the UN General Assembly to vote in favor of a resolution promising self-determination for Tibet. The vote was 56 in favor, 11 opposed, and 29 abstentions. After years of clandestine help for the Dalai Lama's cause, John F. Kennedy had produced a diplomatic victory for Tibetan independence. Unfortunately for Tibet it proved to be the high-water mark of Tibetan efforts to get UN support for their cause.[63]

NEHRU COMES TO NEWPORT

As mentioned earlier Galbraith requested that Kennedy appoint him ambassador to India. Kennedy agreed to do so on the condition that Galbraith would not limit his role to advising on India, but would continue to give the president the benefit of his thinking on all issues domestic and foreign. Kennedy need not have worried:

Galbraith sent the president a constant barrage of letters, memo-
randa, and cables setting forth his views on every issue and many
personalities. This material contained not only substantive advice
and reports on current issues but also humorous anecdotes, gos-
sip, and a few descriptions of beautiful women.

This pattern of Galbraith's deep involvement began even before
the inauguration. Galbraith provided considerable assistance to
planning the administration's economic agenda, and he had a hand
in drafting the president's Inaugural Address. The phrase, "let
us never negotiate out of fear, but let us never fear to negotiate,"
was one of Ken's inputs. He was already emerging as one of the
doves in Kennedy's inner circle, a skeptic of covert action and
military intervention and one of the most liberal of his advisers on
domestic issues as well.[64] After the inauguration Kennedy gave
Galbraith use of the office suite occupied by the wartime secretary
of state, Cordell Hull, in the Old Executive Office Building next
to the White House until his appointment as ambassador was
confirmed by the Senate and he could move to New Delhi.

After Senate confirmation Galbraith and his wife and two children left for India in April 1961, arriving just days before the Bay
of Pigs disaster. Before leaving, Galbraith had written Kennedy a
note that the president should remember how intelligence mistakes
had hurt his predecessors: Truman had been caught off guard by
the large presence of the Chinese in Korea on the Yalu River, and
Eisenhower had been tripped up by the shooting down of the U-2
plane over the Soviet Union. Galbraith urged that Kennedy not
give the Cuban exiles any support, but his advice was too late.[65]

The year 1961 was a very tough one for JFK. After the Bay of
Pigs fiasco he traveled to Vienna to meet with Soviet leader Nikita
Khrushchev in early June. The meetings did not go well; Khrushchev bullied and harangued the young president.[66] Khrushchev,
the son of Ukrainian peasants, had learned the art of politics in the
circle of Russia's ruthless and paranoid dictator Joseph Stalin: He
was a master of intimidation and bullying. The Soviet leader made

clear he wanted more control over West Berlin; the president refused to make any concessions and left Vienna expecting that a crisis would develop over the summer in Berlin. He was correct; the Soviets would build the Berlin Wall later that year. It was a very tense summer and fall in Germany.[67]

For his part Galbraith presented his credentials to the Indian president in an elaborate ceremony. Wearing formal wear and a black silk top hat, which made him appear more than seven feet tall, Galbraith was escorted to the President's Palace, formerly the home of the British viceroy, by Bengal Lancers.

He immediately embarked on wooing Nehru and his cabinet. He was very critical of the Bay of Pigs operation and of some of Kennedy's top aides, including Secretary of State Dean Rusk, in his talks with Nehru. He argued against those urging the United States to send troops to fight communist rebels in Laos and Vietnam, displaying views close to Nehru's own. He was able to persuade India to send troops to serve in the UN peacekeeping mission in the Congo after the death of Lumumba: India became the largest contributor of troops, some of whom flew to Africa on U.S. Air Force transports.

Galbraith and his family also embarked on an extensive series of trips across India to see as much of the country as possible. Ken wanted to see India and be seen by Indians. The ambassador's health was not vibrant, however, and he suffered from a variety of illnesses during his time in India. He was also not partial to the cuisine, preferring old-fashioned American fare like steak and lobster to the exotic Indian meals. It did not help that his chef in the embassy was not very good. Galbraith described his first meal in his residence as "disenchanting."[68]

Galbraith kept a diary during his tour in India that he later edited and had published: It is a marvelous read. In it he shares his opinions about everything and everybody. It not only contains long and careful reports on his meetings with Nehru and other senior Indian officials, extensive excerpts from his letters to JFK, and serious discussions on the Chinese and Vietnamese crises but also very humorous commentaries on his friends and enemies. He often savages Secretary of State Dean Rusk and his department, concluding, "It is hard in this job not to develop a morbid dislike of the State Department. It is remote, mindless, petty and, above all, pompous, overbearing and late."[69] There are also rave reviews of women he met. He describes flying to Los Angeles with the movie actress Angie Dickinson: "I was deeply in love. She has fair pure skin, blond to reddish hair, merry eyes and a neat, unstarved body. The trip went by in a minute."[70]

In 1981 he wrote his memoir, *A Life in Our Times*, which adds a few more details on his India experiences. But his diary is far more enlightening and provides unique insight on what Galbraith and others said and thought at the time, not what they wanted to remember years later in hindsight.

More than a thousand U.S. State Department employees served in India at the embassy and the consulates in Calcutta, Madras, and Bombay. Ken left the duty of managing them to his deputy and focused instead on advising Kennedy. In his memoir he admits that being an ambassador usually took up only two hours of his day. Distrusting the State Department bureaucracy and its communication system, the ambassador kept up his constant stream of messages to Kennedy on all issues; he told Kennedy that trying to operate through State Department channels was "like trying to fornicate through a mattress."[71] He sent these messages directly to Kennedy via the Situation Room.

Under a pseudonym, Galbraith even wrote a number of humorous articles for the U.S. magazine *Esquire* that ridiculed the State Department. One article, titled "The Fully Automated Foreign Policy," suggested that the State Department was run by a computer that automatically generated policy decisions based on previous practice and groupthink. It noted that the State Department had 6,302 employees in 1940 and 40,216 by 1962. Later these essays were published in a book.[72]

Galbraith often disagreed with his instructions from the State Department. He thought it foolish, for example, to try to persuade Nehru to support American efforts to deny Communist China a seat at the UN Security Council; after all Nehru had been pushing for giving that seat to Mao since 1949. Galbraith wrote directly to Kennedy, suggesting, "We take a passive attitude on the Chicoms, making a token vote against them not an impassioned plea." He also sent the same recommendation via State Department channels to Secretary Rusk. He later told JFK that the recommendation "produced one of the rudest responses in the history of diplomacy": The State Department informed him "to the extent your position has any merit it has been fully considered and rejected."[73] In response Galbraith just failed to raise the issue with Nehru, leaving it to his deputy to raise it at a low level in the Ministry of External Affairs. Galbraith thereafter bypassed Rusk on important issues and communicated directly with Kennedy.

What most impressed Nehru and his advisers was the new administration's promise to massively increase assistance to India. Galbraith, Nehru knew, was the moving force in this change. As mentioned, in April 1961 the administration pledged one billion dollars in economic aid to India, half in development loans and half in food assistance, for each of the next two years. It encouraged other countries to increase foreign aid as well, just as Kennedy had suggested in his 1959 Senate speech. India was also a high priority for Kennedy's new Peace Corps, and its first director Sargent Shriver visited India in May 1961 to inaugurate the program. Nehru was very enthusiastic about the Peace Corps, and several hundred volunteers came to work in India in the next few years.[74]

Vice President Lyndon Johnson also visited India in May 1961. Nehru met him at the airport and used his visit to publicly thank Kennedy for the increase in assistance. LBJ also visited Pakistan where he received a much less enthusiastic reception. Ayub Khan told the vice president that Pakistan was deeply concerned about the perceived tilt toward India. Johnson invited the Pakistani leader to Washington to see the president, which led to the Mount Vernon summit in July.

Believing that direct exposure to Kennedy would ease Nehru's lingering suspicion of American foreign policy, Galbraith was eager to get Nehru to visit Washington as well. According to Arthur Schlesinger, "the two leaders shared that address, patrician instinct and long historical view which made them, next to Churchill, the two greatest statesmen on the British model of their day."[75] The Nehru visit came in November 1961. As usual Nehru brought his daughter Indira with him as his chief aide and confidant. He also brought along a second cousin, Braj Kumar Nehru, who was India's new ambassador to the United States.

However, the visit turned out to be a disaster. Born in 1889, "by 1961 Nehru, alas, was no longer the man he had once been," Schlesinger recalled.[76] He had spent thirteen years in jail, imprisoned by the British before partition in 1947 for his pro-independence activism. He had dominated the politics of his country since independence; he was its father figure. He also was its chief diplomat and foreign minister. The workload was enormous for a young man, and Nehru was no longer a young man. The long flight wore him out even more.

Galbraith had pushed for the prime minister's visit to be somehow special, undoubtedly even more so after he learned of the dinner at Mount Vernon for Ayub Khan. So after arriving in New York, Nehru traveled to Newport, Rhode Island, to stay at Jackie Kennedy's family home. The mansion at Hammersmith Farm had been the venue for the Kennedys' wedding reception in 1953 for 1,200 guests and had been a favorite vacation spot for the First Family. It was nicknamed the summer White House by the press and often was the setting for important announcements. For example, McCone's nomination for CIA director was announced there. Nehru concluded the visit by going to Disneyland in California on his way home.

Jackie Kennedy's Secret Service bodyguard was there with the First Lady, and he later described the scene. Hammersmith Farm "was a Victorian style mansion that looked like something straight out of the English countryside. Weathered shingles gave it a cottage-like feel, but you could hardly call this a cottage. Twenty eight rooms were spread out among three levels; countless brick chimneys stuck out of the roof; and there was even a turret."[77] The mansion was set in the middle of forty-eight acres of land overlooking Narragansett Bay. The farm also contained stables, a tennis court, and a dock where the presidential yacht, the *Honey Fitz*, was berthed for the visit.

One day, the Kennedys, Nehrus, and Galbraith sailed on the yacht to Newport.[78] After disembarking, Kennedy drove with Nehru past the enormous mansions of the city's gilded age and remarked, "I wanted you to see how the average American lives," to which Nehru cleverly replied, "Yes, I've heard of your 'affluent society' " (the title of Galbraith's most famous book).[79]

During this visit, Nehru was unusually taciturn, probably because of his fatigue and jet lag. The president tried to engage him in conversation, but Nehru responded in monosyllables or said nothing at all. As Galbraith wrote in his diary, "Nehru simply did not respond. Question after question he answered with mono-syllables or a sentence or two. . . . The President found it very dis-couraging."[80] Ted Sorenson concluded that, although the president liked Nehru, "that meeting convinced him that Nehru would never be a strong reed on which to rely."[81]

After Newport the parties came to Washington for more meet-ings and events with Congress and the press. Again Nehru seemed unwilling or unable to talk or engage with the president and other officials. The state dinner in the White House got off to a bad start when the flue in the Oval Room fireplace had not been opened properly and smoke filled the room after the fire was lit. At dinner Indira Gandhi assailed American policy toward Pakistan and, in

Galbraith's sarcastic words, "otherwise elevated the mood of the evening." As Schlesinger wrote, "It was heavy going; I had the impression of an old man, his energies depleted. It was all so sad: this man had done so much for Indian independence but he had stayed around too long."[82] Kennedy told Galbraith "it was the worst state visit" of his presidency[83] and also felt that Nehru seemed more interested in talking with Jackie than with him.[84]

Jackie Kennedy had already committed to going to India in 1962, a trip Nehru said he was looking forward to very much. Although the First Lady later said that the official "meetings got absolutely nowhere and there was an awful lot of tapping the fingers and looking up at the ceiling," her exchanges with Nehru were "very easy and charming."[85] Her opinion of Indira was less positive. Jacqueline recalled that Mrs. Gandhi was "a truly bitter woman, a real prune—bitter, kind of pushy, horrible woman. It always looks like she's been sucking on a lemon."[86]

In his diary Galbraith portrays the visit as more successful than it had actually been. Much of Galbraith's time during the Washington summit was actually devoted to Vietnam, not to India issues. The president's military adviser and future chairman of the Joint Chiefs of Staff, Maxwell Taylor, had just visited Saigon and reported to JFK that it was urgent to send American combat troops to the country. Galbraith literally grabbed the top-secret Taylor report from the desk of McGeorge Bundy's deputy, took it to his hotel room at the Hay-Adams Hotel across Lafayette Park from the White House, and prepared a detailed rebuttal of its conclusions and recommendations, which Kennedy found very useful.[87]

Kennedy instructed Galbraith to go back to India by way of Honolulu and Saigon to provide him the opportunity to give a first-hand assessment of the situation in Vietnam. The ambassador thus became an informal alternative voice on the Vietnam War to the official team working in Washington and Saigon. As usual, Galbraith's report on his trip to Kennedy was very critical of the strategy recommended by the Pentagon, Pacific Command in Hawaii, and the U.S. Embassy in Saigon. Needless to say it did not endear Galbraith to the hawks.[88]

As he was prone to do (and as he knew the president enjoyed reading), Galbraith shared some lighter comments on life in Vietnam. Saigon reminded him of a shabby provincial French city, but the women enchanted him: "They are tall with long legs, high breasts and wear white silk pajamas and a white silk robe, split at the sides. On a bicycle or scooter they look very compelling."[89]

GOA

Just five weeks after the visit to Washington, the U.S. relationship with India was set back further by Nehru's decision to end Portugal's colonial empire in the subcontinent. In 1947 when India became independent Nehru had asked France and Portugal to peacefully cede their remaining colonies in the Indian subcontinent and give them to India. These small possessions were left over from the age of European imperialism. Paris agreed, but Lisbon refused.

Portugal, starting with the voyages of Vasco da Gama in the late fifteenth century, had been the first European country to build an empire in India. Goa became a colony in 1510; by 1961 it was an enclave on the Arabian Sea coast of about 1,400 square miles with just over 600,000 people, of whom one-third were Christian and most of the rest were Hindu. Two other very small Portuguese possessions—Diu and Daman—also remained outside Indian authority.

Portugal was a dictatorship, but a member of NATO. It regarded its colonies much like France regarded Algeria, as integral parts of the country even though they were denied any voice in choosing their future. Portugal insisted the United States back its claims to all its colonies.

After years of pressing Lisbon to give back Goa and the two other possessions, Nehru decided in late 1961 to take them by force.

Given that he was a leading spokesman for the settlement of all international disputes by peaceful means, this unilateral military action exposed him to charges of hypocrisy that many of his critics were very eager to make. In fact, Nehru had been willing to use military means to unify or maintain the unity of India since independence; he had intervened with force to keep Kashmir a part of India in 1947, and he had used military pressure to compel other recalcitrant Indian princes to join the union.

The U.S. Embassy in New Delhi detected evidence of India's resolve to seize Goa in early December 1961. Galbraith sent "a long elegantly constructed telegram urging our final detachment from Portugal, or at least from its possessions." He admitted he sympathized with India,[90] but the U.S. Embassy in Lisbon not surprisingly took a different view. Galbraith urged Nehru not to use force and Washington to press the Portuguese to provide a timeline for giving up Goa. In contrast, Secretary Rusk sided with the Portuguese even when they suggested that Pakistan send "a couple of divisions to the border to frighten the Indians."[91] It was only as India was making preparations for an assault that the State Department suggested it would pressure Lisbon if Nehru waited six months before taking military action.

That promise was too late. On December 20, 1961, the Indian army implemented Operation Vijay, bombarding Goa and sending in its army. After some sporadic and ineffectual resistance the Portuguese garrison surrendered. The ease of India's victory in Goa had the unfortunate effect of persuading Nehru and his senior civilian advisers that their military was stronger than it really was. Nehru had never given sustained attention to the Indian military nor provided it with the modern weapons it needed. Goa seemed to suggest he did not need to do either. "Encouraged by the Goa incident," one journalist in New Delhi wrote, many Indians ascribed "invincibility to the army."[92] Another Indian journalist later recalled, "Goa was a cakewalk and evoked the mistaken impression, among gifted amateurs in high places, that an unprepared Indian

Army could take on China."[93] The Indian leadership seemed to forget that Portugal was a spent power and, in contrast, China was a rising power.

The U.S. ambassador to the United Nations, Adlai Stevenson, sharply condemned India's use of force, singling out the Indian minister of defense Krishna Menon. Menon was increasingly disliked by many Americans for his own sharp criticisms of American foreign policy. The reaction in the Kennedy White House was similar. Although many in the administration agreed that the Portuguese had been foolish, Nehru's intervention "was a little like catching the preacher in the hen house," as Schlesinger described it. "It was almost too much to expect the targets of Nehru's past sermons not to respond in kind."[94] Jackie called Nehru "awfully sanctimonious" and later said Kennedy had told her, "It's like the town preacher being caught in the whore house."[95] Kennedy's circle regarded Stevenson's speech in the Security Council, especially his jibes at Menon, as "one of Adlai's most effective efforts."[96] Meanwhile Galbraith was appalled by the U.S. reaction, writing in his diary that he could not understand "why this handful of white people emanating from a small European despotism should rule several million Asians and Africans does not seem to impress anyone in the U.S. government."[97]

It was a long way from JFK's brave and strong denunciation of imperialism in Algeria in 1957 to the criticism of India's recovery of Goa in 1961. The first year of Kennedy's administration ended with serious strains in the president's ties to Nehru after the November visit and the Goa affair. Nehru sent the president a long letter at the end of the year complaining that "something that thrills our people in Goa (has been) condemned in the strongest language in the United States."[98] Despite Galbraith's opposition the president was continuing to authorize the CIA to help the Tibetans. It would be left to Mrs. Kennedy to get the relationship back on track in 1962. She would perform brilliantly.

CHAPTER THREE

JACKIE AND INDIA, 1962

The iconic photograph of Jacqueline Bouvier Kennedy posing in front of the Taj Mahal is a part of Camelot's enduring magic. The Taj Mahal is the most beautiful building in India, perhaps in the world. Built between 1632 and 1653 by the Mughal emperor Shah Jahan as a mausoleum for his wife Mumtaz Mahal, it is a monument to their love. Jackie was thirty-two when she visited Agra to see the Taj as part of a trip to India and Pakistan, the first major foreign trip by a First Lady alone that would be televised to a global audience.

Mrs. Kennedy's visit was a public high point of the Kennedy administration's engagement with India and Pakistan. She was remarkably successful in promoting America to the Indian and Pakistani people. In India the crowds shouted, "Jackie Ki Jai! Ameriki Rani!" (Hail Jackie, Queen of America!) She sold the New Frontier to Asians who had been disappointed by the stale cold war paradigms of the Truman and Eisenhower years. She already had won the affection of Prime Minister Nehru before she came to India, but the trip solidified his regard for the First Lady.

Her trip to South Asia also added to her allure at home. Already very popular, Jackie won new respect from Americans by demonstrating her ability to enhance American prestige abroad, especially in a country with a difficult, complex relationship with the United States. The president had always known how valuable Jackie was as a political asset, but during the India trip "the President called me into the Oval Office to look at the headlines and pictures, grinning from ear to ear and saying 'that's our girl!'" recalled his press secretary Pierre Salinger. Salinger described her impact succinctly: "Jackie made you proud to be an American, and that feeling translates into votes."[1]

The trip was planned to take place in the fall of 1961, but was postponed four times—allegedly for Jackie's sinus trouble, but in fact due to her nervousness about traveling abroad "solo" for the first time (i.e., without the president). Of course she was not really traveling alone. She brought along her sister Lee Radziwill, her maid, and her hairdresser; the entourage had sixty-four pieces of luggage for the fourteen-day trip. The Secret Service and sixty journalists including Barbara Walters and Sander Vanocur traveled with her party as well.[2]

Preparation for a visit by a member of the First Family is always a major endeavor both for the White House and the embassies of the host countries, which have competing agendas. There is inevitable competition for where the VIP will visit, where she will rest overnight, and where she will buy souvenirs. The host country will have its own political agenda to advance in a visit, the embassy will be careful not to antagonize local interests, and the White House will want to promote the administration's agenda.

Galbraith was in charge or at least wanted to be in charge of planning the visit. Unfortunately his health was bad in early 1962. He spent much of January in Switzerland recovering from liver trouble, and much of February in Hawaii in the Pearl Harbor naval base hospital and on Kauai recuperating further. He took advantage of being in Honolulu to get briefings on Vietnam from Pacific Command, but he was clearly troubled to be far from New Delhi while planning was underway for the visit. When he got back to New Delhi, Arthur Schlesinger was visiting from Washington so Galbraith got his advice on what the First Lady wanted to do and see in India.

Galbraith's proposed itinerary for Jackie was so packed that the president called him to make sure his wife would have time to sleep and rest.[3] Mrs. Kennedy's Secret Service bodyguard, Clint Hill, found Galbraith both physically and intellectually intimidating. "If he had his way, Jackie would be trekking from one end of India to the other for six weeks," he wrote later.[4]

The ambassador wrote Kennedy on March 2, 1961, that "the rearrangement of Mrs. Kennedy's schedule has gone smoothly." The leaders and people of Calcutta were disappointed she would not be able to visit because of the time constraints, but the rest of the itinerary seemed fine. He added, "She can count on a warm and agreeable welcome. Nehru, who is deeply in love and has a picture of himself strolling with JBK displayed all by itself in the main entrance hall of his house, is entirely agreeable."[5]

MRS. KENNEDY IN SOUTH ASIA

The first stop on the way to India was Rome. As the Catholic wife of the first American Catholic president, Jackie was eager to be received by Pope John XXIII in the Vatican. On March 11, 1962, they met for more than a half-hour in the Vatican Library. All of the members of her traveling party were included, except her sister Lee who was divorced. Mrs. Kennedy also met the president of Italy before taking an Air India jet to New Delhi.[6]

In Delhi the Galbraiths discovered that their young son had inadvertently locked the keys inside the embassy's largest car and they had to rush to the airport in a compact Ford instead. Prime Minister Nehru, Indira Gandhi, Defense Minister Krishna Menon, and a thousand Indian children along with the ambassador and his family were at the airport to greet the First Lady. Then the party went to see the Indian president, occupant of a largely honorific role, before laying roses at the site where Gandhi was cremated.

The advance team discovered that the White House had made one error. Typically on a state visit, there is an exchange of gifts with the hosts. Mrs. Kennedy arrived with several boxes of photo frames to distribute. Unfortunately the frames were covered with cowhide leather, an inappropriate material for a country where cows are considered sacred. Galbraith's staff at the embassy, realizing the problem, "had to scurry around and find some other suitable gifts. The First Lady wound up handing out sterling silver picture frames to her hosts that were made in India."[7]

The embassy had rented a villa for Mrs. Kennedy to stay in, but Nehru insisted after she arrived that she stay in a guest suite at the prime minister's residence.[8] It was the suite often used by Edwina Mountbatten, the wife of India's last viceroy Lord Mountbatten, who had presided over the partition. A frequent visitor to India after independence, Edwina and Nehru were at least close friends if not more.[9] Jackie was getting Nehru's complete attention.

The First Lady was an avid horsewoman who loved to ride. Nehru arranged for her to go riding in the exercise grounds of the President's Bodyguard, the ceremonial cavalry. A mare named Princess was brought out for the occasion.

After several days spent touring the Indian capital, Jackie and her party took the Indian president's special train (previously the viceroy's) to Fatehpur-Sikri to see the ruins of Akbar the Great's Mughal capital city built in 1509. The train included a "drawing room, bedrooms and dining room" and was painted a brilliant red outside. Galbraith said it was "unquestionably the proper way to travel."[10] The Indian government had outfitted the train for the First Lady with "pastel bedrooms, hand loomed curtains, embroidered cashmere bedspreads, sandalwood soaps, even specially installed dressing tables," according to one of Jackie's traveling companions who was making sketches of the trip for later publication.[11] The next stop was Agra and the Taj Mahal.

The visit to the Taj was a photojournalist's dream come true. Galbraith later described the scene in his diary "as a sightseeing tour of the world's most gracious and majestic monument; this was also a bit like making love in a cageful of monkeys. Photographers were jumping everywhere to get into position, reporters crowded in and, all in all, it was pretty much of a riot. But JBK didn't seem to mind and I think rather enjoyed it."[12] On first seeing the Taj, she told the press that "I am overwhelmed by a sense of awe." She returned for a more private visit by moonlight.[13]

The next stop was the Hindu holy city of Benares, today Varanasi, one of the most sacred spots in the subcontinent. Jackie liked the special train so much that the embassy canceled an airplane flight and the group took the train instead to Benares. Wearing a shocking pink dress, Mrs. Kennedy boarded a boat garlanded with marigolds to sail along the Ganges River to view the bathing spots and cremation platforms along the riverside. Later to the delight of the crowds, "Jacqueline walked up a petal strewn path to Sarnath Stupa, the temple from which the Buddha preached his first sermon 2,500 years ago."[14]

From the Ganges the First Lady's party traveled to Rajasthan to visit the White Palace in Udaipur and the Amber Palace in Jaipur. Both are magnificent examples of Indian architecture. The maharajah of Jaipur hosted her for a private visit to the City Palace, his home. The Kennedys would later host him in the White House during the middle of the Cuban missile crisis and Sino-Indian War in a return gesture. There were more photo ops with elephants and strolling through gardens. As Galbraith wrote, "A feature of this trip is beautiful women in beautiful gardens. The combination I find highly agreeable."[15] Jackie's trip to a jewelry store in Jaipur is still remembered today in a proudly displayed letter from the ambassador thanking the owner for helping the First Lady find what she wanted for her husband.

After the tour in Rajasthan, Jackie and Galbraith returned to New Delhi for a final round of meetings and photo opportunities with Nehru and Indian government leaders. It was also the holiday of Holi, the festival of spring when Indians shower each other in colored water and paint, which added to the special joy of the First Lady's visit. Then, after nine days in India, Jackie left in President Ayub Khan's personal jet for Pakistan.

Ayub Khan arranged the schedule in Pakistan. There would be no visit to East Pakistan where a majority of Pakistanis lived: Khan had no affection for the Bengalis or its capital Dacca, where he had been posted after partition. The visit would be limited to West Pakistan and focused on the Punjab.

The first stop was Lahore, the capital city of the Punjab where Jackie visited the Shalimar Gardens. Shah Jahan, the Mughal builder of the Taj Mahal, also built these gardens. They covered forty acres with more than 400 fountains and flowering plants. Mrs. Kennedy spoke briefly to the press, saying, "I'm profoundly impressed by the reverence which you in Pakistan have for your art and culture. As I stand in these gardens, which were built long before my country was born, that's one thing that binds us together and which always will. We'll always share an appreciation for the finer things."[16]

But Ayub Khan had a surprise for the First Lady, a true "finer thing." He gave her a ten-year-old bay gelding named Sardar, or Chief. Jacqueline promptly fell in love with the horse and told her bodyguard, "No one at home will be allowed to ride him but me."[17] In addition to the horse, Ayub Khan gave her a spectacular emerald, ruby, and diamond necklace, both tokens of his appreciation for the dinner at Mount Vernon.[18] Jackie wrote the president immediately to ask that Sardar get special treatment by U.S. customs officials to expedite his arrival at their weekend home outside Washington in Middleburg, Virginia.

Mrs. Kennedy also visited Rawalpindi, the headquarters for the Pakistani army where Ayub Khan spent most of his time, and the Khyber Pass, which leads to Afghanistan. The Khyber Pass trip started with a flight to Peshawar, the city where the U-2s were based (there was no side stop at the air base). The Secret Service had to convince the Pashtun tribesmen at the Khyber Pass not to butcher a lamb in front of Jackie as a way of celebrating her visit. Secret Service bodyguard Hill instructed his advance team, "You guard that lamb with your life; they cannot kill the damn thing until after we leave."[19]

The trip concluded with a visit to Karachi, the country's main port and largest city. Another frenzied photo op took place there when Jackie and her sister rode a camel together. The First Lady stopped briefly in Tehran, Iran, on March 26, 1962, on the flight to London. In London she had lunch with Queen Elizabeth and rested from the fourteen-day journey across South Asia.

The whole trip was a fabulous public relations success. The *Times of India* summed it up by reporting "nothing else happened in India while Mrs. Kennedy was there. She completely dominated the scene."[20] But although the visit helped U.S.-Indian relations to recover from the Goa incident, storm clouds were gathering in the Himalayas between India and China.

INTELLIGENCE ESTIMATES OF CHINA

In the spring of 1962 the president asked CIA director John McCone for an updated assessment of China. On May 2 the DCI delivered *Prospects for Communist China*, a National Intelligence Estimate prepared by the CIA that reflected the views of the entire intelligence community. It drew on earlier studies of the Sino-Soviet split and the Chinese nuclear weapon development program and relied heavily on the PLA documents captured in Tibet in 1961 for insights into the morale of the Chinese people and especially that of the PLA. Declassified in 2004 as part of a larger project to release decades of CIA estimates on China for the use of scholars,

Prospects for Communist China provides an excellent basis for understanding what the U.S. intelligence community knew about China on the eve of the Sino-Indian War.[21]

The NIE reported that Mao's China was in trouble. After delivering a decade of solid economic growth and prosperity between 1949 and 1959, Mao had embarked on a radical socioeconomic policy called the "Great Leap Forward" to modernize China rapidly. Three years of poor weather, combined with that policy's detrimental effects on agriculture and the withdrawal of almost all Soviet economic and military advisers in 1960, resulted in "economic chaos" across the country. "Malnutrition is widespread, foreign trade is down and industrial production and development have dropped sharply," the NIE reported, and "no quick recovery is in sight." China's gross domestic product was down by 10 percent in 1961, the "first decrease since the communists came to power."[22]

However, the NIE stated that the communist regime would survive the "widespread disillusionment and disaffection" produced by the economic crisis because it had a "monopoly on arms, organization and communication" and so could defeat any internal challenge. If the weather improved and the party leadership adopted more cautious policies, China would recover, but it would take years to do so.[23]

According to *Prospects for Communist China* and another NIE on Sino-Soviet relations, Khrushchev and Mao had disagreed so much on how to fight the cold war that the break between the Soviet Union and the PRC was now probably permanent. Virtually all Soviet technicians and advisers, both in economic and military aid projects, had departed suddenly, leading to a virtual cessation of those projects. "Issues of a secret magazine (stolen by the Tibetans) reveal considerable ideological confusion among the regimes troops, mental anguish over the condition of relatives back home, and some outright distrust of the party's leadership." Nonetheless, "the Chinese Communist Army—the world's largest—has a tested capability for prolonged, large scale offensive action."[24]

The NIE assessed that the Tibetan uprising of 1959 was largely suppressed, and only "sporadic armed dissidence continues. The 100,000 Chinese regulars have established effective control and are systematically improving logistical facilities, particularly the road net" in Tibet. It highlighted plans for a major road from Lhasa to Katmandu in Nepal that would greatly expand Chinese commerce and influence in the strategic kingdom.[25] The border dispute with India had soured the China-India relationship, and "it will be very difficult to resolve the border differences."[26] The "continued border dispute with India has drastically reduced Peiping's influence with India and is an embarrassment for Peiping in its relations with the rest of the world."[27]

Most importantly the NIE concluded that the "anti-American aspect of Peiping's foreign policy is deeply grounded," and Washington should expect continued challenges to its national security interests around the world, but especially in Asia. "The Chinese leaders see the US as the epitome of all that is evil in the 'bourgeois capitalist system.' "[28] Despite the withdrawal of Soviet nuclear experts, the NIE predicted "that by the end of the decade the Chinese Communists will have a limited nuclear weapons and missile capability."[29]

Prospects for Communist China was a thorough and thoughtful assessment without political bias. Despite the paucity of intelligence collection inside the PRC (with the one-time exception of the Tibetan windfall), it was a generally accurate summary of the state of the communist regime and its foreign relations. It left little doubt that, despite China's economic setbacks during the Great Leap Forward, Mao was securely in power and determined to challenge American interests. Rather than a monolithic global communist movement, the United States faced two competing communist threats from the Soviet Union and the People's Republic of China.

Kennedy also requested an NIE on India. *The Prospects for India* was sent to the White House on May 31, 1962. It assessed that Nehru was firmly in power and that his Congress Party was likely to dominate Indian elections for the foreseeable future. It expected Nehru to stick to his nonalignment policy, even as relations with the United States had improved in the last year. New Delhi would also seek good ties with Moscow, "especially for help in India's problems with Peiping." The NIE judged India's "major foreign policy problem for the indefinite future will be centered on the threat of Communist China," though the "odds are against any major military escalation"; however, it did anticipate more border clashes.[30]

The two estimates helped inform the administration's policy toward the Tibetan resistance. By mid-1962 the CIA had concluded that the resistance had been largely defeated by the PLA. The Tibet Task Force chief later wrote that the intelligence agency belatedly realized it had underestimated "the Chinese capability and willingness to invest disproportionally large numbers of troops and military aircraft, enough to wipe out the Tibetan resistance. Mao refused to let bands of unruly border tribesmen deny him his dream of reuniting the greater Han empire."[31]

Inside the CIA, Richard Helms, the new chief of operations, took control of the Tibet Task Force from the Far East Division, its principal advocate, and gave it to the Near East Division and the CIA officers in India who were much less enamored of the project. It was in effect "largely emasculated." To ensure that the FE Division did not try to leak to friends in Washington that the program was in trouble, Helms asked the CIA's counterintelligence chief James Jesus Angleton "to report any resistance from Far East types" to the new command system.[32]

The Kennedy administration decided in the summer of 1962 to freeze support for the Tibetans, especially the Mustang force, which was by then the only real fighting force left, pending a decision by India to get more involved and support the resistance.[33] India's involvement, however, was regarded as highly unlikely given Nehru's well-established aversion to such an activist and confrontational policy toward China. Galbraith, it seemed, had gotten his way—but the situation was about to change dramatically.

THE FORWARD POLICY

As tensions with China mounted after the Dalai Lama fled into exile in India in 1959, Nehru and his advisers gradually implemented what became known as the "Forward Policy" of sending Indian military forces forward into contested and disputed territory with China. India had been building up its intelligence presence along the border for more than a decade, but in the early 1960s it began to create military outposts behind the Chinese troops in the disputed land, so as to cut off their supplies and force their return to China. This action led some scholars, most notably the Australian journalist and author Neville Maxwell, to argue, "It was Nehru, not the Chinese, who declared war."[34]

The Forward Policy was never formally reviewed and approved as such by the Indian government; rather it grew from a series of incremental decisions and events. It was also more of a statement of political resolve than a military strategy: The Indian army was never given the means to effectively implement it. Because India's major dispute with China was over territory in the Aksai Chin portion of Kashmir that India claimed and China controlled, it was there that the Forward Policy was most vigorously prosecuted and confrontations with the Chinese were the most volatile. The extremely harsh terrain in Aksai Chin made it a formidable challenge for Indian troops, and the logistics of supplying forward posts was extremely difficult. Later India implemented the Forward Policy in the northeastern region where India occupied the disputed territory claimed by China. Violent incidents became more and more common on both fronts.

Maxwell argues in his study *India's China War* that the crucial meeting on the Forward Policy was held on November 2, 1961. Nehru chaired the session attended by Defense Minister Krishna Menon; Foreign Secretary M. J. Desai; the head of the Intelligence Bureau, B. N. Mullik; and General P. N. Thapar, the recently appointed army chief of staff. Mullik was probably the leading advocate of a tough policy toward China, but the resulting decision was a product of consensus. The instructions to the army were to "patrol as far forward (in Aksai Chin) as possible from our present positions. This will be done with a view to establishing our posts which should prevent the Chinese from advancing any further and also dominating from any posts which they may have already established in our territory."[35]

The process that produced the Forward Policy was not only haphazard but also reflected a seriously dysfunctional understanding of the threat posed by Chinese advances in Tibet and on the border. Nehru was trying to show Indian resolve to Mao and protect his own domestic political position from critics who claimed he was weak on China. Press articles claimed that Nehru had forfeited control of some 2,000 square miles of territory to China in Kashmir by 1962. Editorialists argued that the prime minister had drawn the line against Portugal in Goa in December 1961 and should now do the same to the Chinese (ignoring the enormous power disparity between Portugal and China). For Nehru and Menon the Forward Policy was not a "military challenge to a far stronger power, but the necessary physical extension of a subtle diplomatic game."[36]

The Indian army, which was the service directly affected by the Forward Policy, was given an assignment that its own professional officer corps knew was beyond its means: It did not have the number of troops necessary to engage in a game of chicken with the PLA in the mountains. Despite reinforcements, by mid-1962 the Indian army was outnumbered in the Aksai Chin part of Kashmir by five to one, yet it was trying to staff sixty new forward posts. Even worse, the Indian soldiers were equipped with Lee-Enfield rifles, which had first entered service in the army in 1895, while the Chinese were equipped with modern automatic weapons, artillery, and other equipment. Many of the Chinese commanders were also veterans of the Korean battlefield.[37]

The senior command staff of the army, especially General Thapar, found themselves caught between political leaders with an unrealistic concept of the military situation and local commanders who felt they were being given impossible orders. Unfortunately for India in 1962 the senior command was unfit for the job. As Maxwell argues, "political favoritism put the Army under incompetent leadership which blindly followed the Nehru government's provocative policy."[38]

Mullik's Intelligence Bureau was asked in May 1962 to provide an intelligence estimate of the situation along the border. He later wrote, "We found that all along the frontier the Chinese had further strengthened their military posts by bringing additional troops from the rear and the total strength of their troops on our border and that of Nepal had been raised to nearly seven divisions. The overall strength of Chinese troops in Tibet was in the neighborhood of eleven to twelve divisions." In Aksai Chin the Chinese army was "much further west" than ever before.[39]

Mullik also reported two important intelligence insights to Nehru. First, the Chinese consulate in Calcutta was secretly telling the Indian Communist Party leadership there that "forced by the adamant attitude of the Indian government about the border, the Chinese government was going to adopt a new line of action toward India." The new action would be implemented in the fall, and China wanted its sympathizers in the Indian Communist Party to be ready to back Chinese claims. The consulate was also telling them to expect a change in the Chinese posture toward Pakistan, including a forthcoming resolution of China's border dispute in Pakistan-controlled Kashmir. Mullik found the "report was so authentic and so alarming that we immediately passed this on to the Prime Minister, the Home Minister and the Defence Minister. I talked to them personally about the authenticity of this report and the seriousness of the threat."[40] Mullik believed the report showed "the Chinese had made up their minds to attack India and were giving out propaganda feelers to fellow travelers" like the Communist Party of India.[41]

The CIA monitored the activities of the Communist Party of India closely as it did all communist parties during the cold war. It regarded it as "the best organized and most capably led of the opposition groups" in the Indian parliament.[42] It had long been strong in West Bengal and Calcutta. Mullik's report showed the IB also had kept a careful eye on the communists, who could be a problematic factor in a Sino-Indian conflict.

The second alarming insight that Indian intelligence acquired in May 1962 concerned Pakistan. President Ayub Khan had held a series of meetings with his senior military commanders in the spring of 1962 to consider a "grand strategy" to force India to cede Kashmir to Pakistan. He had become increasingly disappointed in Kennedy and the American tilt toward India. Nor had the SEATO and CENTO alliances delivered the unquestioning American support that Ayub Khan wanted. According to Mullik's report, the field marshal believed "the only solution lay in Pakistan and China forging a grand alliance against the common enemy, India. His strategy would be that whilst Chinese guerillas would attack India from north and east and keep Indian forces heavily engaged, Pakistan would make an onslaught from the west. To make this strategy possible Ayub was willing to go to any length to court China." According to Mullik's sources Ayub Khan had begun sounding out Mao on forming a closer relationship with Pakistan.[43]

Mullik's assessment of "possible military collusion between Pakistan and China" was a bombshell for the Indian leadership. The prospect of a two-front war, as Mullik later wrote, "remained imprinted in the minds of our leaders and the Army Headquarters and explains why during the Sino–Indian War, instead of disturbing the divisions on the Pakistan front" where the bulk of India's army was deployed, they remained in place there, leaving only weaker units to face China and the PLA.[44]

Only one division of the Indian army—the Fourth Infantry Division—had been transferred from the border area near West Pakistan in the Punjab to northeastern India since border tensions arose in 1959. It was a unit with a distinctive history. The Fourth Division had fought with the British Eighth Army in North Africa and Italy during World War II, where it earned a reputation as "one of the finest and greatest fighting divisions of the war." The division headquarters in 1962 still used as its command vehicle the captured command caravan of the famous German Afrika Korps, which surrendered to the Fourth Division in Tunis in 1943.[45]

After its transfer to the North East Frontier Authority (NEFA) in 1961, the Fourth Division became responsible for patrolling the entire northeastern portion of India, including the length of the Mc-Mahon Line in dispute with China, which stretched 360 miles from Bhutan to Burma. It also had responsibility for defending against East Pakistan, today's Bangladesh. Yet in light of the perceived West Pakistan threat India felt that no additional forces could be spared for the area then known as NEFA.[46] As in Aksai Chin, Indian army forces in NEFA and Assam were stretched far too thin to face the Chinese forces. Moreover, the Indians had not invested sufficient effort in building roads and airfields near the border so their supply lines were inadequate in getting ammunition and other equipment to the frontline troops in combat.

The Chinese, by contrast, had made the building of roads and other supply facilities a high priority since they entered Tibet in 1950, seeing their construction as a means to entrench their occupation of the province. As mentioned earlier the building of major roads in Aksai Chin connecting the Chinese regions of Tibet and Xinjiang had been a precipitating factor in the buildup of tensions in the late 1950s.

In May 1962 the Chinese began a major buildup of forces facing the weak Indian positions in NEFA. Arms, gasoline, and ammunition supply depots were filled behind the lines; road construction was completed; prisoner camps were built; and the troops were indoctrinated and trained for combat against India—all this according to one of the commanders of the Fourth Division, Brigadier John P. Dalvi, who was captured in the fighting in October 1962 and thus gained involuntary access to behind the Chinese lines and the opportunity to talk to Chinese commanders. Dalvi also reported that senior Chinese officers who had fought in Korea had been reassigned to the Tibet battlefield in May 1962. In his account of the war Dalvi concluded, "It is ludicrous to suggest that India provoked the Chinese, forcing the Chinese to launch self defense counter attacks. The war was coldly and calculatingly planned by the Chinese."[47]

By the fall of 1962 Nehru made clear he would refuse to trade Chinese control of Aksai Chin for Indian control of NEFA up to the McMahon Line, the compromise Mao and Zhou had suggested they would accept. With a diplomatic solution ruled out, Nehru implemented the Forward Policy of pressing India's territorial claims aggressively on the ground both in Kashmir and NEFA— but without providing the military with the forces needed to defend those areas should China choose to go to war. This despite the fact that the Intelligence Bureau had told him in May to expect a Chinese move in the fall.

The threat from Pakistan hovered over all Indian plans and strategy. Nehru had based his diplomacy on the belief that China and India were brothers, if not allies, in the great struggle against imperialism and that the main threat was coming from Pakistan in the west. In the fall of 1962 Nehru still hoped that China would be reasonable and avoid war. His hopes were about to be dashed.

UNDERSTANDING CHINESE PERCEPTIONS

We know far more about Indian decisionmaking and involvement in Tibet, the border dispute, and the origins of the 1962 Sino-Indian War than we do about Chinese decisionmaking. There is a rich literature on the Indian side about the war and how it came about, but no such literature exists on the Chinese side. In part this disparity reflects the outcome of the war: India lost badly and spent many years trying to understand why. Much of the voluminous literature about the war, such as Mullik's *The Chinese Betrayal* and Dalvi's

Himalayan Blunder, is made up of scathing books intended to apportion blame and responsibility for what went wrong in 1962. Accounts of the campaign contain more than their fair share of mudslinging and bad-mouthing, either exonerating or pillorying Nehru. Another reason for the much more extensive material on Indian involvement is that India is the world's most populous democracy with a free press. The country engaged in a spirited and healthy debate about the 1962 war.

Unfortunately, the official history is a stale and boring read, more a defense of India's diplomacy than a study of the conflict. The government prepared a lengthy official postmortem called the *Henderson Brooks-Bhagat Report,* but it has never been published. The Australian scholar Neville Maxwell provided an excerpt from the first of two volumes of the report to the Indian press in 2014, but even that excerpt has a significant gap in it. The fact that the *Henderson Brooks-Bhagat Report* is still unpublished for security reasons underscores how devastating and wrenching the war remains for Indians more than a half-century later.

In contrast, China won the war and felt no remorse nor any need to engage in self-criticism. Mao remained in power for another fourteen years, and he was unlikely to open up any serious discussion of his war aims or planning. The Communist Party has allowed many changes in the country since Mao died, but it has not given up control of its archives nor allowed a free debate about its diplomacy: China is still a communist dictatorship more than a half-century after the war. Its territorial claims are still major sources of tension with Japan, Vietnam, and India. China's alliance with Pakistan is still intact today; in fact, it is stronger than ever.

Consequently we have to be more speculative about the Chinese government's motives and intentions in 1962 than about the Indian and American decisionmaking process and outcome. Western scholarship on China's side of the war has gone through a learning curve as China and China's role in the world have changed since 1962.

At the time of the war the analysis seemed simple: China was the aggressor and its goals were part of a global communist conspiracy to take over the world. China had proved its hostile intentions in Korea, and as the Dalai Lama wrote in his widely read memoir, the conquest of Tibet was a completely unprovoked act of aggression against an innocent and peace-loving people. In his account Tibet had achieved de facto independence in 1912 and enjoyed that independence until the world "abandoned Tibet to the hordes of the Chinese army."[48] Thanks in part to the CIA's propaganda efforts in the 1950s and 1960s the Tibetan struggle was widely publicized around the world.

In the American popular mind in the 1960s, China and Mao were seen as fanatics more dangerous than the Soviet communist menace. As the Vietnam War escalated steadily during the decade, China came to be perceived as a malevolent adversary willing to sacrifice millions of its own people to achieve its goals.

By the end of the 1960s, however, American perceptions of China began to change. President Richard Nixon, once the leader of the China alarmist camp, decided to open a communications path to Mao. Pakistan became the secret intermediary for Nixon's overture to China. Henry Kissinger, Nixon's national security adviser, secretly traveled from Islamabad to Beijing in 1971 to open the door to a new, favorable relationship and was received cordially by Mao. As a consequence of this backdoor diplomacy, Nixon tilted toward Pakistan in the 1971 war that India won and that resulted in the creation of Bangladesh.

The new approach stopped demonizing China and Mao and instead recognized that China's actions were guided by a deliberate and calculating foreign and national security policy, not a maniacal urge for world domination. Mao was rehabilitated as a statesman not an ideologue. Thanks to the Sino-Soviet split, China could be an ally against the USSR. Nehru's successor, his daughter Indira, became for Nixon and Kissinger the threat to peace in South Asia.

The first important revisionist history of the conflict was Neville Maxwell's book *India's China War*, which was published in 1970. The Australian journalist was the South Asia correspondent for the *Times* of London from 1959 until after the 1962 war. In the late 1960s he spent two years at the University of London researching the war and its origins before writing his book.

His book put the blame for the war squarely on Nehru and India: Nehru had refused to negotiate a compromise territorial deal that would give China what it wanted in the west (Aksai Chin) and India what it wanted in the east (the McMahon Line). Then India provoked the war with its poorly thought through Forward Policy. In this account India was no longer a victim; it was the aggressor. Even the Tibetan cause was recast as an example of Indian meddling in China's internal affairs.

Unsurprisingly, the revisionist school was poorly received in India. Dalvi's book was received more favorably. Based on his firsthand experience in the Fourth Division and as a POW, it claimed that China had begun planning the war in 1959 and needed three years to build the roads and infrastructure for its offensive; therefore it was a preplanned war of aggression.[49] Although the Forward Policy was widely denounced as ineffectual within India, there was no agreement that it provoked Mao to war.

The United States and other Western countries were more accepting of the revisionist argument. Indeed, Maxwell was a beneficiary of the changed view of China. The cover of the 2013 edition of *India's China War* quotes Henry Kissinger as telling Zhou Enlai that "reading this book showed me I could do business with you people." It also quotes Zhou Enlai telling Maxwell that "your book has done a service to the truth and China benefitted from that."[50] Book cover blurbs sell books.

Other scholars have argued for a more nuanced assessment of Chinese motives and policies. Allen Whiting, who was an analyst on China in the State Department, wrote a 1975 study on Chinese policy in India and Indochina that portrayed China as a very rational state actor with a clear understanding of deterrence theory and the limits of power.[51]

After Mao's death in 1976 and especially after the crackdown on political dissidence in Beijing in 1989, the perception of China took another turn. China continued to be seen as a rational actor, but Mao came to be rightly characterized as a very dangerous and paranoid dictator who was responsible for the deaths of millions of his own people in his nearly continuous purges and corrective movements. Belgian scholar Pierre Ryckmans wrote early accounts of the horrors of Mao's Cultural Revolution. In 1994 Mao's personal physician, Dr. Li Zhisvi, published *The Private Life of Chairman Mao*, which painted a devastating portrait of the leader. In this account, Mao was a paranoid who isolated himself from reality. Living with a closed circle of admirers and bodyguards, Mao "spent much of his time in bed or lounging by the side of a private pool, not dressing for days at a time. He ate oily food, rinsed his mouth with tea and slept with country girls." Indeed, the Communist Party apparatus literally "served women to him like food. Mao's sex life was a central project of his court."[52] Convinced that his many enemies were trying to kill him, Mao was sealed off in what "must have been the most protected place on earth" where he was "waited on by a harem of young girls."[53]

The Private Life of Chairman Mao is not a detailed chronicle of Chinese foreign policy under Mao, but it does recount that in October 1954 Mao told Nehru that the Korean War proved the atom bomb was a "paper tiger. The atom bomb is nothing to be afraid of, Mao told Nehru, China has many people. If someone else can drop an atomic bomb, I can too. The death of ten or twenty million people is nothing to be afraid of." According to Dr. Zhisvi, Nehru was shocked by Mao's statement.[54]

CHINESE MOTIVES IN THE CONFLICT

Whatever the peculiarities of Mao's private life, China's involvement in the border conflict with India in the late 1950s and early 1960s was driven by two interrelated concerns: its control of Tibet and India's Forward Policy. Tibet was probably the more crucial factor. New research on Chinese sources about the war has clarified Mao's motives and intentions. "The 1962 war with India was long China's forgotten war. Little was published in China regarding the process through which China decided for war—unlike the Korean war, the Indochina wars" and other conflicts, notes one American specialist. But that changed in the 1990s, and since then a stream of studies and articles have been published in China.[55]

In the late 1950s Mao increasingly came to see India as the principal cause of the difficulties China encountered in conquering Tibet. Rather than blaming the emergence of Tibetan resistance on the occupation itself, Mao found it more useful to blame Nehru and India. "There is unanimous agreement among Chinese scholars that the root cause of the 1962 war was an Indian attempt to undermine Chinese rule and seize Tibet. The official PLA history of the 1962 war argues that India sought to turn Tibet into a 'buffer zone'"; it saw Nehru as a "complete successor" to the British Raj, who sought a "great Indian empire" in South Asia, "filling the vacuum" left by partition in 1947. This history saw the control of Tibet as one of Nehru's ambitions.[56] Other studies in China concluded that India was seeking a colony or protectorate in Tibet.[57] They agreed with the official PLA history that India inherited the aggressive intentions toward China in Tibet that the British Empire had during its peak. Like the British, Nehru allegedly sought to keep Tibet a buffer between India and China. His willingness to let the Dalai Lama live in exile in India was proof of that intention. Of course, this perception of Indian hostility was greatly exaggerated, but nonetheless formed the crucial backdrop to Mao's decision for war.

A key moment in Mao's decisionmaking process came in 1959 when the Tibetan uprising flared up. Mao ordered the official Chinese news agency, Xinhua, to publish an article on May 6, 1959, titled "The Revolution in Tibet and Nehru's Philosophy"; Mao himself revised its wording before its publication. The article said that Nehru was encouraging Tibetan "reactionaries" to fight China in order to restore the old feudal system in Tibet. It pilloried Nehru as a bourgeois Indian who had taken on the strategic aspirations of British imperialism. On the day the article attacking Nehru was published, Zhou Enlai said in a public forum that Nehru "had inherited England's old policy of saying Tibet is an independent country" and that this mentality was "the center of the Sino-Indian conflict."[58]

Mao made this argument after the war as well, telling a visiting delegation from Nepal in 1964 that the issue was not the border in Kashmir or the McMahon Line. Rather the problem that forced China to go to war was that Nehru and the Indian government believed Tibet belonged to India. Mao made the same argument to the Soviets before and after the 1962 war.[59]

Because Mao totally dominated Chinese decisionmaking, his views of Nehru, whether they were right or wrong, determined Chinese policy. Once he had publicly proclaimed Nehru to be the source of China's difficulty in consolidating control of Tibet and ending all Tibetan resistance inside and outside Tibet, war was probably only a matter of time.

The failure of Indian and Chinese negotiations on the border issue in 1959 and 1960 and the increasingly rancorous India press reports about Chinese atrocities in Tibet and in the border clashes with India only strengthened Mao's determination to teach Nehru a lesson. Nehru's refusal to accept a compromise in which China would keep Aksai Chin and India would accept the McMahon Line was a major provocation, because the road China had built in Aksai Chin "was very important to the PLA logistic capabilities in Tibet. Chinese abandonment of that road would have significantly diminished PLA capabilities in Tibet, further increasing pressure on Beijing to compromise with India regarding Tibet."[60] The Forward Policy that India began to implement in late 1961 heightened Mao's paranoia about Nehru's goals in Tibet.

Mao took personal charge of the "struggle with India." According to Chinese accounts of the war's origins, he instructed the PLA to respond aggressively to the Forward Policy and accelerate road construction and other preparations for a showdown with India. Nehru's aggressive patrols in Aksai Chin and NEFA convinced Mao that "India had not learned the lesson that the Americans had learned in Korea—to respect the power of New China." Therefore, "a very strong jolt [was] necessary to cause Indian leaders to acquire a sober appreciation of Chinese power."[61]

In July 1962 Mao issued a directive to the PLA to forcefully resist the Forward Policy; firefights on the border then intensified. Chinese diplomats told their Indian counterparts that New Delhi was risking increased conflict if it did not stand down. Nehru's refusal to accept a territorial compromise, his Forward Policy, and his public demand that China evacuate Aksai Chin solidified Mao's view that he had to teach Nehru a painful lesson.

The Chinese view greatly misperceived India's posture on China's takeover of Tibet. In 1950 Nehru acceded to the Chinese advance into Tibet, albeit with some publicly stated concerns about the use of force. He even worked to keep the issue out of the UN Security Council. In the mid-1950s Nehru sought to work with China to create the nonaligned movement and to build Sino-Indian cooperation. The Dalai Lama writes in his memoirs that it was Nehru who persuaded him to return to Tibet in 1956 and accept Zhou's promises that China would respect Tibetan rights.[62] Even after the 1959 Tibetan revolt and the Dalai Lama's decision to take permanent exile in India, Nehru still acknowledged China's right to control Tibet.

Mao's misconceptions about Nehru's intentions stemmed from the paranoid dictator's isolation from outside opinion: He was surrounded by sycophants who told him what he wanted to hear. But these misconceptions probably also reflected Mao's deep frustration that Tibet would not accept, quietly and submissively, Chinese communist rule. The 1959 uprising and the Dalai Lama's flight to India had to be blamed on outside agitation. When Nehru refused a territorial compromise, it strengthened Mao's conviction that Nehru was a born-again British aggressor who was harboring designs on Tibet.

A crucial question is how much the CIA's activities in Tibet played into Mao's thinking. The Chinese communists expected that the Americans were trying to undermine their domestic control of China in general and Tibet in particular. Having captured and tortured many of the Tibetans whom the CIA parachuted into Tibet, the Chinese undoubtedly had a good appreciation of the CIA's role in Tibet.

Mao probably assumed that Nehru was a partner with the CIA and Washington in these covert operations to assist the Tibetan resistance. In fact, as described in Chapters One and Two, the Indians and Americans were not cooperating: The CIA's partner was actually Pakistan. But from Mao's perspective, collusion between Nehru and the CIA seemed self-evident. John Garver, the American sinologist who has looked most carefully at Chinese plans for war in 1962, concludes that "whatever the actual extent of Indian complicity with U.S. covert operations, Beijing believed that Nehru knew of and cooperated with CIA efforts."[63]

Indeed Nehru and his intelligence chief Mullik had some understanding of the CIA operation, especially after Mullik met with Richard Helms in Hawaii in 1960. In addition, Mullik had his own intelligence sources in the Tibetan community in India and elsewhere who undoubtedly kept him informed about Tibetan-American cooperation. As one expert surmises, "Nehru, Mullik and perhaps a few other people in the Indian government understood at least the broad contours of U.S. covert action into Tibet, but chose to turn a blind eye to them."[64]

From Mao's perspective, outsiders were stirring up resistance to China's historic right to recover control of Tibet. Nehru was giving sanctuary to the Dalai Lama and abetting CIA clandestine efforts to encourage armed resistance against the PLA. Probably as early as 1959, Mao decided that he would have to take a firm action against Nehru. The border clashes since then and the Forward Policy in 1962 strengthened the rationale for fighting back and hitting India hard. The final decision to go to war was made in the early fall of 1962, as we see in the next chapter.

SOVIET-INDIAN RELATIONS

In May rumors circulated in Washington and London that Defense Minister Krishna Menon had agreed to a Soviet proposal to purchase advanced jet fighters, MIG-21s. Although India had bought Soviet weapons before, the sale of these planes would significantly strengthen Soviet-Indian military relations and displace the United Kingdom as the main source of aircraft for the Indian Air Force. Kennedy pressed Prime Minister Harold Macmillan to offer the Indians a better deal and so undercut the Soviets.

Kennedy had great faith in Macmillan, whose war record he admired. In World War I, Macmillan had been wounded in the battle of the Somme and calmly waited for medical attention while reading classical Greek. After the Vienna summit with Khrushchev that so rattled him, Kennedy stopped in London and got a supportive hearing from the prime minister. JFK said of Macmillan, "I am lucky to have a man to deal with whom I have such a close understanding." Seeing Macmillan was like being "in the bosom of the family."[65]

Macmillan sent a team to New Delhi to propose a British sale, but the Soviet deal was much sweeter. On August 17, 1962, the USSR and India announced the signing of the Indo-Soviet Treaty of Peace, Friendship and Co-operation. It gave twelve MIG-21s at no cost to India and the right to build additional Soviet aircraft in Indian factories under the supervision of Russian advisers. Nehru explained the deal as necessary to counter the F-104 aircraft the United States was providing to Pakistan.[66]

China was angered by the Soviet MIG deal. For Mao the Soviet decision to arm India by providing high-performance aircraft to China's enemy was yet another demonstration that Moscow was neither a true ally nor a true revolutionary state.

PAKISTAN AND JFK

At this time Ayub Khan wanted to change Pakistan's image as a military dictatorship. In March 1962 he lifted the martial law regime imposed by his 1958 coup. The Pakistani Constitution of 1962 allowed limited political activity and the return of political parties. One of the junior ministers in his new government, Zulfikar Bhutto, suggested to General Khan that one way to ensure his senior standing with the generals and the public, despite the façade of change, would be to promote himself to field marshal. Ayub Khan thought the idea was "brilliant" and promptly became President Field Marshal Ayub Khan.[67]

The field marshal was becoming increasingly disillusioned with JFK. The massive increase in economic aid to India, talk of possible arms sales in the press, and—despite its disapproval of India's incursion into Goa—the administration's tilt toward India had added to Ayub Khan's doubts about Kennedy that he felt in the 1961 Mount Vernon visit. Ayub Khan looked back fondly on Eisenhower, a fellow general, and on Nixon with his pro-Pakistan outlook.

Still the fundamentals of the American-Pakistan embrace remained intact. American military aid "by the early 1960s was finally getting the Pakistani Army close to the quarter million size that Ayub and his planners had conceived as just right to counter

India's large and well established force." American weapons and training had made the Pakistani army much stronger and more modern, equipped with late-model Patton tanks and F-104 Starfighter jets.[68]

The Pakistan bases remained critically important to the United States. U-2 missions over China still departed from the Peshawar air base, about four miles south of the city of Peshawar. The facilities were supposed to be top secret, but they were part of the life of that city. The Americans stationed there shopped in the city's bazaars and hotels. They "even had special shoulder badges made by local artisans with a colorful shield with a Punjabi curved shoe (khussa), an oil lamp, a bolt of lightning, and two clasped hands, with the motto Khair Sagalie inscribed beneath it, meaning 'good will.' "[69]

Ayub Khan's second visit to Washington in the Kennedy years in September 1962 was intended to try to restore the goodwill that seemed to be ebbing away. Kennedy treated this second trip with as much fanfare as the first. It included stops at Hammersmith Farm, the summer White House in Newport, and at the Kennedys' weekend home in Middleburg, Virginia, called Glen Ora. The Middleburg home was also a farm, and it was where Sardar, the horse Ayub Khan had given Jackie during her visit to Pakistan, was stabled. Jackie and Ayub Khan, both accomplished horse riders, rode together across Glen Ora. The "mutual love of horses was the bond they shared, and Sardar was the emblem of that bond."[70]

But the behind-the-scenes discussions between JFK and Ayub Khan were troubled. On September 24 in Newport, in a meeting alone with Kennedy, Khan kept stressing the threat that India posed to Pakistan and the unresolved Kashmir dispute. He made clear Pakistan's strong objections to any arms sales to India and received further reassurances that Washington would not sell arms to India without consulting with Pakistan. Before the September visit to Newport and Washington, the Soviets, at India's behest, had vetoed a UN Security Council draft resolution on Kashmir that called for a negotiated solution to the dispute, and Ayub Khan wanted Kennedy to press Nehru to accept outside mediation. Kennedy knew that Nehru would never agree to that proposal. Ayub Khan became increasingly convinced that the "most allied ally" of the 1950s was being jilted in the 1960s and that he needed a new ally against India.

Afghanistan also was on the agenda in Newport. Afghanistan had never accepted the border with Pakistan that was drawn by the British at the end of the nineteenth century after they won the Second Anglo-Afghan War. The Durand Line divided the homeland of Afghanistan's largest ethnic group, the Pashtuns, into two. When the 1947 partition resulted in the creation of Pakistan, Kabul demanded the return of what it called Pashtunistan and refused to accept Pakistan's legitimacy. In fact, Afghanistan voted against giving Pakistan membership in the United Nations.

By 1962 relations had deteriorated between the two countries, and Pakistan had closed its borders with Afghanistan, effectively cutting off Afghanistan's main trade route through Karachi to the world. Kabul was forced to depend on the Soviet Union and Iran for trade at considerable extra expense. The Afghan monarch appealed for Kennedy's help to mediate the crisis. When JFK pressed Ayub Khan at Hammersmith to be flexible, the field marshal saw this as one more sign that Pakistan was no longer America's special ally.

As Mullik's intelligence suggested, Pakistan was starting to look to China for help against Nehru. An early sign of Ayub Khan's move toward China was his 1961 vote on the annual UN General Assembly motion to admit Communist China to the UN and give it the Security Council seat still held by the Nationalist government on Taiwan. In the Eisenhower years Pakistan was a consistent supporter of the American "no" vote. In 1961 Pakistan voted yes.

China and Pakistan began negotiations in Beijing in May 1962 to settle their own border claims. Pakistan had seized the northern half of Kashmir in the war following partition in 1947. As a consequence it had a common border with the PRC north of Aksai Chin and the Indian-administered portion of Kashmir. The land link between Pakistan and China was over very difficult terrain, but had become strategically important. Because of India's position that all of Kashmir belonged to it and that Aksai Chin was part of Kashmir, it would view as very alarming any negotiations on resolving the two countries' different claims about the border they inherited from the British. The Beijing talks got off to a slow start, but did raise alarm bells in India.[71]

MOSCOW AND HAVANA

On the other side of the world, in late July 1962 the National Security Agency (NSA) detected an increase in the number of Soviet ships traveling to Cuba and published this finding in a report titled "Unusual Number of Soviet Passenger Ships en Route Cuba." It noted that the ships were receiving "high precedence messages," which indicated they were "engaged in other than routine activities." It was a crucial intelligence tip.[72]

Fidel's brother Raul spent two weeks in Moscow in July. We know now that the talks between Raul Castro and Nikita Khrushchev set the stage for the Soviet deployment of some 50,000 troops to Cuba and the stationing of nuclear weapons on the island. In his memoirs Khrushchev said the idea to send the missiles came to him earlier, in May 1962 during a visit to Bulgaria, and preliminary conversations within the Kremlin may have occurred even before then in April 1962. The discussions with Raul in the summer resulted in a formal agreement on the deployment of the Soviet expeditionary force to Cuba.[73]

In late August and early September 1962 the CIA found evidence of the arrival in Cuba of new surface-to-air missiles (SAMs), missiles similar to those that had shot down Gary Powers's U-2 plane in 1960. These were defensive weapons, but DCI McCone was convinced that the SAMs were the front end of a larger deployment that would include offensive weapons. Such a deployment would be absolutely contrary to repeated Soviet assurances to Kennedy that Moscow would not provide offensive weapons to Cuba; Khrushchev had made this assurance in writing several times. McCone began "a stream of communications stating his personal opinion that the Soviets might be planning to base medium range ballistic missiles in Cuba." The attorney general, Bobby Kennedy, became convinced that McCone was correct.[74]

However, McCone's analysts were not entirely convinced. The CIA's Office of Current Intelligence (OCI) prepared an analysis on August 22, 1962, on "Recent Soviet Military Aid to Cuba," which noted that as many as twenty Soviet vessels had already arrived in Cuba since late July carrying military cargo and that more were en route. Perhaps 5,000 Soviet personnel had arrived in Cuba in the last month. The OCI paper concluded that "the speed and magnitude of this influx of Soviet bloc personnel and equipment into a non-bloc country is unprecedented in Soviet military aid activities: clearly something new and different is taking place." However, it suggested that the most likely explanation for the buildup was that it was for defensive purposes: Moscow was putting defensive SAMs on the island and communications intelligence collection facilities.[75]

The intelligence community prepared a Special National Intelligence Estimate (SNIE) on September 19, 1962, for the president on "The Military Buildup in Cuba" after U-2 missions had confirmed the deployment of the SAMs. It agreed with the conclusion of the August analysis, noting, "The Soviets evidently hope to deter" a possible U.S. attempt to overthrow Castro "by enhancing Castro's defensive capabilities and by threatening Soviet military retaliation." The Soviets were probably eager not to "provoke US military intervention and thus defeat their present purpose." Deploying offensive weapons, either intermediate-range ballistic missiles or a submarine base, would "be incompatible with Soviet practices to date and with Soviet policy as we presently estimate it. It would indicate a far greater willingness to increase the level of risk in US-Soviet relations than the USSR has displayed thus far," the SNIE concluded.[76]

Before he left on his honeymoon to southern France in late summer, McCone pushed for more U-2 flights to collect intelligence over Cuba. However, on September 10 National Security Adviser Bundy and Secretary Rusk ordered the cessation of U-2 flights over Cuba because they worried the new SAMs would shoot them down in a repeat of the Gary Powers debacle. McCone's deputy protested this decision, as did McCone in cables sent from his honeymoon. When he returned from France he pushed for at least a limited U-2 flight over the western half of Cuba. The mission was flown on October 15, 1962, and the images collected set the missile crisis in motion.[77]

McCone was proven right: Khrushchev was upping the ante. And so was Mao Zedong, yet neither communist leader coordinated his plans with the other. Russian sources indicate that Khrushchev did not tell Mao that he was sending missiles to Cuba, nor did Mao tell Moscow he was going to war with India until two days before the attack.[78] On opposite sides of the globe the two communist giants were each planning military action, but were so antagonistic to each other that they operated on separate paths. The world was heading toward perhaps its most dangerous days ever.

CHAPTER FOUR

JFK, INDIA, AND WAR

he U.S. Embassy in New Delhi is one of the Department of State's most ambitious architectural projects. Sitting on twenty-eight acres of land in the capital's diplomatic quarter, the embassy was designed by Edward D. Stone, one of the premier architects of his generation. Stone would later design the John F. Kennedy Center for the Performing Arts in Washington, the nation's most important monument to the president. Chief Justice of the Supreme Court Earl Warren laid the cornerstone for the embassy in 1956, and Nehru and then Ambassador Ellsworth Bunker formally dedicated the embassy chancery building on January 5, 1959.

The ambassador's residence, which Galbraith named Roosevelt House, was not completed until 1962. Galbraith and his family moved in on November 8, 1962, in the middle of the Sino-Indian War. The move was far from smooth. Galbraith wrote in his diary that after putting everything in boxes at the old residence "a vast army of peons by nightfall had dumped the contents into the new house. Being immediately adjacent to the Chancery [the embassy], the house is much more convenient and certainly not without grandeur. It is also in a sad state of confusion. For dinner, an emergency detachment had to be sent out for dishes, none being locatable in the unopened boxes." However, Galbraith did enjoy his "newest luxury"—the large swimming pool in the garden behind Roosevelt House. He characterized his new home as "lacking in warmth but not in beauty, with high ceilings and wide porches, so white that one needs snow glasses. A fountain runs constantly below the stairway and gives the impression everywhere of a toilet out of control."[1]

John Kenneth Galbraith was a very busy man in October and November 1962 because India was at war. On October 20, China made two simultaneous major attacks on the border 1,000 kilometers apart. In the western theater, the PLA sought to expel Indian forces from the Chip Chap valley in Aksai Chin, whereas in NEFA they attacked near the McMahon Line. Just days earlier, on October 16, National Security Adviser McGeorge Bundy had opened his daily briefing book in his West Wing office to find two urgent memos. In the first the State Department warned that "fighting on the Sino-Indian border has become much more serious" than normal and that India might soon need U.S. assistance.[2] In the second, the CIA reported that U-2 imagery had confirmed the delivery of offensive intermediate-range missiles to Cuba. On October 22, only two days after the Chinese invasion of India, the president told the American people and the world that he was imposing a naval quarantine on Cuba. The twin crises were thus joined. Because the Cuban crisis was so dangerous and critical, the Kennedy national security team in Washington devoted all their energy and time to managing it, leaving Galbraith virtually alone to handle the China-India crisis. After summoning him from London back to New Delhi, Kennedy gave his friend remarkable latitude to engage with Nehru. For his part Galbraith relished the independence and the challenge, and Kennedy would find his ambassador was up to the task.

BUILDING UP TO WAR

India's implementation of the Forward Policy served as a major provocation to China in September 1962. India's Fourth Division was stationed near the juncture of the western end of the McMahon Line with the small kingdom of Bhutan. As in many other parts of the border, the exact demarcation of the McMahon Line was unclear here; the British had never traced it out on the ground in detail. In principle the border was supposed to run along the ridge-line separating the Himalayas from the descent into Assam, but in this area the McMahon Line did not align with the ridgeline, but ran south of it. In keeping with the Forward Policy, the Fourth Division was ordered to move forward to the Thag La ridge (also called Thagla) in territory the Chinese regarded as theirs.

Brigadier John P. Dalvi commanded the Seventh Brigade of the Fourth Division that was instructed to move to the Thag La ridge. He reported to New Delhi that his forces were outnumbered and poorly supplied. While the Chinese soldiers had winter clothing and a supply depot immediately behind their front lines, the Indian troops were dressed in summer uniforms and depended on air drops to get needed food and ammunition. He urged caution.

Instead Nehru and Defense Minister Krishna Menon decided to press the Indian claim and ordered the army high command on September 9, 1962, to carry out Operation Leghorn to take control of Thag La ridge. "This order was typical of the approach that the Army HQ was to take throughout the war. It responded dutifully to the political requirements of the government, but disregarded elementary military considerations."[3] Dalvi, who was a veteran of World War II battles in Burma against the Japanese, initially re-sisted the order, but was instructed to carry out the plan regardless of the reality on the ground. The Chinese could see the Indians reinforcing their positions and consequently further strengthened their own, thereby outnumbering the Indian forces even more. A senior Indian general, B. M. Kaul, was given overall command in

NEFA and came to the ridge front to oversee Dalvi's Seventh Brigade. Kaul was a cousin of Nehru and was not highly regarded by his fellow officers, who regarded him as a political appointee without serious military experience.

Mao probably finalized the decision to go to war in a meeting in Beijing on October 6 with his senior generals. Mao told them that China had defeated Chiang Kai-shek and the Nationalists, Imperial Japan, and the United States in Korea. Now "Nehru sticks his head out and insists on us fighting him; for us not to fight with him would not be friendly enough. Courtesy demands reciprocity."[4] The People's Liberation Army was ordered to impose a "fierce and painful" blow on India and expel India from the territory China claimed in Kashmir west of the Johnson Line and in NEFA south of the McMahon Line.[5] On October 8 the Chinese Foreign Ministry informed the Soviet ambassador in Beijing that a massive attack by China was imminent.[6] Because the Soviets were engaged in their own high-stakes gamble in Cuba, Moscow did not discourage the Chinese, despite Khrushchev's close relations with Nehru. Even though the Soviets had just promised to sell India advanced jet fighters, MIG-21s, they had little choice but to back their fellow communists in China now that war was imminent. Khrushchev needed the support of China in his global gamble in Cuba.

Mao's focus was on Nehru, but a defeat of India would also be a setback for two of Mao's other enemies: Khrushchev and Kennedy. Humiliating India would demonstrate that China's hardline foreign policy and ruthless determination to "communize" itself on its own without the aid of Soviet advisers was a superior strategy to Khrushchev's more moderate policies. Mao knew that Moscow's half-hearted support for his war with India was likely to last only as long as the Cuba crisis, and humiliating India would send a tough message to Moscow.

At the same time defeating India would answer the question Kennedy had raised in his 1959 speech in the Senate about which country, democratic India or communist China, was poised to win the race for great power status in Asia. For Mao the conflict with India provided a surrogate for his rivalry with Moscow and with Washington.

On October 10, 1962, the PLA struck first, pushing back Dalvi's patrol with superior force. Dalvi later reported that Kaul said, "Oh my God, you're right; they (the Chinese) mean business," and he rushed back to New Delhi to report the situation.[7] The very next day Kaul met with Nehru and the senior Indian leadership, proposing that "India should seek speedy and copious military assistance from the United States." Kaul was agitated and close to a breakdown. His proposals included setting up a temporary dictatorship in India, asking South Korea and Taiwan to attack China, and requesting that the United States "launch massive air attacks on China from bases in India."[8]

Nehru rejected these hysterical ideas and insisted that Operation Leghorn continue. The next morning Nehru left for a three-day visit to Ceylon. At the airport Nehru told the press, "Our instructions are to free our territory, I can not fix a date; that is entirely for the army." Thus Nehru ignored the advice of his generals on the scene and instead listened to the top brass in New Delhi. This was a serious mistake. Having surrounded himself in New Delhi with "courtiers" who told him "only what his top military advisers believed he wished to hear," Nehru took their bad advice.[9]

The Indian and international media interpreted Nehru's remarks at the airport en route to Ceylon as an ultimatum to China. The *New York Herald Tribune* headline, all in capital letters, was "NEHRU DECLARES WAR ON CHINA." The *People's Daily* in Beijing reported, "A massive invasion of Chinese territory by Indian troops seems imminent." It urged Nehru to "pull back from the brink of the precipice."[10] Meanwhile the Indian press demanded action to "free" Indian territory from Chinese invaders.

THE WAR BEGINS

The war began at dawn on October 20 with simultaneous attacks, 1,000 kilometers apart, on India's western and northeast borders. Near the McMahon Line, PLA forces attacked the exposed brigade of the Fourth Division at the Thag La ridge commanded by Brigadier Dalvi. Outnumbered by at least three to one, the brigade was routed, and Dalvi was taken prisoner on October 22. The PLA took control of the border region near Bhutan in NEFA, quickly driving the Indians south. PLA forces also attacked in the far eastern portion of NEFA at an Indian stronghold at Walong where India abuts Burma.

At the same time, the Chinese launched a major offensive in the west in Kashmir, sweeping the Indians out of Aksai Chin and taking control of the territory China claimed in the western sector. Over the course of the next eight days, PLA forces overran all the posts established as part of the Forward Policy.[11] The reaction in New Delhi to these setbacks was complete surprise. Back from Ceylon, Nehru began having daily decisionmaking meetings with his inner circle and the top military command.

Galbraith's and Kennedy's Response

On October 20 Ambassador Galbraith was in London to give a speech. He was staying at the Ritz Hotel when "a lad" from the U.S. Embassy in London arrived at his room in the middle of the night with a "TOP SECRET EYES ONLY" message from President Kennedy instructing him to immediately return to New Delhi. In his diary he wrote, "My lectures sponsors were unhappy but naturally did not argue with a war."[12] He was back in New Delhi on October 22.

Galbraith did not know that a week before, on October 15, a CIA U-2 flight over Cuba had photographed Soviet soldiers building launch facilities for medium-range ballistic missiles. The CIA had orally briefed National Security Adviser McGeorge Bundy late that day about the findings. By the next morning a CIA report on the imagery had been written and Kennedy briefed. The president then instructed Bundy to convene an urgent meeting of his national security advisers, a group called the EXCOMM; it would continue to meet several times a day throughout the thirteen days of the Cuban missile crisis, in the Cabinet Room immediately adjacent to the Oval Office.

The White House kept the news of the Soviet missile bases in Cuba secret until the president addressed the nation on October 22. Kennedy's earlier EYES ONLY message for Galbraith in London related to the Cuban crisis, not the Sino-Indian War; he wanted his friend Ken to return to India to explain to Nehru U.S. policy on the placement of missiles in Cuba. It was a useful coincidence that this order also put Galbraith back on the scene as the first major Chinese attack was getting underway.[13]

At the time Americans believed that the Cuban missile crisis was the most dangerous moment in the cold war, the closest that the United States and the USSR came to a direct military clash that would precipitate nuclear war and global Armageddon. Decades later we know from Soviet records that it was even more dangerous than was thought in 1962. At the time the CIA estimated there were from 6,000 to 8,000 Soviet troops on the island; in fact, there were 50,000. Unbeknownst to the CIA and JFK, the Soviets had sent not only medium- and intermediate-range ballistic missiles to Cuba but also tactical missiles called FROGs loaded with nuclear warheads. Soviet forces on Cuba were ready to fire nuclear weapons at the U.S. Naval Base at Guantanamo Bay with its garrison of 5,000 Marines if the Americans decided to bomb the longer-range missiles and warheads that threatened its cities.

The president had ordered the Pentagon to draw up plans to invade Cuba. The main plan, Operation Scabbard, involved 120,000 troops from eight divisions going ashore in a D-day–like assault. In addition, two Army airborne divisions would parachute into

Cuba, and the First Marine Division would conduct a separate landing. Three aircraft carrier battle groups, including the first ever nuclear-powered carrier, USS *Enterprise*, would provide air support. Undoubtedly in response, the Soviets would have used tactical nuclear weapons to defend the beaches. Thus if Kennedy had accepted the advice of most of his military advisers and attacked the island, nuclear war would have begun immediately.[14]

The Cuban crisis reached its peak on October 27 when Soviet air defense forces shot down a CIA U-2 aircraft flying over Cuba, killing the pilot. Another unrelated U-2 mission in the Arctic Ocean went badly off course and flew inside Russian Siberia. Fortunately on October 28 Khrushchev agreed to remove the missiles from Cuba in return for a public American pledge not to invade Cuba and a private promise from Kennedy to remove American medium-range missiles from Turkey.

The Cuban crisis was not completely resolved by October 28, although the worst was over. Kennedy demanded that Khrushchev also withdraw IL-28 bombers that could target American cities and wanted on-site inspections of all offensive weapons systems to ensure their complete withdrawal. Castro resisted any inspections and felt that Khrushchev had let him down in agreeing to withdraw the missiles. Not until November 20 did Khrushchev agree to remove the IL-28s. Kennedy lifted the quarantine and announced the crisis at an end.

Although it did not meet as frequently or for as long as it did during the first thirteen days of the crisis, the EXCOMM continued to meet throughout October and November. The president secretly tape recorded those meetings, having installed microphones to record conversations in the Oval Office and the Cabinet Room in the summer of 1962. He and his brother Bobby were the only ones who knew about the secret recordings. Since the Kennedy Library made the tapes available to the public in the 1990s, scholars have studied them extensively, and a transcript has been published.[15] There have also been an extensive series of oral history projects that have brought together the EXCOMM participants to discuss their memories of the crisis.[16] In both the transcript and the oral histories, there is little or no mention of the other crisis going on in India or that the president ever asked the EXCOMM team to study the China crisis.

We can only speculate why Kennedy did not use the EXCOMM to assess the second crisis underway on the other side of the globe. Perhaps he did not think he needed the advice of the team or that it should be kept narrowly focused on Cuba and not diverted from its primary task. Perhaps by the time he was making decisions relating to India and China he had come to find the EXCOMM too hawkish and doctrinaire in its thinking. Indeed Kennedy told Galbraith privately in December 1962 "with much feeling and some anger of the recklessness of much of the professional advice he had received during the missile crisis, in particular the proposal to bomb the missile sites." The president told Ken, "The worst advice as always was from those who feared that to be sensible made them seem soft and unheroic."[17]

It is clear that Kennedy felt that Galbraith and he made up the right team to tackle the war in India largely on their own. Once back in New Delhi Galbraith got to work immediately. In his diary Galbraith writes that he got "rather meager communications from Washington as a result of the Cuban crisis." Late on October 22 he did receive an "execrably drafted letter from the President to the Prime Minister (Nehru) which had been so badly drafted for the President that I had to get permission from Washington to make some changes in the interests both of reasonable tact and syntax."[18] Armed with the letter on Cuba, Galbraith went to see Nehru the next day.[19]

Despite some concerns about the legality of a quarantine, Nehru assured Galbraith of Indian support for the U.S. position on Cuba. However, his main focus naturally was on China and the disaster on the Thag La ridge. There was increasing political pressure to remove Menon as the minister of defense; before the month was over he was gone, first demoted to a more junior cabinet job and then removed from government service altogether. Menon was the symbol of anti-Americanism in India, and his departure was welcome in Washington.

Galbraith offered U.S. political support to India, but not any military aid in its fight with China. In his view it was better for India to take the first step on the question of American assistance: "My general line is to give quiet sympathy and encouragement to the Indians, let them know who are their true friends, be receptive to requests for aid, but also to have decently in mind the pounding we have been taking from Krishna Menon."[20] Anticipating that such a request for help would be forthcoming, Galbraith asked the embassy staff to study what type of assistance could be best provided by the United States. "It would take Washington far too long to decide on this matter," he felt, so better he and his team be prepared to tell Washington exactly what made sense.[21]

On October 24, the ambassador had another urgent meeting, this one with the prime minister of Bhutan, who told Galbraith that Chinese forces were massed on his tiny kingdom's border. The miniscule army of Bhutan could not hope to stop a Chinese attack. If the Chinese broadened their offensive to include Bhutan and its even smaller neighbor Sikkim, they could easily drive south to cut off India's entire northeastern section—made up of NEFA and Assam—and link up with East Pakistan.

At this time, India regarded Bhutan and Sikkim as its protectorates, not as independent countries. A Chinese advance through them toward the narrow corridor connecting India to its northeastern states—the Siliguri Corridor, so named after the West Bengal city located in the corridor—would be a disaster for India. Undoubtedly the Indians encouraged the Bhutanese prime minister to make his concerns known to the Americans.[22]

On the same day that Galbraith met with the Bhutanese prime minister, the Chinese decided to halt its offensive operations and make a diplomatic gesture. Mao and Zhou offered India a three-point plan: (1) India and China would agree to settle their dispute peacefully, (2) both would withdraw their troops to twenty kilometers behind the previous line of actual control (LOAC) along the McMahon Line, and (3) the two prime ministers would meet to negotiate a final border deal. Nehru rejected the plan immediately. The Indians saw it as affirming Chinese control of Aksai Chin and opening up a negotiations process for the McMahon Line.[23] In fact it was the same Chinese proposal that Mao and Zhou had offered as early as 1959: China would get what it wanted in Kashmir, thereby protecting its supply line to Tibet, and India would get withdrawals of Chinese soldiers behind the McMahon Line in the east. Nehru had rejected this proposal before, and it would be political suicide to accept it now after the defeat at Thag La.

Behind the scenes Nehru was already thinking about a new strategy for dealing with China—providing aggressive support for the Tibetan resistance. Menon and Kaul, the two men most responsible for the defeat of the Seventh Brigade, now urgently suggested the arming of Tibetan guerillas to strike at the PLA's supply lines and depots in Tibet. They nominated a recently retired army officer, Brigadier Sujan Singh Uban, for the job of organizing the campaign. Tibetan exiles in India were approached and agreed to fight, but wanted the operation to be run by Mullik's Intelligence Bureau with Uban under his control; their recommendation was accepted. The plan would not bear any fruit immediately, but it was to have important consequences later.[24]

Meanwhile, as Galbraith wrote in his diary, Washington remained "totally occupied with Cuba. For a week, I have had a considerable war on my hands without a single telegram, letter, telephone call or other communication of guidance" from Washington. The embassy was sending "off telegrams on various urgent matters without the slightest knowledge of whether they are being received or acted upon. It is like marching troops out of the trenches and over no man's land without knowing whether they get through or get shot down en route."[25]

During this period Galbraith did receive one message from the State Department, but characteristically chose to challenge it. It instructed him that, because Nationalist China did not accept the McMahon Line as the legitimate border, neither should Galbraith and the United States. Ignoring the only guidance he had gotten so far from the State Department, Galbraith issued a statement endorsing the Indian claim to the McMahon Line, but only after getting permission from Bundy and the White House to do so. As soon as Ken got approval to endorse India's claim the embassy released a statement, thereby putting the United States clearly on India's side in the border dispute. Soon after that the U.S. Embassy in Taiwan complained, "protesting bitterly" Galbraith's end-around of the State Department and the Nationalist government.

On October 28, on the same day that the Cuban missile crisis began to abate as Khrushchev announced the withdrawal of Soviet missiles, Kennedy wrote a letter to Nehru assuring him that the United States fully backed India against the Chinese attack. The letter promised both moral and tangible support if India sought help. The next day Nehru summoned Galbraith to a meeting where the Indian leader congratulated Kennedy and Khrushchev for finding a peaceful settlement and then told him that India "indeed had to have aid and it would have to come from the United States." Nehru also told Galbraith that the Soviets would not be supplying the MIG-21s as promised, signaling that the USSR was siding with Mao.

Asking for American arms was a humiliating moment for the prime minister, who had prided himself on Indian independence and neutrality. He knew he needed JFK's help, but did not want to be seen to be abandoning his principles. Nehru especially did not want to join a military alliance such as SEATO, but he desperately needed arms. Galbraith assured him that Kennedy would not impose the condition of joining any military alliance. Menon, who was also at the meeting with Nehru and Galbraith, provided the details on exactly what weapons India wanted. Galbraith told the

British and Canadian ambassadors in New Delhi that India had requested military aid and that Kennedy had agreed to provide it; they both asked their respective governments in London and Ottawa to join the effort.[26]

Prime Minister Harold Macmillan agreed to join the supply effort. As mentioned earlier, Macmillan fought in World War I with the Grenadier Guards in France. Severely wounded in the Battle of the Somme in September 1916 he read Aeschylus in the original Greek as he lay in his trench until the medics could take him to the rear. Kennedy admired Macmillan's toughness and was fond of the British ambassador in Washington, David Ormsby-Gore, who was a close family friend of the Kennedys.

The United States and United Kingdom responded very quickly to Nehru's request for armaments. U.S. Air Force (USAF) Boeing 707 aircraft, flying from bases in Europe and Thailand, began airlifting weapons and ammunition to India; by November 2, eight flights a day were each bringing in twenty tons of supplies to Calcutta. USAF C-130s then transported the arms from Calcutta to airfields near the front line. Basic infantry equipment was thus flowing rapidly to help the Indian army,[27] and the press was reporting on the U.S. airlift. The Royal Air Force (RAF) also soon began airlifting supplies to India, and London was consulting with Australia, New Zealand, and Canada on providing aid from the British Commonwealth.[28]

In addition to providing material support, the airlifts also led to a fundamental change in military-to-military relations. Previously the Indian military had held the American defense attaché and his staff in New Delhi at arm's length, giving them almost no information about conditions at the front. Likewise at Galbraith's daily staff meeting the only information available was what was reported in the Indian press. Once the airlift began, however, the Indian Defense Ministry started to provide briefings on the battlefield situation and, most importantly, on Indian requirements for arms, winter gear, and other equipment. The two bureaucracies did not always interact smoothly, but they were at least talking to each other. The removal of the controversial Menon facilitated the interaction.

As mentioned earlier, in the end of October there was a three-week lull in Chinese military operations that gave the Indian military a chance to regroup and regain their self-confidence. By this time the Indians had built a new defensive line south of the Thag La ridge at a pass in the mountains named Se La. At an altitude of 14,600 feet, the pass would provide a strong position from which to stop further PLA advances if the Chinese resumed their offensive. Yet, by retreating to Se La the Indians abandoned the town of Tawang, an important Buddhist center. To make matters worse, the Chinese found it easy to outflank the position at Se La, which India still found difficult to supply.

Nehru asked Intelligence Bureau director Mullik for an updated assessment of Chinese military strength and battle plans. Mullik reported large-scale Chinese troop movements from Xinjiang and other parts of China to Tibet to reinforce their offensive maneuvers along the McMahon line and in Aksai Chin. The eleven PLA divisions at the start of the crisis had been reinforced by at least an additional three divisions. The Indians had roughly half as many divisions deployed along the entire border from Kashmir to NEFA; several were guarding the Bhutan-Sikkim front where the narrow Indian connections between NEFA and mainland India were so vulnerable. The estimate also warned that China had overall superiority in the air and could defeat the Indian air force. The only way to reinforce the Himalayan battlefield was to draw down troops facing Pakistan, "which would expose Punjab and Kashmir to great danger," Mullik warned Nehru.[29]

During the lull in fighting Kennedy also asked for an intelligence estimate from McCone. The Special National Intelligence Estimate, which was delivered to the Oval Office on November 9, 1962, concluded that the "Sino-Indian quarrel has become a serious military struggle which is already causing a change in India's foreign and domestic attitudes favorable to the West." The PLA had "a distinct military advantage." In Tibet the Chinese had more than 100,000 troops, and many more could be added from the rest of China. The Chinese air force was four or five times larger than India's, with more than 2,000 jet fighters to India's 315, and 460 bombers to India's 320. China could deploy an attack force of 400 jet fighters and 200 bombers to Tibet. The principal restriction on the Chinese was the difficult terrain, but the PLA had a proven track record of overcoming logistical constraints in Korea and elsewhere. The American intelligence community expected China to wait for spring and better weather to resume the offensive, which could well expand into Bhutan and Sikkim.[30]

The SNIE also reported that "Pakistan's reaction to the West's support of India has been a bitter one." The Goa incident had already exacerbated Pakistan's endemic worries about Indian attitudes toward its neighbors. U.S. aid to India had eroded Pakistan's confidence in its treaty ally. If the United States increased arms assistance to India further, the SNIE predicted that "Ayub would be unwilling to agree to any expansion of special US facilities in Pakistan, and might demand the elimination of some of them." The facilities in Peshawar were now at risk in the CIA's view. For its part, India was keeping substantial numbers of troops on the Pakistani front because it feared a Pakistani attack.[31]

AYUB, PAKISTAN, AND KENNEDY

For Galbraith "the nightmare of a combined attack by Pakistan and China, with the possibility of defeat, collapse and even anarchy in India, was much on my mind. My concern was about equally divided between helping the Indians against the Chinese and keeping peace between the Indians and the Pakistanis."[32] The ambassador was right to be concerned. From the beginning of hostilities Ayub Khan began pressing for some kind of Indian "compensation" in

Kashmir in exchange for Pakistani neutrality. As the United States began to back India publicly on the McMahon Line and then to send it arms, Ayub Khan felt betrayed by Kennedy. The promise he had gotten in July 1961 that Washington would not arm India, even if China attacked, without Pakistan's agreement seemed to be a dead letter: The "most allied ally" was being forsaken to help its bigger neighbor.

On October 28, the day before Nehru asked for American military help, the U.S. ambassador in Pakistan, Walter McConaughy, met with Ayub Khan. The ambassador urged him to send assurances to Nehru that Pakistan would not take advantage of India's war with China. McConaughy later told Galbraith that Ayub Khan's reaction to this request was "stiff." Following up on a suggestion Galbraith had given McConaughy before this meeting, the U.S. ambassador asked Ayub whether a letter from Kennedy himself requesting such assurances would be helpful. The Pakistani leader liked the idea and suggested that such a letter include a promise that, in return for assurances of Pakistani restraint during the war, Kennedy would promise to "take a strong stand on behalf of Ayub on Kashmir." As Galbraith wrote in his diary, Ayub Khan was proposing that "the Americans and Pakistanis work together to seek the surrender of Indian territory just as the Chinese were grabbing land. All would seem to be grabbing." For Galbraith this amounted to Pakistani "blackmail," and he told the Pakistani ambassador in India just that. Galbraith was convinced that his counterpart Mc-Conaughy was a typical State Department career diplomat who was inclined to favor Pakistan and was thus capable of giving Ayub Khan too much. Galbraith immediately sent an "alarming telegram" to Washington and Karachi "asking for God's sake that they keep Kashmir out" of any American messages to Pakistan.[33]

Walter McConaughy was in fact a career diplomat, one of the State Department's old China hands. Born in Alabama and educated at Duke University, he spent seven years in Japan before being posted to Beijing in early 1941, then under the control of Japan.

After Pearl Harbor was attacked, he was interned by the Japanese before being released in an exchange of diplomats. As consul general in Shanghai, he closed the last State Department office in China in May 1950, a year after the People's Liberation Army arrived in that city. He also served in Hong Kong, Burma, and South Korea before Kennedy appointed him ambassador to Pakistan in 1962. Of course, McConaughy did not have the personal and political connections to JFK that Galbraith enjoyed.[34]

Washington sided immediately with Galbraith on Kashmir, but thought it would be useful for McConaughy to be able to tell Ayub Khan that Nehru would welcome reassurances of Pakistani neutrality. Galbraith that evening saw the prime minister and wrote later in his diary, "Nehru was frail, brittle, and seemed small and old. He was obviously desperately tired." When asked if the United States could tell Ayub Khan that Nehru would welcome a Pakistani assurance of neutrality, the prime minister said he would not object. Galbraith then "moved in very hard saying this would not be sufficient, that we must be able to say that Nehru would warmly accept such assurances. He looked a little stunned."[35] Nehru relented and agreed that such a letter would be helpful. Galbraith pressed further and asked Nehru to promise that he would positively respond to a Pakistani assurance. Nehru said "on some appropriate occasion he would." Galbraith pressed hard again and said, "This was a time for generosity and he should be immediately forthcoming. Again Nehru agreed."[36] Thus Galbraith was increasingly becoming a key policy counselor to the Indian prime minister behind the scenes.

The next day, on October 29, Nehru formally asked Kennedy via Galbraith to supply arms to India. Kennedy had just sent a letter to Ayub Khan describing the Chinese attack on India as an act of aggression and informing him that the United States would provide support to India. Kennedy asked for Pakistan to reassure India that it would not take advantage of the Chinese attack to pressure India. Kennedy's message was, in essence, that the Chinese communists were now threatening a neighbor and that Pakistan, as a member of two alliances built to fight communism, needed to be on the right side. This was why the Pakistanis and Americans were treaty allies: to fight communism.

Nehru did write to Ayub Khan on October 29 to explain the situation as Galbraith had suggested and Ayub wrote back. Nonetheless, throughout late October and November Ayub Khan and his aides publicly criticized U.S. and British military aid to India. After all, Pakistan was an ally of the United States, whereas India was a neutral nonaligned state. As Ayub Khan recalled later, "I expressed concern over the western decision to rush military aid to India on a scale based apparently on an assumption that India was faced with a major war with China. It made no sense militarily, I said, that China should decide to launch an invasion of India over the Himalayas at the height of winter."[37] His argument was that Chinese aims were limited, Nehru had provoked the war by his Forward Policy, and Washington and London were overreacting. In addition, Kennedy was not consulting Pakistan about aid to India, but was just informing it after the fact without taking into account its interests, especially in Kashmir.

On November 7, Ayub Khan followed up his public comments with a long letter to Kennedy. Ayub Khan began by writing that India "for the last fifteen years has posed a major military threat to Pakistan. She has built up her forces three or four times our strength and had openly declared that Pakistan is her enemy number one. Eighty per cent of Armed Forces have been earmarked against us." He blamed Nehru's obstructionism for the Kashmir problem. He then shared his military assessment that China had limited objectives in the border conflict. Ayub Khan reminded Kennedy that it was Nehru who had hoisted "the white flag of neutralism to appease communism," not Pakistan, and that Nehru had also been the aggressor in seizing Goa. "In the eyes of many people in Asia, Indian intentions are suspect and India continues to pose a serious threat to our security."[38]

The Pakistani president then responded directly to American suggestions that he provide "an assurance to Mr. Nehru." Ayub wrote, "I am surprised that such a request is being made to us." India was a threat to Pakistan, not the other way around, and was already "moving forward their reserve armored formations to battle locations against Pakistan." The Indian navy was concentrated in Bombay harbor "to pose a threat to us." "No, Mr. President, the answer to this problem lies elsewhere . . . in a settlement of the question of Kashmir."[39]

Finally Ayub Khan turned to Kennedy's assurance that "the arms you are now supplying to India will not be used against us." He reminded Kennedy "of the promise you were good enough to make, namely that we shall be consulted before you gave any military assistance to India, and we did expect to be consulted on the types and quantities of weapons now being supplied to them. It is regrettable that none of this has been done." Ayub Khan refused to give Kennedy any assurances, accusing him of failing to live up to his promises of 1961. Then he raised the Kashmir gambit: Pakistan would stay out of the war if it got "an equitable and an honourable settlement" in Kashmir."[40]

Ayub Khan's letter to the president seemed to justify all of Galbraith's fears of Pakistani collusion with China against India. The United States and Pakistan had diametrically opposed views of the Chinese attack on India. Ayub Khan saw it as a border war that was largely a product of India's arrogance toward all its neighbors, whereas Washington saw the Chinese attack as a major communist move in the cold war. The State Department told the Pakistani ambassador in Washington that it "regarded the Chinese move as the biggest since Korea. In Korea the U.S. decision to go to war in 1950 had been taken with great rapidity and the same speed was necessary to meet the present situation."[41] The State Department gave the Pakistani ambassador lists of the equipment to be provided to India, divided into two categories: the material that would be airlifted immediately and that which would be sent later.

The department assured the ambassador that the rules for this equipment's use would be same as those for the U.S. weapons received by Pakistan: The military equipment was to be used against communist aggression, not India's neighbor.

Yet, the American expectation that India would not use U.S. arms to fight Pakistan nor would Pakistan use U.S. arms to fight India was completely unrealistic. Pakistan had allied itself with the United States in the SEATO and CENTO alliances to strengthen its armed forces to fight India, not Russia or China. As the architect of Pakistan's military buildup since independence, Ayub Khan was well aware of the hollow nature of such previous Pakistani commitments to Washington and suspected Nehru's assurances were equally hollow.

Nehru continued his correspondence with Ayub Khan by sending a long letter to Karachi on November 12. It began with a compliment to the field marshal: "With your experience as a distinguished soldier you will no doubt realize that the Chinese aggression is not merely a border incident, but is an invasion of India on a massive scale." China was threatening the security of all South Asia, and India had asked for help from the United States and United Kingdom to stop a "powerful and unscrupulous invader." Nehru thus completely rejected Ayub Khan's assessment of China's intentions. The letter made no mention of Kashmir.[42]

Galbraith wrote Kennedy a long letter on November 13 reviewing the crisis. Ken said the invasion had "brought great change here—no doubt the greatest change in public attitudes since World War II." Indians now saw China as their top enemy. The Soviet Union had failed India, and so had the nonaligned world. The United States and United Kingdom had been its only reliable allies. Galbraith wrote that accepting this Western support "hurt Nehru's pride" because Nehru had fought for independence for so long from the West. Galbraith wisely urged Kennedy "to be generous on this."[43]

"The great question is what the Chinese intend" to do next, Galbraith wrote JFK. Initially Galbraith had thought their intentions were limited and that the Chinese were focused on Aksai Chin and securing their position in Tibet and Sinkiang and their road network there. "I have not entirely discarded the above theory," Galbraith told Kennedy, but he was very worried now that Mao had more dangerous and expansive ambitions. Galbraith was especially concerned about the narrow neck connecting all of northeastern India to the nation's core. The Siliguri Corridor was India's great vulnerability. U.S. intelligence in New Delhi reported that the PLA was massing forces north of Sikkim and Bhutan, and Galbraith worried that "a drive down here would cut off all of eastern India—North East Frontier Agency, Assam, Tripura, and Manipur." Galbraith told Kennedy that the Indians "have consistently underestimated Chinese intentions."[44]

Finally Galbraith told Kennedy that "we do have a serious problem next door and this has been much on my mind": Ayub Khan wanted Kashmir. Galbraith acknowledged that the United States had not consulted with the field marshal before implementing the airlift of military aid, "an action not too gracefully cleared with the Pakistanis." He had pressed Nehru to write "a long and friendly letter to Ayub on the situation," and Nehru had followed this counsel. Galbraith wrote the president that "McConaughy has been doing noble work in Karachi to calm the Pakistanis and make them see the threat" from China. Once the crisis had passed it would be time to "propose meaningful negotiations on Kashmir," but not under the threat of Chinese-Pakistani collusion.[45]

A Pakistani attack in Kashmir in the fall of 1962 would have stretched India's military to the breaking point. Three years later in 1965 Ayub Khan did attack India. In a plan code-named Operation Gibraltar, Pakistani commandos infiltrated into Kashmir to provoke a popular uprising; then Pakistan launched Operation Grand Slam to deliver a decisive armored attack severing Kashmir from India. Both operations, especially Grand Slam, failed primarily because of the improved weapons and equipment India had acquired from the United States after the 1962 war.

Pakistan was clearly capable of initiating war with India, but decided in 1962 not to take advantage of India's vulnerability. One reason it did not attack was that most of India's army and air force, and its entire navy, remained concentrated on the western border with Pakistan. The forces that were moved eastward to reinforce the endangered NEFA battlefield were infantry, and they moved slowly. For the Indians this meant that they had to build an entire new force and supporting infrastructure to defend themselves against China. This new force would need to be trained and equipped for mountain warfare, while the core of the existing Indian army would remain focused on armored warfare against Pakistan. Only the United States and United Kingdom could provide the needed equipment for the new force. Ayub Khan was already worrying about this aid, as his memoir makes very clear.

The Americans thus played a decisive role in forestalling a Pakistani attack on India. Kennedy's messages to Ayub Khan, reinforced by similar messages from Prime Minister Macmillan, left little doubt that the United States and the United Kingdom would view a Pakistani move against India as a hostile and aggressive action inconsistent with the SEATO and CENTO treaties. The Americans told Pakistan that the Chinese attack was the most dangerous move made by Mao since Korea in 1950 and that they intended to respond decisively. They asked for his assurance of neutrality. To have acted militarily would have left Pakistan isolated from its treaty allies and totally dependent on China—and Pakistan was unsure about China's military intentions. Any Pakistani attack on India in the west would need to be based on the assumption that China would keep up the pressure in the east and in Kashmir. Ayub had no concrete reason to believe that would be the case. Like everyone else he did not know what Mao planned to do next.

CHINA STRIKES AGAIN

As mentioned earlier, during the lull in fighting in late October Nehru gathered his advisers to assess the risk from Pakistan. His intelligence chief, Mullik, warned, "Ayub was on the prowl and, if our Punjab defenses were weakened, he would certainly try to carry out his grand strategy of which we had given a detailed report a few months before." But he also told them that Chinese forces were massing on the Sikkim border and posed a threat to the Siliguri Corridor connecting India's northeastern region to the core of the state. After much deliberation Prime Minister Nehru decided to take a modest risk in the west and move some infantry forces to face the immediate danger from Mao. The Indian Air Force flew one division of Indian troops from the Punjab to Siliguri to protect India's most vulnerable point.[46]

The Indian army also decided to stage a counterattack at the extreme far eastern end of the battle line on the Burma border. On October 22 some fighting had taken place there around the town of Walong. Unlike at Thag La ridge the Indian defense had held the PLA back for the most part, losing only a small amount of territory. On November 14 the Indians attacked to regain the land they had lost in October. The attack went poorly, partly because General Kaul was back in command and temporized. The PLA sent reinforcements, and the second major Chinese offensive began on the night of November 17–18.

The Chinese offensive in mid-November 1962 was much larger and more devastating than its attack in October. The PLA forces outnumbered the Indians at least two to one at the point of attack and were better armed and equipped for battle; their supply lines were also more efficient and well stocked. Most of all, their leadership was well trained and experienced, with many having fought in Korea. In contrast, the Indian leadership too often temporizing and panicked easily.

The Chinese also attacked again in the western part of Kashmir, pushing the Indians out of their few remaining positions in Aksai Chin. The PLA took control of the entire region—an area of 14,380 square miles that India had claimed now came completely under Chinese control, as it remains today. The Chinese appeared to be ready to move farther into Kashmir and threaten the city of Leh, the capital of the Ladakh district of Kashmir. The Indian forces in the west, however, had retained their cohesion and were still capable of combat.

At around the same time, the first blow nearly 1,000 kilometers to the east came at Walong, where Chinese artillery overwhelmed the Indian position, decimating a brigade of the Indian army. Kaul left the scene in one of the last flights out by the Indian Air Force. The entire western portion of NEFA fell into Chinese hands, and there were no reservists to stop the PLA from moving south into Assam. Kaul told Nehru "some foreign armies should be invited to come and assist the Indian Army to mount a major offensive over the Himalayas." He sent out another urgent call for more American help.[47]

The main attack came at Se La on November 17, the position to which the Indians had retreated after losing the Thag La ridge in October. The Indian Fourth Division was entrenched here and had been reinforced to make up for the loss of Dalvi's brigade in October. Approximately 10,000 to 12,000 Indian troops faced two PLA divisions numbering 18,000 to 20,000 men. The Indians had World War II–vintage field artillery and light tanks and were still equipped with ancient Lee-Enfield rifles from World War I. Modern American automatic rifles had arrived at the front, but were still in their packing crates; in any event, the troops were not yet trained to shoot them. Both the Chinese equipment and their front-line commanders were far superior to those of the Indian army.[48]

The Chinese victory was swift and decisive. By early morning on November 20 the Fourth Division had ceased to exist as an organized combat formation. The PLA seized the Se La pass and then moved south past the town of Bomdila. The Indians' heavy equipment and artillery were captured, as were the American automatic rifles still in their crates.[49] The eastern portion of NEFA was also in Chinese hands, as was all of the territory that Beijing claimed in the eastern sector south of the McMahon Line. More than 32,000 square miles of Indian territory was lost to the PLA.

There was little to prevent further Chinese advances. As the official postwar inquiry into the disastrous war—the still classified *Henderson Brooks-Bhagat Report*—concluded, the "Fighting Fourth" division was all but destroyed. It noted that "the lull between the two Chinese offensives brought about a sense of complacency" that ended in catastrophic failure for India.[50]

News of the "Black November" disaster began to arrive in New Delhi on November 17, but its full extent only became apparent two days later. In his diary Galbraith wrote that November 19 "was a day of unbelievably dismal developments. The Chinese had taken over most of NEFA and with incredible speed. The Indians at all levels are in a state of shock." All Indian Airlines flights across the country were canceled to divert the aircraft to military use.[51] In his memoir written years later, Galbraith writes that not only Assam but also Bengal and Calcutta were at risk, although in retrospect he acknowledges that attacking them would have posed formidable logistical challenges to the PLA.[52]

On the evening of November 19, the ambassador was hosting a delegation of U.S. senators, including Mike Mansfield (D-Montana) and Claiborne Pell (D-Rhode Island), for dinner at Roosevelt House. The Indian finance minister Morarji Desai was the guest of honor. Galbraith recalled that Desai "was sunk in gloom. Into the conversation came the most improbable rumors. A Polish ship had been seen in Calcutta with suspicious maps of the Bay of Bengal. This affirmed some design by Poland in the area" because Poland was a communist state. Galbraith concluded that "it was a hideous evening and I brought it to an end as quickly as possible."[53] The ambassador's diary makes clear he was close to exhaustion by this point; he could not sleep and was extremely tired. He later told a biographer that he relied on "large amounts" of barbiturates and sedatives to get any sleep.[54] The experience of managing a major crisis was fatiguing but also exhilarating; he later wrote that "an exhausting government crisis has this in common with a sex orgy or a drunken bat: the participants greatly enjoy it although they feel they shouldn't."[55]

Also on November 19, Nehru summoned Mullik, the intelligence chief, to a briefing. Mullik told Nehru that the Army Headquarters staff was preparing a plan to "withdraw troops entirely from Assam" and would give him that plan in the afternoon. Should the army's withdrawal plan be approved by Nehru, Mullik said, "I would not like to continue any longer as the Director of Intelligence and would like to quit that post that very day and go to Assam to organize people's resistance movements and not return until this area was reconquered for India." According to Mullik's account, Nehru "reacted very favourably to the idea of a people's resistance and asked me exactly what my plans were." Nehru told Mullik he wanted him to do both jobs: to remain as director of the Intelligence Bureau and to command the resistance movement behind Chinese lines as the "leader of guerillas in Assam."[56] In short, the prime minister and his intelligence chief were fully expecting to lose control of all of northeastern India to China east of the Siliguri neck.

NEHRU'S APPEAL TO KENNEDY

At the peak of the crisis on November 19, Nehru wrote two letters to Kennedy. They were delivered immediately by the Indian embassy in Washington to the White House and also to Galbraith in India. The existence of these two letters, especially of the second one, was not made public at the time. In his diary Galbraith makes only a cursory mention of them, writing that "not one but two pleas for help are coming to us, the second one of them still highly confidential."[57] For years afterward, successive Indian governments denied that the letters existed. Nehru's successor Lal Bahadur Shastri said he had conducted a thorough review of the prime minister's secretariat and the Ministry of External Affairs, but found no evidence of them.[58]

For its part, the U.S. Department of State archives acknowledged that two letters had been received by JFK from Nehru, but kept the contents secret. For years, copies of the letters held at the John F. Kennedy Presidential Library and Museum were heavily redacted, allegedly in part at the request of the government of India. Then in 2010 the library made available the original letters in full, giving scholars the opportunity to analyze the exact text.

The first, "EYES ONLY," letter begins with an expression of Nehru's gratitude for what Kennedy had already done since the attack began in October. "We are extremely grateful to you and the Government and people of the USA for the practical support given to us," Nehru wrote, and "we particularly appreciate the speed with which the urgently needed small arms and ammunition were rushed to India." Nehru then told the president that during the lull in fighting in early November, the Chinese had "made full preparations" for a second attack. Two Indian divisions were now "fighting difficult rear guard actions" in NEFA and might not last much longer.

Nehru described the grim battlefield situation: "The Chinese are, by and large, in possession of the greater part of the North East Frontier Agency and are poised to over run Chushul in Ladakh" in the Kashmir. "There is nothing to stop them till they reach Leh, the headquarters of the Ladakh Province of Kashmir. We are facing a grim situation in our struggle for survival . . . against an unscrupulous and powerful aggressor."

Then Nehru came to the point of the letter: India needed "air transport and jet fighters to stem the Chinese tide of aggression. A lot more effort, both from us and from our friends will be required to roll back this aggressive tide." Nehru then made his pitch, writing, "I hope we will continue to have the support and assistance of your great country in the gigantic efforts that have to be made." The prime minister closed by telling the president he was also writing a similar message to British prime minister Macmillan.[59]

Almost at the same time as the White House received this first letter, Galbraith sent an urgent telegram classified TOP SECRET EYES ONLY FOR PRESIDENT, SECRETARY AND SECRETARY DEFENSE.[60] It began, "I have just learned under conditions of the greatest confidence that another" letter from Nehru is "in preparation." Having been briefed on the second letter by Finance Minister M. J. Desai in great secrecy,[61] Galbraith wrote that it reflected the "new disasters and further large Chinese advances today and will ask for some form of back up support to the Indian Air Force by USAF amounting to joint Air Defenses to deter attacks on cities and lines of communication while the Indians commit IAF to tactical operations and attacks on Chinese communications which they believe is now the only chance of stopping Chinese and preventing cutoff of eastern India or more." The Indian leadership had decided that India could only stop the Chinese advance and prevent the loss of all of northeastern India by launching air strikes on the PLA's lines of supply and communications back to Tibet. To ensure the defense of India's own cities and supply lines, Nehru was asking the president to send American pilots and aircraft to back up the Indian Air Force by flying defensive missions over India.

Nehru was thus asking Kennedy to join the war against China by partnering in an air war to defeat the PLA. It was a momentous request that the Indian prime minister was making. Just a decade after American forces had reached a cease-fire with the Chinese Communist Forces in Korea, India was asking JFK to join a new war against Communist China. Galbraith sent the telegram in advance of the letter because he knew he had to buy some time for the president to consider the huge commitment India was seeking.

He said he would urge Nehru not to start any air strikes prematurely and for the Indians' "careful consideration of the acceleration of the conflict in the air." Yet he warned the president that the "Indian mood is desperate and the situation indeed grim." Galbraith's urgent telegram concluded, "I have learned of this move under conditions of greatest confidence even senior Ministers not being yet informed. My staff is not informed. You must protect the fact of my knowledge and this warning now and indefinitely."

India's ambassador in Washington, Braj Kumar Nehru, delivered the second letter late in the evening of November 19. It began with a dire assessment of the situation facing India: "Within a few hours of dispatching my earlier message of today, the situation in the NEFA command has deteriorated still further." Nehru wrote that "the entire Brahmaputra Valley is seriously threatened and unless something is done immediately to stem the tide the whole of Assam, Tripura, Manipur and Nagaland would also pass into Chinese hands." Even worse, Nehru warned that the Chinese had "massive forces" north of Sikkim and Bhutan, and "another invasion from that direction appears imminent." He repeated his concerns about Kashmir and feared "increasing air activity by the Chinese air force in Tibet." The letter's assessment of the crisis concluded, "The situation is really desperate. We have to have more comprehensive assistance if the Chinese are to be prevented from taking over the whole of Eastern India." Without American airpower Nehru believed India faced "a catastrophe for our country."

India's only hope was to counter China's gains on the ground with the use of airpower, but India lacked "air and radar equipment to defend against retaliatory action by the Chinese." Nehru made his request specific: "A minimum of 12 squadrons of supersonic all weather fighters are essential. We have no modern radar cover in the country. The United States Air Force personnel will have to man these fighters and radar installations while our personnel are being trained." The Indian prime minister spelled out the implications of his request, writing that "U.S. fighters and transport planes manned by U.S. personnel will be used for the present to protect our cities and installations" from the Chinese. Moreover, American pilots and fighters would "assist the Indian Air Force in air battles with the Chinese air force over Indian areas," while Indian aircraft attacked Chinese PLA troops and supply lines on the ground. Air attacks inside Tibet would be undertaken by the Indian Air Force alone.

In addition to the fighters and radar installations manned by Americans, Nehru also requested "two squadrons of B-47 Bombers" to strike in Tibet. India would "like to send immediately our pilots and technicians for training in the United States" to operate these sophisticated long-range jet bombers. The prime minister assured JFK that the equipment would not be used against Pakistan, but only for "resistance against the Chinese." The stakes were "not merely the survival of India," Nehru told Kennedy, "but the survival of free and independent Governments in the whole of this subcontinent or in Asia." India was ready to "spare no effort until the threat posed by Chinese expansionist and aggressive militarism to freedom and independence is completely eliminated."[62]

In this second letter Nehru was, in fact, asking Kennedy for some 350 combat aircraft and crews: twelve squadrons of fighter aircraft with twenty-four jets in each and two bomber squadrons. At least 10,000 personnel would be needed to staff and operate the jets, provide radar support, and conduct logistical support for the operation. If the RAF shared the task the American numbers would be lower, but it still would be a substantial force, large enough to make it a numbered air force in the American order of battle.

Ambassador B. K. Nehru was so stunned by the contents of the messages from Prime Minister Nehru that he did not show them to any of his staff and kept the only copies in his own desk. Many years later he told an American historian that Nehru must have been exhausted and psychologically devastated by the news of India's defeats when he sent the two letters.[63] The British prime minister received similar letters that Harold Macmillan referred to briefly in his memoirs as "agitated."[64]

In Roosevelt House Galbraith wrote that November 20, 1962, "was the day of ultimate panic in New Delhi, the first time I have ever witnessed the disintegration of public morale. The wildest rumors flew around the town." He convened his embassy planning team to send three immediate recommendations to Washington, "which I came up with overnight with the benefit of insomnia": cranking up the airlift of supplies, sending twelve more C-130 air transports immediately, and most importantly, sending "elements of the Seventh Fleet . . . into the Bay of Bengal." The Indians had not asked for a demonstration of American naval power, but Galbraith felt it was essential to have a very visible symbol of U.S. support for India. He also thought that a U.S. Navy carrier battle group would signal China that America was serious. Washington immediately agreed with Ken's suggestion and Pacific Fleet Headquarters in Honolulu was tasked to send one at once.[65]

Galbraith also had advice for the Indians. He urged them not to start air operations against China until an answer to Nehru's second letter arrived from Kennedy. He noted, "There is no technical chance that we could accord them immediately the protection that Nehru asked." It would take time to get the U.S. Air Force on the scene. Galbraith was also skeptical of the impact of airpower on the PLA based on America's experience in Korea ten years before where "we learned in Korea that even with complete control of the air, we could not keep them from applying their forces or advancing."[66] Air attacks would prompt retaliation, including attacks on Indian cities like Calcutta and perhaps a drive down from Sikkim to the Siliguri neck.

The ambassador and the visiting U.S. senators called on Nehru the morning of November 20 and then shared lunch with the prime minister. After lunch Galbraith hoped for a nap, but instead "a message came from President Kennedy" replying to Nehru's two urgent letters. Kennedy proposed to send immediately a high-level mission led by Ambassador Averell Harriman, a longtime friend of Galbraith's, to assess India's needs. He also promised to immediately increase the airlift of supplies and to deploy the U.S. Navy to the Bay of Bengal. An aircraft carrier was dispatched to sail to Madras, but was later recalled when the crisis eased.[67] Galbraith informed the Indians of Kennedy's promises and then "had dinner with the children" before a long telegram arrived from Secretary Rusk "asking questions I had answered before" about the "second midnight letter." Galbraith's diary reports that he "dictated a lengthy answer to all points and then ended with the prediction that the Chinese would not, as the Indians assumed, press forward on all fronts."[68]

MAO HALTS

In his diary Ken Galbraith reports that, on the morning of November 21, "like a thief in the night peace arrived."[69] Just before midnight on November 20 the Chinese government declared that a unilateral cease-fire along the entire Sino-Indian border would begin within twenty-four hours. In addition, beginning on December 1, Chinese forces would "withdraw to positions twenty kilometers behind the line of actual control (LOAC) which existed between China and India on November 7, 1959." The Chinese statement further clarified that in the eastern sector the withdrawal would be "north of the illegal McMahon line." In short, in the east China was withdrawing from the territory it had conquered by force in NEFA. In Kashmir the Chinese would stay in Aksai Chin, but would pull their combat forces twenty kilometers behind the LOAC (they did not in the end do so). India was expected to also keep its forces twenty kilometers from the LOAC in both sectors. Thus Mao was unilaterally imposing the border offer he had made to Nehru before the war in November 1959: China would keep the strategic but uninhabited land in the west, and in the east retain its claim to NEFA, but adhere to the de facto border situation that existed before the 1962 war.[70]

China warned that there would be grave consequences if India did not honor the cease-fire or resumed the Forward Policy of challenging China's claims, especially in Kashmir. The Chinese conveyed their proposals formally to India through diplomatic channels as well as by a public announcement. A week after that announcement, Zhou Enlai wrote to Nehru appealing for India to accept the new situation and warning that Indian refusal to cooperate would jeopardize the cease-fire. The 1962 war was over on China's terms. India had lost.

In 1965 India released final casualty figures for the short war: 1,383 soldiers had died, 1,696 were missing, and 3,968 had been captured. Twenty-six of the prisoners died in Chinese POW camps from their battle wounds; the rest of the prisoners, including Brigadier Dalvi, were repatriated to India by May 1963. Ninety percent of the Indian loses were on the NEFA front. The Chinese losses are unknown, because Beijing never provided any accounting of its casualties. Judging from what the Indians found on the battlefield after the PLA withdrew to the LOAC, the Chinese had also suffered significant dead and wounded. Yet, the Indians did not capture even one Chinese soldier, perhaps the best illustration of the rout that India's army suffered in NEFA.[71]

The Chinese withdrawal from NEFA to the McMahon Line, now termed by both sides the "line of actual control," took place throughout the month of December. The Indians advanced cautiously north from their positions slowly, but did not abide by the condition of moving twenty kilometers south of the LOAC; instead, regular Indian army units maintained a discrete distance from the LOAC, allowing Indian police and militia to occupy sensitive sites. Most importantly India did not restart the Forward Policy.[72]

Why did China abruptly impose a unilateral cease-fire and then withdraw its forces? Two reasons seem most important. First Mao had accomplished his goal of humiliating Nehru: China had prevailed over its Asian rival. A short war had demonstrated Chinese military superiority to the world. From Mao's perspective it was clear that the communist system was the stronger in the contest for Asia between the People's Republic of China and democratic India. Nehru was forced to accept the border proposal Beijing had been advocating since at least 1959. By withdrawing from NEFA, Mao also demonstrated restraint. China would later point to its restraint in November 1962 as a sign that it was a responsible member of the international community and should be given its seat in the UN Security Council. This was a key message Zhou conveyed to Henry Kissinger in 1971 when their secret talks began on opening a dialogue between Beijing and Washington, as Kissinger attested in his endorsement of Neville Maxwell's book.

Undoubtedly other logistical issues motivated Mao's decision to withdraw from NEFA. Winter was approaching, and the PLA's supply lines over Tibet and the Himalayas would have been stretched, making very difficult the provision of food, ammunition, fuel, and other supplies south of the infrastructure and to its bases in Tibet. Ayub Khan was correct that it would be challenging to move supplies across the Himalayas in the winter. Mao's generals were doubtless worried about fighting so far from their base camps.

But there must also have been a temptation to take further advantage of India's humiliation and Nehru's plight. Moving into Assam and assaulting the Siliguri neck were real options open to Mao in later November 1962. By doing so, his forces would have grabbed valuable territory and brought China's army to the border of East Pakistan. In a worst-case scenario Calcutta would have been at risk.

Yet Mao must have realized that such blatant aggression would have forced Kennedy's hand. The second reason for China's restraint was undoubtedly U.S. support for India. JFK had made clear from the start of the crisis that the United States was on India's side. Regardless of the ill-advised Forward Policy, Kennedy blamed the war on China. The United States endorsed the Mc-

Mahon Line as the rightful boundary; by crossing it China was the aggressor.

The airlift of supplies by the USAF and the RAF was the visible manifestation that Washington and London were offering not only moral support to India but also concrete and tangible military assistance. By mid-November, the aid was arriving on the battlefields, albeit not yet in decisive amounts to change the balance of power, but the trend was clear. Mao Zedong knew by late November 1962, if not earlier, that India was not alone and that the longer the war continued the more American and British aid would arrive.

The Americans were also characterizing the Chinese attack on India as comparable to the Chinese attack on UN forces in Korea in 1950. Although the CCF had scored a huge victory in Korea that winter, Mao knew well that they had not defeated the Americans decisively and that the war had gone on for three more years. China had suffered huge loses in the Korea conflict, and despite Chinese claims of defeating the United States and UN in Korea, Mao knew the price had been very high.

Following the Chinese announcement of a cease-fire, wild rumors were still circulating in New Delhi. One came from Indira Gandhi whom Galbraith only identifies in his diary as a "highly placed leader" who had just come back from the northeastern front. Indira was the only senior Indian official who bravely went to NEFA in the thick of the fighting, earning a much-deserved reputation for "remarkable courage." Indira traveled twice to Tezpur in Assam on November 19 and 20 to deliver Red Cross supplies to the local population, only thirty miles from the Chinese front line.[73] On returning she shared with Ken a rumor that China had secretly agreed to give Assam to East Pakistan and that this had been conveyed to local Muslims in Assam. The ambassador replied he thought it unlikely that Pakistan could communicate "a secret deal to illiterate Muslim villagers."[74]

Galbraith found the cease-fire announcement suspicious. "My first reaction was to suspect small print and hidden clauses" in what

China was saying, he wrote that day in his journal, adding, "It would all have been extremely confusing to Napoleon" himself. But the fact was "India has no army left in the area and has lost extensively of material, so any breathing space is incredibly important." Both Galbraith and his British counterpart together urged the Indians "to maintain silence." Galbraith feared that in the "present aroused mood there seemed to me a danger of outright rejection of the cease fire: Indeed that was a strong possibility."[75]

At noon on November 22 Galbraith met with Nehru to compare notes. The prime minister "was inclined to think the Chinese offer of a ceasefire and withdrawal was real," Ken reported. Nehru cited two factors that convinced Mao to halt the war. First was the "anger of the Indian people when aroused" and the risk of an open-ended conflict that anger would produce. The second factor in Nehru's judgment "was the speed of the American response."[76] Nehru was not alone in crediting U.S. help with deterring further Chinese military advances. From his POW camp where he was held in solitary confinement by the PLA, Brigadier Dalvi credited Kennedy as a "big brother and true friend of India." He later wrote that the Chinese withdrawal was the direct result of President Kennedy's decisive action.[77]

Not all Indians were as grateful. Intelligence chief Mullik described foreign assistance as "meagre" and conditioned on "India making up her differences with Pakistan on Kashmir." The record shows this was not the case. Kennedy's aid was never conditioned on Kashmir. He advised Nehru through Galbraith to maintain a steady dialogue with Ayub Khan, but not to offer any assurances of future Indian concessions. In fact, Galbraith was insistent throughout the crisis that American diplomacy steer clear of the Kashmir question and that no Pakistani "blackmail" be tolerated. Mullik did credit Nehru for asking for and accepting U.S. military aid despite his nonalignment policy. There was thus a bit of duplicity in his characterization of the American role: Mullik did not want to give JFK credit for providing the aid, but he did give Nehru credit for asking for it.[78]

This raises the great "what if" question about the 1962 forgotten crisis. What if the Chinese had not issued their unilateral cease-fire and withdrawal? How would Kennedy have answered Nehru's desperate appeal for American pilots to start flying combat missions to fight the Chinese and defend India?

Almost certainly Kennedy would have responded positively to India's request. His track record on India in general and the 1962 crisis in particular shows he believed that the rivalry between India and China was an existential issue for the United States. He had expressed this belief earlier in his 1959 speech on the race between China and India for leadership in Asia. "We want India to win," he said then. As president he had greatly stepped up economic aid to India. When the Indian prime minister made an urgent request for arms and equipment in October 1962 Kennedy said yes. When Pakistan complained and asked for compensation, he refused to be blackmailed.

The immediate dispatch of Averell Harriman and a large mission of American experts and advisers to assess Indian needs after receiving Nehru's second letter on November 19 was the action of a president preparing for war. Harriman and two dozen senior Kennedy officials arrived in New Delhi at 6 p.m. on November 22. Galbraith took them immediately to see Nehru, who was "very grateful for our prompt reaction."[79]

Kennedy would have gone to the American people at some point to explain why the United States was going to help India in its conflict with China. The Chinese invasion of India had been so overshadowed by the Cuban missile crisis that it was not until late November that the president spoke publicly about the stakes in South Asia. Before then Galbraith was his public voice, and it was the ambassador's statements and actions that had warned Mao of American resolve. Yet Kennedy could confidently tell the American people that U.S. ground troops would not be necessary, that India had enough soldiers to fight its battle: What India needed were arms and air support. The situation would not have evolved into another Korea or Vietnam.

Of course, we will never know what the specifics of American assistance to India would have been if the war had continued. Recommendations for the type and amount of support would have been spelled out in the urgent consultations conducted by Harriman and Galbraith, and Kennedy would have subsequently acted based on these recommendations. As we see in the next chapter the Harriman visit had significant consequences. Just a week after Harriman arrived in New Delhi, Kennedy sent Galbraith a private message asking him to stay on as ambassador and offering to personally intervene with Harvard to exempt Galbraith from its rule that professors could only get a two-year leave of absence without jeopardizing tenure.[80] Galbraith almost certainly would have wanted to give Nehru a positive answer to his appeal for help. Thus, we can be reasonably certain that America, India, and probably Great Britain would have been at war together against China.

CHAPTER FIVE

FROM JFK TO TODAY

Sardar, the horse that Ayub Khan gave to Jacqueline Kennedy in Pakistan, trotted slowly and gracefully along Pennsylvania Avenue. Riderless, he was following the caisson that carried John Fitzgerald Kennedy's body. The nation was in mourning. Just a year after the peak of the crisis in India the president was assassinated in Dallas on November 22, 1963. Jackie decided to have Sardar, with an empty saddle, follow JFK's body to symbolize the nation's loss.

Sardar also symbolized the importance that South Asia had played in Kennedy's one thousand days in office. From the state dinner at Mount Vernon in July 1961 to the crisis days of October and November 1962, India and Pakistan had been very much on the president's agenda. If Mao had not unilaterally declared a cease-fire in late November 1962, Kennedy almost certainly would have spent much of his last year in office dealing with a major war between India and China, with the ever-present threat of Pakistan joining the conflict. Even with the cease-fire, Kennedy said in one of his last press conferences in 1963, "I can tell you that there is nothing that has occupied our attention more than India in the last nine months."[1]

We now know that the war ended in November 1962, but Kennedy and his national security team expected the war to be renewed when better weather came, in the spring of 1963. They assumed that the war would begin again at a time and occasion chosen by Mao and China. Indeed the specter of another Sino-Indian war would linger on long after the Kennedy administration. In 1965 and 1971 India and Pakistan fought two major wars, and in both Washington was concerned that China might intervene on Pakistan's behalf. Pakistan certainly sought China's help during those conflicts. Again in 1999, during the Kargil War, Pakistan turned to China for help against India. The development of a China-Pakistan axis was one of the major enduring consequences of the 1962 crisis and of Kennedy's decision to help India with an airlift of military supplies.

HARRIMAN'S MISSION AND ITS RESULTS

As described in the previous chapter, in a meeting at the White House on November 19, 1962, when the situation in India was most bleak, Kennedy made the decision to send Ambassador Averell Harriman to India to assess its needs. Nehru's first letter and Galbraith's urgent cable previewing the second letter had already been received; the second letter arrived in the White House later that evening. Meeting with Kennedy were Secretary of State Dean Rusk, Secretary of Defense Robert McNamara, DCI John McCone, National Security Adviser McGeorge Bundy, and several of their key aides, including Robert Komer from the NSC staff and Phillips Talbot and Harriman from the State Department.

McCone opened the meeting with an intelligence briefing. He warned that Assam was defenseless and at risk. The CIA estimated that China could amass as many at 300,000 troops in Tibet and 170,000 combat troops inside India to undertake a major invasion to seize Assam and Bengal. The question under discussion was what did India need to do to stop the "Chicoms." McNamara wondered why India did not use its airpower, saying, "They would certainly tear up Chicom roads." The meeting's summary also notes that "there was some discussion of the desirability of using Tibetan rebels" to harass the PLA. McNamara suggested sending Harriman and an interagency team to urgently assess India's requirements and recommend to Kennedy what assistance to provide. Kennedy agreed.[2] The team was assembled rapidly and left from Andrews Air Force Base in a USAF KC-135 air-to-air refueling jet that had been converted to passenger service with eight portable bunks and twenty seats. After an eighteen-hour flight with a brief stop in Turkey for refueling, the plane arrived at 6 p.m. in New Delhi.[3]

Averell Harriman was an icon of American diplomacy. Roosevelt had sent him to London during the Battle of Britain in 1941 to implement the lend-lease program to aid the British and then to Moscow to coordinate the war effort with Stalin. He served as ambassador to the Soviet Union and the United Kingdom. Later he would be the chief negotiator at the 1975 Paris peace talks with North Vietnam. Sending such a high-level diplomat as Harriman was an important expression of American resolve.

At around the same time, the British government sent its own team from London led by Commonwealth Secretary Duncan Sandys. Prime Minister Harold Macmillan had received the same two urgent appeals as had Kennedy and wanted to be in the action. Even though Kennedy had kept Macmillan informed throughout the thirteen days of the Cuban missile crisis and also had met with the British ambassador to keep London in the loop, Britain had no direct role in the showdown. However, it had more influence in South Asia with its two former colonies and was determined to be a player in the Sino-Indian-Pakistani crisis.

The British were particularly convinced that, with at least the temporary cessation of hostilities, the moment was ripe to address the Kashmir issue. Macmillan believed that "if in the aftermath of the Chinese invasion we could bring about a solution of the Kashmir problem it would greatly ameliorate both the military and the economic situation, and this would be one of Sandys's main objectives." Macmillan also consulted with Australian prime minister Sir Robert Menzies, who disagreed with Macmillan and thought the prospect of war would make Nehru more reluctant than ever to consider a Kashmir deal; however, he did offer Australian troops for any possible Commonwealth peacekeeping force and for any military force to help India against China.[4]

The composition of the American team reflected the Harriman mission's three goals. The most immediate goal was to get India the military aid it needed to defend itself against China. The ceasefire gave the team some time to review Nehru's urgent requests for USAF fighters and bombers without the need for an immediate response. General Paul Adams, head of the Air Forces Strike Command, and Paul Nitze, then assistant secretary of defense for international security affairs, represented the Pentagon. The second goal was to address Pakistan's concerns about American military aid to India and the Kashmir problem. Like the British, the State Department, represented by Harriman and Talbot, was eager to get movement on Kashmir to keep Pakistan from tilting toward China and to eliminate Kashmir as a flashpoint before it sparked another war. The third goal, which was clandestine, was to secure Indian support for the CIA's covert action operations in Tibet, thereby strengthening resistance to the Chinese occupation of Tibet. The CIA component of the team was headed by Desmond FitzGerald, chief of the Far East Division, and John Kenneth Knaus, director of the CIA Tibetan Task Force. The chief of the Near East Division, James Critchfield, was in Lebanon at the time and was told by Richard Helms, overall director of CIA operations, to fly immediately to New Delhi to join what Helms called "the hottest ticket in town"—the Harriman team.[5]

First Goal: Increase U.S. Military Aid

Galbraith met the Harriman team at the airport on November 22, Thanksgiving Day, and took the senior team members immediately to see Nehru, who was "very grateful for our prompt reaction" but also very tired. In his diary, Ken wrote that the "mission is so large that there doesn't seem to be any way of arranging conferences with the Indians short of hiring a church. However, I have hit on the idea of scheduling a great number of conferences at the same time. This cuts down the number that can attend any one." Galbraith hosted all of his guests for dinner that night at Roosevelt House.[6] He was fond of Harriman, to whom he later dedicated a novel about life in the State Department, although the book is not a flattering portrait of Foggy Bottom.[7]

Nitze's discussions with the Indians centered on the need to increase aid to their armed forces and to plan for a major air defense exercise in India to take place in 1963. The air defense exercise would send American, British, Canadian, and Australian pilots and jet fighters and bombers to carry out precisely the mission Nehru had requested in his November 19 letters. As JFK told Macmillan, "If the Chinese were to make a large scale attack upon India, and especially if undefended Indian cities were put at risk, the reaction of American opinion would be serious."[8] That such a training exercise was planned makes clear that Kennedy undoubtedly would have sent the USAF to fight alongside India, had Mao not declared a cease-fire in 1962.

National Security Action Memorandum No. 209, approved on December 10, 1962, by JFK, authorized a new military aid package for India in response to Nitze's recommendations. The United States would (1) assist in creating and equipping six new mountain divisions to work with the Indian army to guard the Himalayas, (2) help India increase its own arms production facilities, and (3) prepare for a U.S.-UK air defense program for India. The first two missions were to assist India develop its capabilities, and the third was a joint American-British military exercise in India. Kennedy wanted the funding for the program to be split 50–50 with the United Kingdom and its Commonwealth partners. On December 20 Kennedy and Macmillan met in Nassau in the Bahamas and agreed on a $120 million short-term aid package ($70 million had already been spent during the crisis), to be split evenly, to address India's immediate needs.[9] Galbraith, who joined Kennedy at the summit in Nassau, was unimpressed with the British prime minister; he felt that the British paid too much attention to Kashmir and too little to China and that both London and Washington missed the opportunity to provide even more support to India on air defense and military cooperation.[10] Galbraith was correct: The Kennedy administration was already showing a lack of urgency that would become more apparent over the next year in meeting India's needs.

Nehru was likewise disappointed by the proposed aid package: He wanted a much larger and more long-term package of military aid. In May 1963 the new Indian minister for defense production, T. T. Krishnamachari, came to Washington and proposed an aid program with a price tag of $1.3 billion to Kennedy. Further discussions in New Delhi and Washington led to agreement on a $500 million program over five years. A final decision on the aid program was to be made at a White House meeting with JFK on November 26, 1963, but Kennedy was assassinated in Dallas several days earlier.[11]

The air defense exercise did take place in November, before Kennedy's death. The USAF and the RAF each sent a squadron of jet fighters, Australia provided some bombers from the Royal Australian Air Force, and Canada sent some pilots from the Royal Canadian Air Force. The Chinese got the message and denounced the exercise. Macmillan later wrote that it was "curious to compare British skepticism with American alarm" about the risk of another attack. London expected Chinese restraint, but "Washington was more nervous than London" about a "wholesale invasion."[12] That the exercise did deliver a clear message of deterrence was clear, however: The United States, United Kingdom, and the Commonwealth were ready to defend Indian airspace.

Second Goal: Start India-Pakistan Negotiations on Kashmir

Pakistan remained a thorny problem. After the Nassau conference held on December 20, Ayub Khan wrote to both Macmillan and Kennedy. Ayub Khan warned that the military aid that the United States and United Kingdom planned to give to India "is fraught with serious consequences to the maintenance of the present ratio of military strength in the sub-continent and hence to the security of Pakistan." The field marshal scoffed at the idea that China intended to invade the subcontinent. He pushed for Macmillan and Kennedy to link any military aid to a settlement of Kashmir, suggesting that "if the flow of your arms is so regulated as to influence India to be in a more amenable frame of mind (on Kashmir), positive results are bound to follow from negotiations now under way." If there were no linkage of arms to Kashmir, the Indians would be under no compulsion to make a deal on Pakistan's terms.[13]

The British were convinced that the war offered an opportunity to use India's need for military help to leverage Nehru to make concessions on Kashmir. Many in the White House and State Department shared the view that there was a unique opportunity to move Pakistan and India toward a settlement of the Kashmir dispute, which would then unite both countries in the anticommunist global alliance against the Soviet Union and China.

Galbraith, however, was skeptical about that possibility. He believed that the war had made Nehru less likely, not more, to make concessions to Pakistan. Nehru was a hardliner on Kashmir, and his political position at home had been badly eroded by the humiliating defeat by China. In a letter to Kennedy on December 6, 1962, Ken began with the good news. Polls by the U.S. embassy public relations office showed Indian approval of the United States had jumped from 2.5 percent in October 1957 to 7 percent in 1962, and then surged to 62 percent in December 1962 because of Kennedy's support for India.

Then he told the president that Nehru would never accept a territorial settlement of Kashmir; at most Nehru might allow Muslims in Kashmir some cultural autonomy within the Indian state. This arrangement would be similar to that in in the Saar region in Germany, which was German sovereign territory, but where French was commonly spoken and French culture was evident. He predicted that a diplomatic effort to coax a settlement on Kashmir would not only fail but also erode the positive Indian image of the United States. He warned that the Chinese were still the main danger and that an attack in the Siliguri neck could place Chinese forces on the East Pakistan border quickly, separating India from Assam and uniting its two enemies against it.[14]

Ignoring Galbraith's recommendation and yielding to pressure from Britain, Kennedy decided to try to bring about a Kashmir settlement. This decision suited his administration's preference for activism in foreign policy. Harriman and his British counterpart Sandys shuttled between Nehru and Ayub Khan and secured an agreement to start bilateral negotiations on December 27 in Rawalpindi. However, on the eve of the talks, Pakistan announced that it had reached a border agreement with China on their common border in Kashmir. Under the deal Pakistan gained control of almost 2,000 square kilometers that China had been occupying since the late 1940s; in turn China got formal accession and official title to a slightly larger amount of territory. By making a formal border treaty Pakistan and China set the stage for their future infrastructure projects in the area, such as the Karakorum Highway, which would bind the two countries closer.

The Indians cried foul: Pakistan was preparing to negotiate with India on the future of Kashmir, but then secretly made a deal with China on the borders of the same state. India claimed that the territory Pakistan was ceding to China was Indian land, not Pakistani or Chinese. It had just fought a war to keep China from gaining Kashmiri land, and now Pakistan agreed to a deal that would give part of Kashmir to China. Galbraith noted in his diary that the prospects for the Indo-Pakistani talks were now even more hopeless.[15]

Despite India's sense of betrayal by the Pakistan deal with China, the Kashmir talks went on for a total of six sessions, alternating between Pakistan and India. The president wrote to both leaders more than once to try to persuade them to reach a compromise. The Americans and British considered putting forward their own proposed compromise, but in the end neither London nor Washington was prepared to link arms assistance to the two states directly to a diplomatic solution—thus undercutting the most significant leverage the mediators had available. Instead vague linkages were insinuated that had no real benefit, but instead had the effect of undermining India's confidence in the reliability of London's and Washington's promise of military aid.

The third round of the talks, held in Karachi on February 8–10, was the most critical. The Pakistanis finally put their demands on the table: They wanted all of Kashmir, except a small corner in the southeast that was entirely Hindu. The territory in Ladakh that India had just fought to keep from China was to be ceded to Pakistan along with the Kashmir Valley and Srinagar, the capital. The Indians counterproposed some border adjustments along the cease-fire line, but insisted on retaining most of the territory they already held. Implicit in the Indian offer, however, was acceptance of Pakistan's control of the part of the state it had occupied in 1947. Galbraith had cynically predicted that Pakistan would claim all of Kashmir, wryly predicting its proposed border line would fall just short of Tokyo. After Karachi, Ken told the State Department he was proven right yet again.[16]

To make the situation worse Pakistan's foreign minister Zulfikar Bhutto announced he would go to Beijing on February 22, 1963, to sign the border deal with China. The deal symbolized Pakistan's new entente with Communist China, the enemy of America and India. As Galbraith wrote in his diary, "the Chinese have moved with great skill and audacity to drive a wedge between the Indians and Pakistanis."[17] Just before the planned visit, Nehru wrote to Kennedy that "instead of showing sympathy to us, Pakistan has utilized this opportunity by supporting China in the conflict and they have even suggested that we were the aggressors."[18]

In the White House Kennedy met with his advisers the day before Bhutto's announcement to discuss the talks. The State Department conceded that the talks had not gone well and put the blame primarily on Pakistan. Kennedy agreed to put forward a joint American-British proposal for a territorial division of the Kashmir Valley, the most populous and economically important part of the state. Secretary of State Dean Rusk went to the region to try to sell the idea, which neither Nehru nor Ayub Khan accepted. The talks ended after a fruitless sixth round in May 1963. Galbraith, who was soon to depart India to return to Harvard, felt the effort had damaged Nehru's confidence in Kennedy and the relationship for no gain. He told the State Department that "letters from the President have been issued like Confederate currency and with similar results."[19]

In August 1963 China and Pakistan signed an aviation agreement, in which Pakistan International Airways began regular service between Dacca and Shanghai. This broke an American-led effort to keep China isolated from the outside world. In response Kennedy canceled a deal to upgrade the Dacca airport with $4.3 million in American economic aid, the first of what would become many U.S. sanctions on Pakistan.[20]

A few months after the breakdown of the talks, Ayub Khan threatened to restrict CIA operations at the Badabar communications facility in the air base near Peshawar. Kennedy sent Undersecretary of State George Ball to Karachi to persuade Ayub Khan to actually increase CIA activity at the facility and McCone weighed in as well. Ball found Ayub Khan "obsessed" with India and the

American arms aid to New Delhi, but he reluctantly agreed to an expanded CIA program at Badabar in a secret agreement in September 1963.[21]

Zulfikar Bhutto visited Washington in October 1963. The foreign minister had deservedly earned a reputation in the United States as being pro-China and anti-America. In a bid to flatter the young Bhutto, Kennedy remarked that if Zulfi (Bhutto's nickname) were an American, he would be serving in JFK's cabinet. Zulfi responded that if he was really an American, he would be president and JFK would be in his cabinet. This response was the final irritant in Kennedy's relations with the Pakistani leadership.[22]

Third Goal: Secure Indian Support for Tibetan Clandestine Operations

The third goal of Harriman's mission was the most sensitive. Galbraith made only a few allusions in his diary to the talks on Tibet, such as a note that he saw Nehru on November 28 to discuss "matters that are top secret for even these confessions."[23] Long a skeptic on the Tibet covert action program, Galbraith now was a supporter because it could be a joint American-Indian project. However, he wanted the project under the control of the Near East Division of the CIA because its priority was Indian relations. Galbraith was also very suspicious of FitzGerald, the Far East Division chief, who was a very enthusiastic proponent of clandestine armies not just in Tibet but also in Vietnam and Laos. Galbraith thought FitzGerald "irresponsible" and his ploy of playing the NE Division against the FE Division a brilliant way to have "a spy watch a spy" to avoid mischief.[24] So Galbraith kept FitzGerald busy with protocol meetings, while the chief of the NE Division, Critchfield, worked with Mullik.[25]

After being given a thorough briefing on the CIA's covert program and especially the Tibet force in Mustang in Nepal, Mullik agreed to work together with the Americans to support the Tibetan resistance. This support took three forms. Mullik's Intelligence Bureau recruited its own Tibetan force—initially called Establishment 22 and later the Special Frontier Force (SFF)—to be commanded by former general Sujan Singh Uban, the man Nehru had tapped to lead Tibetan clandestine operations during the war.[26] The CIA agreed to support the SFF with a clandestine air force. Eight C-46 aircraft and four smaller planes with their pilots were deployed to a secret Indian air base, code-named Oak Tree, at Charbatia in Orissa (now Odisha), a state in the east of India. The secret air force worked with a special branch of the IB, the Aviation Research Centre.

The SFF recruited hundreds of Tibetans and trained them with CIA support to patrol along the line of actual control (LOAC) with China. The Tibetans were eager to join the SFF, hoping it would someday become an army to liberate their homeland. Mullik shared their long-term hopes of driving out the PLA from Tibet, but his immediate plans were more modest: He wanted to use the Tibetans to patrol the front lines and collect intelligence on the PLA. As Knaus recalled, the SFF "conducted cross border reconnaissance operations to place sensors for detecting nuclear and missile tests and devices for intercepting Chinese military communications."[27] Nehru was an enthusiastic supporter of the project. He visited the main SFF training camp in the Himalayas on November 14, 1963, and the secret air base Oak Tree on January 2, 1964, to see the covert action firsthand.[28]

The second project for which India provided support was the training of Tibetans in Colorado and other CIA installations and then getting them into Tibet. Camp Hale in Colorado was reopened in February 1963, and 135 Tibetans were trained there to operate behind Chinese lines in their homeland. The Indians were not eager for them to be parachuted into Tibet, however, because this action would be very provocative. Instead the resistance fighters would infiltrate across the LOAC with help from the Intelligence Bureau. Between 1964 and 1967 twenty-five teams of fighters were sent into Tibet. The members of one team survived for two years inside Tibet, but the rest of the teams were either captured, killed, or came back to India almost immediately after crossing the LOAC. The project was abandoned in 1968.[29]

The CIA played the lead role in the third project, which was to revitalize the Tibetan force in Mustang. To coordinate all three projects a Special Center within the IB was set up in New Delhi in November 1963, enabling CIA and IB officers to be in daily contact. Knaus was the CIA representative. Despite much prodding by Knaus, however, the Mustang force carried out almost no missions across the border into Tibet. It would gradually be shut down by the CIA and the fighters helped to find new jobs in rug factories and hotels in Pokhara in Nepal.[30]

Galbraith was briefed weekly on the clandestine operations until he departed New Delhi to return to Harvard. JFK was also fully briefed on them. In 1964 the CIA was authorized $1,735,000 for the joint projects, a significant amount for covert programs.[31] But except for the SFF patrols, the project had little success.

The joint IB-CIA program's one notable success came in a project not related to the Tibetans. In 1963, as the Tibetan covert assistance programs were gearing up, the United States asked for permission, which Nehru granted, to fly U-2 missions over Tibet and Xinjiang from Indian air bases. The missions over Tibet provided intelligence on the PLA that proved useful to the Indian army and to the covert planners. Those over Xinjiang provided the best available information on China's nuclear test site at Lop Nur. In the spring of 1964 a U-2 detachment moved onto the Charbatia air base, with support from the IB Aviation Research Centre. Several missions over western China followed that produced imagery showing that the Chinese nuclear program was on the verge of testing a bomb.[32] On August 26, 1964, a Special National Intelligence Estimate told President Lyndon Johnson that "on the basis of new overhead photography, we are now convinced that the previously suspect facility at Lop Nur in Western China is a nuclear test site which could be ready for use in about two months."³³ Imagery collected by these flights enabled the CIA to predict that China would test its first atomic bomb on October 16, 1964, at its Lop Nur test facility in Xinjiang.³⁴

It is, of course, deeply ironic that the Chinese invasion of India prompted close American-Indian intelligence cooperation, because in part Mao's paranoia about American-Indian collusion in Tibet prompted the invasion. By making China a threat to India in 1962, Mao created the partnership he had feared, bringing India closer to the United States than anyone would have thought possible before October 1962.

The final year of Kennedy's administration saw a dramatic improvement in American relations with India in the military arena as well. In 1963 American, British, Australian, and Canadian pilots were training in India on bombers and jet fighters supplied by those countries. Six Indian mountain divisions were being equipped by American and British arms, and a robust dialogue was underway on further military cooperation. The Kashmir gambit failed, but the president felt that the effort had been worth trying. As described earlier, American and Indian intelligence officers were cooperating on assisting the Tibetan resistance and collecting intelligence on China, although this relationship gradually atrophied in the late 1960s and early 1970s as tensions arose between India and Pakistan that culminated in the 1971 war.

Galbraith left for Harvard in the summer to resume teaching. Kennedy tried to persuade him to stay or even to become ambassador in Moscow and deal with the Soviets, but Ken was eager to get away from the government bureaucracy and return to scholarly pursuits. In the White House Kennedy was planning a trip with Jackie to Asia in early 1964 to include stops in India and Pakistan, as well as Japan, the Philippines, and Indonesia.³⁵ Tragically, that trip was not to be.

LOST OPPORTUNITY

Galbraith's successor as ambassador was Chester Bowles, a Democratic Party stalwart from Connecticut who had been Harry Truman's ambassador to India in 1951 for two years. Just as with Kennedy's first encounter with Nehru, Bowles's first meeting with the prime minister was memorable, but not for the right reason. While JFK only bored Nehru, Bowles actually put him to sleep in their first official encounter. In time the two, however, became good friends.[36]

Kennedy first brought Bowles into his administration from the House of Representatives in 1961 as undersecretary of state working for Dean Rusk. It was not a happy arrangement. Like Galbraith, Bowles thought Rusk was unimaginative and too hawkish. When JFK offered him the opportunity to go back to India, Bowles was eager to get out of Washington and be "10,000 miles away" from its "stifling bureaucracy." He asked for a commitment from Kennedy that he could go around Rusk and the State Department bureaucracy and communicate directly with the White House, as Galbraith had done; JFK promised he would give Bowles the same access Galbraith had enjoyed. Rusk was not pleased, but went along with the appointment.[37]

Bowles returned to India as ambassador in July 1963. He found Roosevelt House to be "a magnificent piece of architecture," but "its formal grandeur and vast spaces made us feel uncomfortable." Bowles and his wife moved back into the house they had occupied in the early 1950s, and Roosevelt House was used for ceremonial purposes and to host visitors. Its large swimming pool was opened to the embassy community.[38] Bowles and his wife would stay in India until 1969 and the end of the Johnson administration.

When he arrived in 1963, Bowles believed that the combination of the Chinese attack on India in 1962 and the split between Moscow and Beijing opened the door to a new American approach to India and to Asia: India could become a partner with the United

States and other democracies, especially Japan, in containing Communist China until it became a more moderate nation. Bowles was a harsh critic of Pakistan's military dictatorship and believed that U.S. military aid to Pakistan was "misguided." As an ambassador who had "a clear mandate from the President," he sensed a major opportunity was in front of him to forge a new American posture in Asia.[39]

Bowles's first task as ambassador was to wrap up the five-year, $500 million military aid package agreed to by the Kennedy administration more than seven months earlier. In the interim, the emergency aid provided by America to India during and immediately after the war had totaled $70 million. The final decision on the aid deal was to be made on November 26, 1963, at a National Security Council meeting chaired by JFK. Bowles returned to Washington for the meeting and told Kennedy that another Chinese attack could come at any time "on a larger scale" and that Pakistan "could not be depended upon to remain neutral if the Chinese launched another attack." Rusk reluctantly came around to supporting the deal, and the president was enthusiastically in favor of it. Four days before the scheduled NSC Principals meeting Kennedy was shot dead in Dallas, and that meeting was never held.[40]

The new administration led by President Lyndon B. Johnson postponed a decision on the military aid package and engaged in a review of the proposal for several months. As Bowles recalled, "The new Administration soon found itself under heavy pressure from the Pakistan lobby in the State and Defense Departments and in Congress." The White House wanted to go forward and approve the deal, but "the State Department and Pentagon were not yet prepared to risk our base in Peshawar by providing the kind of military assistance that India needed." They feared that Ayub Khan would throw the CIA out of the Peshawar base if a new arms deal were signed with Nehru. In response Bowles argued that India, not Pakistan, was the strategic prize in Asia.

It was not until May 28, 1964, that a final meeting to approve the agreement was scheduled at noon in the White House.[41] Again Bowles came back to Washington to make his case. In his memoirs Bowles writes, "Once again fate intervened. On Wednesday, May 27, I was awakened at 6 a.m. by a telephone call and was told that Nehru has suddenly died. Three hours later I left for India on the President's plane to attend the funeral with Dean Rusk and most of the Indian team who had come to Washington to negotiate the agreement." Once again the decision was postponed. President Johnson was persuaded to let the dust settle in New Delhi, and "the fears and confusion at high levels in Washington created by the possibility that Pakistan would cancel our agreement on the Peshawar air base were no doubt the most immediate cause for the delay."[42]

India's new prime minister was Lal Bahadur Shastri, a close Nehru aide who had never traveled outside of India, but was eager to close an arms deal. In August 1964 Shastri's defense team, the same team that had come to Washington in May 1964 to close the deal with LBJ, traveled to Moscow. The Indian-Soviet talks there led to the resuscitation and considerable expansion of the earlier MIG-21 deal, with no linkage to the Kashmir issue. India and the Soviet Union signed a multiyear deal that provided "all India has asked for and more," as Bowles wrote later. That India never signed an arms deal with the United States was "a lost opportunity" in Indo-American relations.[43]

Over the course of the next few decades the Indian military would become increasingly dependent on Soviet arms and equipment. Indian military officers were trained in the Soviet Union, and Indian civilian defense planners counted on Soviet military assistance to structure their arms acquisitions. The unforeseeable events of Kennedy's assassination and Nehru's death, combined with Pakistan's threat to cut off the intelligence operation in Peshawar, stymied Kennedy's goal of building a new long-term strategic partnership with India.

THE INDO-PAKISTANI WAR OF 1965

Ironically the lost opportunity in Indo-American relations did not keep Pakistan from embarking on a plan to attack India. By early 1965 Ayub Khan had decided that he had to force the Kashmir issue to a final resolution by recovering the entire province by war and thereby humiliating India. His young foreign minister Zulfikar Bhutto helped design an ambitious two-part plan. The first step would be to infiltrate Pakistani army commandoes and Kashmiri irregulars into the Kashmir Valley to instigate an uprising by the Muslim majority. This part of the operation was called Gibraltar and was implemented in August 1965. Then the Pakistani army would strike to sever Kashmir from India in a major armored offensive called Operation Grand Slam, beginning on September 1. By mid-September India and Pakistan were engaged in the largest tank battles in the world since the end of World War II.

Operation Grand Slam, however, rested on several incorrect assumptions. The field marshal believed that time was not on his side. The more time India had to absorb the new weapons it had acquired from the United States, the United Kingdom, and the USSR, the more difficult would be Grand Slam's mission. So Pakistan needed to act sooner rather than later. But by mid-1965 India had already absorbed the new equipment from the United States and Britain, and its army and air force were much better prepared to fight Pakistan than they had been prepared to fight China in 1962. Pakistan was already too late. Ayub Khan also assumed that Johnson would keep U.S. arms and ammunition flowing to Pakistan in any war with India because it held the trump card of the Peshawar base. If the war moved swiftly to a Pakistani victory, perhaps LBJ would even help with resolving the diplomatic aftermath and back a winner.

What is still unknown about Ayub Khan's plot is what role he thought China might play in the war. Ayub visited China in March 1965 and was given a hero's welcome, "the most enthusiastic welcome given any visitor" yet to the People's Republic. Zhou visited Pakistan in April and again in June, discussing the plans for Operations Gibraltar and Grand Slam. The details of the Chinese-Pakistani cooperation remain secret, but the evidence is clear that Ayub told the Chinese he intended to force a crisis in Kashmir that fall.[44]

In Washington the CIA suspected that a "secret Sino-Pakistani military arrangement" existed. Its Office of Current Intelligence (OCI) told the White House as the crisis developed that "a series of clandestine reports received since early 1964 indicates a possible secret Sino-Pakistani mutual defense agreement of some kind" existed; however, the analysis concluded that it was likely "a very loose" arrangement that provided "Peiping maximum latitude in deciding when or whether it might come into force."

Most importantly the OCI report warned that "we believe some secret understanding exists between Peiping and Rawalpindi," which "Rawalpindi can consider an 'ace in the hole' in the present confrontation" in 1965. The CIA suggested that this understanding "could produce a feeling of greater confidence in Rawalpindi," or even worse, "it could make Pakistan utterly foolhardy."[45] Ambassador McConaughy, still posted in Pakistan, was instructed by Washington to ask Ayub Khan directly if Pakistan had a secret arrangement with China by which the Chinese forces would engage in diversionary action on the northeastern border with India. The field marshal "did not answer the question directly," merely replying, "What the Chinese and the Soviets would do in the future, I do not know."[46] This denial only raised LBJ's suspicions that Pakistan was colluding with China to dismember India.

When the war started on September 1, the Chinese publicly supported Pakistan and castigated India as the aggressor. On September 17, China gave India an ultimatum to dismantle installations on the border between them that allegedly violated the LOAC within three days or China would do so unilaterally. The Chinese ultimatum focused on the Sikkim-China border, implicitly threatening the

Siliguri Corridor connecting Assam to Bengal.[47] It seemed to set the stage for a Chinese attack. The White House asked for an urgent CIA estimate that day. The CIA Special National Intelligence Estimate concluded that China "will avoid direct, large scale military involvement in the Indo-Pakistani war," but that "there is an even chance it will make small scale military probes across the Indian frontier." The CIA expected China also to issue threats and propaganda to intimidate the Indian leadership both politically and psychologically.[48] Sikkim seemed to be the point of greatest risk and vulnerability.

Ayub Khan and Bhutto flew secretly to China on September 19, 1965, as the Chinese ultimatum was due to expire. What happened in that mission is still largely a secret. According to the two accounts Ayub Khan later gave to confidants, the Chinese leadership promised support to Pakistan, urging it to fight a long war of attrition to wear India down and not to agree to a cease-fire. Pakistan should be prepared to lose major cities in the conflict, Mao and Zhou reportedly told Khan. Because Lahore was already threatened by Indian troops, in effect China was telling Ayub Khan to let the country's second-largest city fall into Indian hands and fight a long war like China's war with Japan. Ayub Khan's cryptic comments on his trip do not reveal whether Mao promised active PLA support by opening another front to take the pressure off of Pakistan.

But Ayub did not want a long war—his plan had been predicated on a quick victory—and he certainly was not willing to sacrifice Lahore. Instead he settled for a cease-fire on September 23.[49]

The Soviets negotiated the peace agreement that followed. Ayub Khan and Lal Shastri met with the Soviet leadership in Tashkent to agree on an exchange of captured territory and prisoners. On January 10, 1966, the Tashkent peace agreement was signed. A few hours later Shastri died of a heart attack at 3 a.m. Indira Gandhi would become India's third prime minister.

Washington was largely a bystander to the 1965 war. Johnson sought to keep American involvement in the war as minimal as possible; by that time his administration was completely preoccupied with the Vietnam War. LBJ chose to cut off military assistance to both sides to pressure them to accept a cease-fire. Both countries were astonished: Pakistan that the United States would halt military aid to a treaty ally during a war and India that its aid partner since 1962 would halt aid when India was being attacked by an aggressor backed by China. The aid cutoff affected Pakistan much more than India because the former depended much more on American arms and resupply than India.

Bowles believed that Johnson cut off aid to both sides because he knew Pakistan was at fault, but was desperate to appear even-handed to help ensure continued access to the intelligence base at Peshawar: "The possibility of losing our Peshawar base still dominated American policy in South Asia. Our government was clearly determined to duck the implications of our pledge to keep the Pakistani from using U.S. weapons in aggression against India."[50] Yet more than 100 U.S.-supplied Patton tanks were captured by the Indians intact on the battlefield. "Over and over again it was pointed out to me that every Indian casualty had been caused by an American bullet, an American shell or an American hand grenade," Bowles recalled.[51]

The cutoff in aid in 1965 was another major missed opportunity for strengthening U.S. relations with India. Had Kennedy lived, it almost certainly would have been a different story. JFK would have concluded an arms deal with New Delhi in 1963, and he would have been far more inclined to side with India in 1965 than did Johnson. Kennedy had much less patience with Ayub Khan than did LBJ.

In the very last days of his life in 1963 Kennedy met with his secretary of defense, Robert McNamara, in the Oval Office to review options for responding to various international crises. The secret tape recording of that meeting captured McNamara telling JFK that "we should recognize that in order to carry out any commitment to defend India against a substantial Chinese attack, we would have to use nuclear weapons." Kennedy responded, "We should defend India, and therefore we will defend India if she were attacked."[52]

Bowles later gave this "what might have been" assessment: "The consequence of our failure in 1963 and 1964 to persuade Washington to respond affirmatively to India's request for military assistance was clear. I believe that a moderate five year program of military aid to help modernize India's Army and Air Force following the 1962 Chinese attack might have made a decisive difference in the course of events in Asia."[53]

THE INDIA-CHINA-PAKISTAN TRIANGLE

The events of the autumn of 1962 created the balance of power, the alliance structure, and the arms race that still prevail today in Asia. The competition between Asia's two giants ended in China's victory and India's defeat. According to the Stockholm International Peace Research Institute, India today is the largest arms buyer in the world, followed by China and then Pakistan. Together the three countries account for one-quarter of the world's arms purchases. Russia remains India's top source of arms, but it is increasingly buying weapons from Israel, the United States, and Europe. Pakistan secures its arms from China and the United States.[54]

India's concerns about China and about the Chinese alliance with Pakistan have been the driving force behind India's development and acquisition of nuclear weapons. When he was prime minister, Nehru was adamantly against developing nuclear weapons, believing that they were immoral and criticizing the United States for using them on Japan in 1945. Before 1962 there was virtually no debate in India about the issue, but the Chinese invasion that year opened the door to their consideration; opposition politicians began to call for an Indian nuclear deterrent. As one expert noted, "The 1962 war with China fundamentally altered the Indian discourse over nuclear weapons. In a very real sense this war began the process that culminated in the Indian nuclear tests of 1998."[55]

After the CIA obtained U-2 imagery—generated from flights from the secret Indian air base—that detected preparations for China's first test of a bomb in 1964, Secretary Rusk publicly warned that a test was imminent in September. Nehru addressed a non-aligned conference in Cairo on October 7, 1964, urging it to send a delegation to China to dissuade Mao from testing a bomb. He also asked the UN secretary-general to take action to discourage China from developing the bomb. The Chinese replied on October 9 with a "blistering public attack on Nehru's slanders and distortions." On October 16 they tested their bomb.[56]

Yet Nehru continued to oppose development of an Indian nuclear weapons program, as did his successor Shastri. Nehru's daughter Indira took a more nuanced approach. In 1971, five years after she became prime minister, India and Pakistan fought another war, precipitated by a savage Pakistani crackdown on its own citizens in East Pakistan, millions of whom then fled into India. Ayub Khan's successor, Yahya Khan, again solicited Chinese help as the crisis developed, but China was preoccupied with its own internal problems in the wake of the Cultural Revolution and tensions with the Soviet Union in Siberia. Richard Nixon and Henry Kissinger, both of whom despised Gandhi, urged China to help Pakistan, but to no avail. The president tilted toward Pakistan throughout the crisis despite the humanitarian disaster in East Pakistan, because he wanted to safeguard his emerging overture to China.

During the crisis Senator Ted Kennedy led the opposition to Nixon's policy, denouncing Pakistan's repression as "genocide." Ted traveled to India in August 1971 to tour the refugee camps and was appalled by what he saw and by the fact that American weapons were making the massacre possible. He called Nixon's Pakistan tilt "shabby and shameful" and invoked his brother's policy of supporting India against China. Ted became so popular in India that opposition leader Atal Bihari Vajpayee asked in parliament,

"When is Senator Kennedy going to become the President of the United States?" Ted said, "I like this kind of question."[57]

The war was a disaster for Pakistan. India quickly defeated the Pakistani army in the east, which surrendered, leading to the creation of Bangladesh. China briefly threatened again during the war to take military action on the Sikkim-Tibet border if India did not withdraw from certain areas, a repeat of its 1965 threats, but Indira rightly judged Mao was bluffing this time.[58]

After the 1971 Indo-Pakistani war that humiliated Pakistan, Indira authorized development of a so-called peaceful nuclear explosive device. It was exploded on May 18, 1974, demonstrating that India had indeed been in the process of developing nuclear weapons. Indira did not embark on building a nuclear weapons arsenal, however, and was content with only one nuclear test. For the next twenty-four years no further Indian nuclear tests were conducted; neither did Pakistan engage in any nuclear tests.

On May 11, 1998, I was in my office at the Old Executive Office Building next to the White House when my deputy told me that CNN was reporting India had just tested nuclear weapons. There had been no warning from the CIA that a nuclear test was even likely in India. I had just returned from a trip to South Asia that included meetings in New Delhi with Prime Minister Atal Vajpayee (Ted's admirer in 1971) and his top national security advisers. They had assured us that there would be no strategic surprises by India and that the new Indian People's Party (BJP) government was carefully studying its nuclear options and strategy.[59]

After the nuclear test, Vajpayee sent President Bill Clinton a letter explaining why his government had chosen to test nuclear weapons. It began, "I have been deeply concerned at the deteriorating security environment, specifically the nuclear environment, faced by India for some years past." India has "an overt nuclear weapons state on our borders, a state which committed armed aggression against India in 1962." Vajpayee admitted the Sino-Indian relationship was not as hostile in 1998 as it had been in 1962, but argued, "An atmosphere of distrust persists mainly due to the un-resolved border problem."

Yet China was only part of the problem. Vajpayee wrote, "To add to the distrust that country (China) has materially helped another neighbor of ours (Pakistan) to become a covert nuclear weapons state. At the hands of this bitter neighbor we have suffered three aggressions in the last fifty years." The prime minister concluded by noting that Pakistan was engaged in "unremitting terrorism and militancy" against India, especially in Kashmir and the Punjab. India's nuclear tests were a response to this dangerous entente of China and Pakistan.[60]

Following the May tests India and the United States engaged in an intensive dialogue on nuclear proliferation and arms control. Deputy Secretary of State Strobe Talbott chaired the American team, and Foreign Minister Jaswant Singh led the Indian team. Fourteen meetings were held in seven countries over two and half years. Singh summed up India's view in an interview with the *New York Times*: "Our problem is China. We are not seeking parity with China. We don't have the resources, and we don't have the will. What we want is a minimum deterrent" against China.[61] Singh was deeply affected by his participation in the 1962 Sino-Indian War on the northeastern front. In his memoirs he wrote, "1962 was traumatic; it left an imprint so deep we still have not shaken free of it. . . . 1962 almost defines the relationship (with China) and certainly influences it deeply."[62] Singh repeatedly also argued that Pakistan, as well as China, posed nuclear threats to India, which required a deterrent.

In 1999 Pakistan initiated yet another military operation intended to force India to give up Kashmir. Pakistani soldiers crossed the line of control (LOC) around Kargil, a town in central Kashmir, and seized control of key mountaintops overlooking the main highway linking Ladakh to Srinagar. India responded with a large air and ground counteroffensive. As the crisis threatened to escalate, Pakistani prime minister Nawaz Sharif flew to Beijing to solicit

Chinese assistance. What happened in Beijing is unclear, but Sharif next flew to Washington and reluctantly agreed to withdraw the Pakistani army behind the LOC. A year after India tested nuclear weapons, China did not want to side with Pakistan in a military confrontation.

Yet for India's deterrent to continue to be credible, it had to have the means to deliver its nuclear weapons to China's capital Beijing and other major Chinese cities. On April 19, 2012, India's Defense Research and Development Organization (DRDO) in the Ministry of Defense announced, "The nation's dream has become a reality. India's long range missile with a range of more than 5000 kilometers AGNI-V was successfully test fired at 0807 hours from the Wheeler's Island, Orissa." Prime Minister Manmohan Singh said, "DRDO scientists have made the country proud." National Security Adviser Shiv Shanker Menon said the test launch was "a milestone in the long range missile era of India." No one needed to make the bottom line explicit: Beijing was now in range of Indian nuclear-tipped intermediate ballistic missiles fifty years after the humiliation of 1962.[63]

China had achieved the capability to target India's cities much earlier, and its nuclear weapons arsenal is motivated by a much larger threat assessment than just India. China has been a key player in assisting Pakistan's nuclear program for decades, seen as a cheap way of offsetting India's nuclear capability. China provided Pakistan with its first design for a nuclear weapon and two nuclear reactors. Three more Pakistani reactors are currently under construction.[64] The driving force behind the Chinese-Pakistan nuclear partnership was Zulfikar Bhutto, who had been the main actor behind the border negotiations with China and the 1965 war with India.

Ironically the United States helped start Pakistan's nuclear research project by building a small research reactor in the 1960s in the Pakistan Institute of Nuclear Science and Technology (PINSTECH) near Islamabad. PINSTECH's main building was designed by the American architect Edward Durell Stone, who also designed Roosevelt House and the Kennedy Center; he called PINSTECH his "greatest work." The Pakistanis call it the "Taj Mahal of Nuclear Pakistan" for its graceful mixture of Mughal design and modern architecture. The reactor went critical in December 1965, just after the war with India ended.[65]

Pakistani officials often contrast their relationship with the United States to their Chinese connection. They consider Washington a fair-weather friend, whereas China is an "all-weather friend," as reliable as the Himalayas are tall. This characterization is literal, as China has invested heavily in extensive efforts to develop an all-weather highway connection over the Himalayas to allow year-round road traffic between the two states. In April 2015 Chinese President Xi Jinping visited Pakistan and announced plans to invest $46 billion in infrastructure projects to build an economic corridor connecting western China, Tibet, and Xinjiang, with ports on the Arabian Sea in Pakistan. One of these ports will be a warm-water port on the Indian Ocean at Gwadar, a Pakistani dream project for decades, which will be on the doorstep of the Persian Gulf.[66] The staggering size of the projects, much larger than any ever contemplated in Pakistan, underscores the continuing geostrategic importance of Pakistan for China.

China also continues to project its military power into the Indian Ocean surrounding India. In February 2014 the director of the Defense Intelligence Agency (DIA) told Congress that a Chinese nuclear-powered fast attack submarine had just made its first foray into the Indian Ocean.[67] The DIA expects China to deploy nuclear submarines in the Indian Ocean on routine patrols in the coming years.

In 2013, after fifty years playing defense, India established a Mountain Strike Corps in West Bengal to give it the capacity to undertake offensive military operations in the east. Expected to cost $10 to 12 billion over seven years to train and equip, the Mountain Strike Corps is another manifestation of the arms race begun in 1962.[68]

Tensions also remain high in the Himalayas. No one expects a return to war as in 1962, but skirmishes are common along the LOAC. Despite seventeen rounds of talks since 2003 on resolving the border issue, India and China have still not come to an agreement: Their border dispute is the longest unsettled border in the world. Road construction in the border area also remains a hot issue. After winning a landslide election victory in 2014 Prime Minister Narendra Modi announced plans to build a new network of modern roads in Arunachal Pradesh, formerly NEFA, along the McMahon Line. As part of the road network, Modi plans to build a 1,800-kilometer highway along the LOAC to improve India's ability to respond to any incursion; it "will be the biggest single infrastructure project in the history of India."[69] China protested the plan and urged India not to "further complicate" the border dispute. A Chinese government spokesman said, "The border issue between China and India is a problem left over by the colonial past."[70] India's Home Minister Rajnath Singh responded, "No one can give warning to India. We are a very powerful country."[71]

China and India also remain at loggerheads over Tibet. India still grants the Dalai Lama refuge in India, where he leads a global struggle to keep the Tibetan cause alive. China refuses to allow India to open a consulate in Lhasa, a request India reiterated as recently as April 2014.[72] A border incident marred the visit of Chinese president Xi Jinping to New Delhi in September 2014.

China and India are not in a state of near conflict. Neither country wants a war or even a border skirmish. They are competitors, not enemies, with a booming bilateral trade relationship. In 2011 bilateral trade topped $75 billion. Because of the global economic downturn, it declined to $65 billion in 2013, but is still sizable. China is India's largest trading partner.

Yet China and India are not equivalent powers, as indicated by India's $31 billion trade deficit in 2013.[73] India's defeat in 1962 is not the only or even the major reason for the disparity in power between India and China, but it did mark a turning point for each country.

China went on to have several decades of unprecedented growth and development. Since then India's economy has grown, but not nearly as dynamically as China's. China's per capita income in 2013 was more than twice that of India: $11,850 compared to $5,350. Foreign direct investment in China from 2010 to 2012 averaged $119.5 billion annually versus a more modest $27 billion a year in India. The Indian gross domestic product is a mere 22.5 percent of China's.

In military terms the two Asian giants each devote about 2 percent of their GDP to defense spending. That translates into a defense budget of $47 billion for India and $188 billion for China. China has a significant advantage in airpower and missile development. Jaswant Singh was right to tell Strobe Talbott that India lacks the capability to match China's nuclear arsenal, at least for the foreseeable future.[74] The shadow of 1962 still lies across the race between the two most populous countries in the world.

The last three presidents of the United States have followed in Kennedy's footsteps and recognized the crucial importance of India. Clinton tilted toward India in the 1999 Kargil War and then had a breakthrough visit to India in March 2000, the first by an American president in a quarter-century. George W. Bush took the relationship to a new strategic level with his civil nuclear agreement with India that recognized its status as a nuclear weapons state, ending years of dispute on nonproliferation issues. Bush did not offer Pakistan a similar agreement. Barack Obama traveled to India in 2010 and endorsed India's request to become a permanent member of the United Nations Security Council. Unlike Clinton and Bush, Obama did not visit Pakistan on his voyage to India.

In January 2015 President Barack Obama traveled to India again to attend the Republic Day celebration marking Indian independence. It was an unprecedented second visit by a president to India and a strong signal of U.S. support for the country. He sat with Prime Minister Narendra Modi in the reviewing stand in the heart of New Delhi to watch the annual military parade. Again Obama did not travel to Pakistan.

On the same day that Obama was watching that parade, Pakistan's chief of army staff, General Raheel Sharif, the most powerful man in Pakistan, was in Beijing. His picture was broadcast on Pakistani and Chinese television to contrast it with the ceremony in Delhi. The Chinese foreign minister met the general and called Pakistan and China "irreplaceable all weather friends." Sharif said China and Pakistan are "iron brothers."[75]

LESSONS LEARNED ABOUT PRESIDENTS AND THEIR RELATIONSHIP TO THE INTELLIGENCE COMMUNITY

There are important lessons to be learned from Kennedy's experiences about how the president and the intelligence community can interact most effectively. The White House is rightly the central player in American intelligence policy; the CIA and other intelligence agencies should see the president as their top boss and top consumer. John F. Kennedy had a very close but complex relationship with the CIA and American espionage. In the 1960s there was no congressional oversight of the intelligence community, no Senate or House intelligence committees reviewing the budget, no process for notifying the congressional leadership of covert operations. As a consequence the president's control of the intelligence process and community was even greater than it is today.

Kennedy made a bad mistake in keeping Allen Dulles on as DCI in 1961, in an effort to appear bipartisan on national security issues. As a result, before the disaster at the Bay of Pigs, the Kennedy administration undertook no serious review of the Cuban operation planned by the Eisenhower team. Nor did Dulles and Bissell adequately brief the new administration on the invasion plan and on the likely reaction of the Cuban people. JFK incorrectly assumed he was authorizing a clandestine operation, not a miniature D-day, and Dulles incorrectly assumed that Kennedy would send in the Marines if the operation faltered. Kennedy's administration suffered a humiliating and self-inflicted setback in its first hundred days that also set in motion the events leading to the missile crisis a year later.

The first lesson is that presidents need to handpick their top intelligence leadership from among their most trusted aides. The intelligence chief needs to be able to tell truth to power, to tell the president not what the commander in chief wants to hear, but what he or she needs to know. Often, that may be bad news, but it is the responsibility of the intelligence experts to be the bearers of bad tidings. "The truth will set you free" should be more than a motto: It must be continually be put into action, as a reminder to spies that their first responsibility is to discover bad news and unpleasant secrets, assess them, and report them to the Oval Office.

Kennedy selected a replacement for Allen Dulles who was from outside his own party and his inner circle, but he was fortunate that John McCone was prepared to tell truth to power. McCone's dogged conviction that the Soviets would put offensive weapons in Cuba, when even his own analysts disagreed, ensured that intelligence collection efforts over Cuba were in high gear. When the NSC shut down U-2 missions over Cuba, his honeymoon cables got the U-2s flying again; one of those missions discovered the Soviet missiles before it was too late. As a biographer of McCone has written, "Telling the President and his top advisors what they preferred not to believe is not a job for the faint of heart."[76] McCone also provided excellent intelligence on China to Kennedy in early 1962. He deserves to be counted among the best directors of the CIA in its history. The distinguished Harvard historian of American diplomacy and espionage, Ernest R. May, assessed McCone as one of the two best DCIs ever.[77]

Another key lesson of the Kennedy administration is that intelligence operations can become their own ends, rather than means to an end. The intelligence collection capability built in

Pakistan by Dulles to collect information on the Soviet Union and China, as well as to support the Tibetan resistance, was later perceived to be so important that its maintenance became a key source of leverage for Ayub Khan to exert influence over U.S. policy. Rather than being a means to an end—a way to collect intelligence—it became America's most crucial asset in Pakistan, and keeping that capability operational became more important than pursuing the right policy toward India.

This became very clear in the Johnson administration when LBJ failed to take advantage of the opportunity created by the 1962 Sino-Indian War to build a military relationship with India. At the Nassau summit with the British a year before his death, JFK had asked his national security team, "What do we get from Pakistan? In return for the protection of our alliance and our assistance, what do they do for us?"[78] Ironically Eisenhower asked much the same question at the end of his second term in office. Bowles's account makes clear that by 1964 the preservation of the Peshawar facilities, the answer to that question, had become an end in itself that trumped all other policy objectives in South Asia.

Intelligence operations should be constantly evaluated for their continued utility and usefulness. However, this periodic reevaluation should not be done entirely in-house by the intelligence professionals themselves. It should be done in the White House by an interagency team and then be subject to congressional oversight and questioning.

A third lesson is that presidents often must manage the alliance diplomacy that makes covert action effective. Kennedy personally raised the Tibet operation with Ayub Khan at Mount Vernon in 1961. He sent Harriman with a CIA team to develop a joint U.S-India covert operation in 1962. Later he sent George Ball to meet with Ayub Khan to pressure him to expand the operations at the Peshawar base when the prime minister was threatening to shut them down. Kennedy also had to take the heat for the Bay of Pigs debacle with allies, enemies, and the public, just as Eisenhower had to take the heat for the shooting down of the U-2 plane.

Often the president's aides and intelligence professionals try to keep the commander in chief and the White House distant from covert operations so they can have plausible deniability if a project fails or is uncovered by the media. That is a laudable goal but not a very realistic one. All too often the lights come on, illuminating a covert affair, when the parties are least prepared for the glare of publicity.

Moreover, presidents themselves may have to be engaged directly with foreign leaders to get their support for a covert program. In Tibet the Kennedy team first needed the Pakistanis for help and then, after the 1962 war, the Indians. Intermediaries can play a role in talks, but sometimes the president is the only official who can convince a foreign head of state to help.

A final lesson is that intelligence operations often have unanticipated consequences. The Tibet covert operation played a role in Mao's decision to invade India. How big a role it played is hard to discern in the absence of access to China's archives, but there is little doubt that Mao believed that Nehru was conspiring with Washington to destabilize Tibet and help the resistance.

It is puzzling that Kennedy did not listen to the sage advice of his ambassador to India on the Tibet project. After being briefed on it by Dulles and Bissell in early 1961, Galbraith believed it was a dangerous folly. He made his dissent clear to the president and other senior officials, but was overruled. Galbraith only changed his view when India became a partner in the operation, but even as a joint CIA-IB project it had virtually no chance of success.

Indeed the Tibet operation never had any real chance of achieving its aims. At most it was a nuisance to Mao and the Chinese Communist leadership. China was determined to take Tibet and make it part of the Chinese state, no matter how many Tibetans resisted. The

Nationalist government would have done the same thing if it had won the Chinese civil war instead of the communists.

The best argument for helping the Tibetans is that they would have fought the occupation with or without U.S. help. The CIA did not create a Tibetan resistance, nor did it convince the Dalai Lama to fight Mao. The Tibetans made their own decisions; the Americans simply tried to help them win what was a hopeless fight. Nehru had been right when he told the Dalai Lama that resistance was futile.

Two decades after the 1962 war the United States assisted another Himalayan people, the Afghans, in resisting occupation. The covert war against the Soviet invaders of Afghanistan turned out to be the final and decisive battle of the cold war. In the late 1980s the Russians lost in Afghanistan, and within months the Berlin Wall collapsed, the Warsaw Pact imploded, and the Union of Soviet Socialist Republics became history. When President Jimmy Carter started the covert action in Afghanistan in 1979 he had no reason to believe it would end in such complete victory, but it is hard to argue that the Tibetans ever had the opportunities that the Afghans made so much of. Of course, the price for the Afghan people was staggering: More than a million died in the war against the Red Army.

HOW KENNEDY HANDLED CRISES

John F. Kennedy made serious mistakes in his handling of the intelligence operations he inherited from Eisenhower. He should have asked more questions about the Bay of Pigs plan; he should have listened to his instincts and doubted the "experts" as he said later. He probably should have listened to Galbraith and shut down the Tibetan venture as well. JFK was inclined to activism and was enthralled with espionage and 007 spycraft, as was his brother.

But in the fall of 1962 JFK performed brilliantly. Once the Soviet missiles were discovered in Cuba Kennedy was resolute that the United States had to proceed by diplomacy, not by a military action that would escalate to Armageddon. He did not listen to the generals and experts who advised him to go to war in Cuba. That summer he had read Barbara Tuchman's masterpiece about the start of World War I, *The Guns of August*, and was resolved not to repeat the mistakes of 1914 and to let war plans dictate decisionmaking. Kennedy was so impressed by the book that he gave a copy to Macmillan.

Kennedy's handling of the Cuban missile crisis has rightly won him universal praise from historians: It was his finest hour without any doubt. His masterful handling of what was the most dangerous moment in the cold war, perhaps in all American history, overshadowed his mistakes at the Vienna summit and at the Bay of Pigs. The hawks who argued for air strikes on the Soviet bases in Cuba would have taken the world to nuclear war. The more we have learned about the Soviet expeditionary force in Cuba, especially since 1992 because of our greater access to Russian documents and officials, the more Kennedy's reputation for cool and steady leadership and diplomacy in the crisis has been enhanced.

The forgotten crisis, the Sino-Indian War in 1962, adds more to the Kennedy legacy and the Kennedy touch. Kennedy rightly did trust his expert on India, John Kenneth Galbraith, and gave him wide authority to react in October and November 1962 when the rest of the national security bureaucracy was preoccupied with the Soviet challenge in the Caribbean Sea. JFK gave Nehru the support he needed to signal Mao not to go too far. He wisely worked with London to present a united front in support of New Delhi that discouraged Mao from pressing his military advantage.

Kennedy also handled Ayub Khan well. His hours spent meeting with the Pakistani dictator at Mount Vernon and Newport undoubtedly helped him understand the field marshal better in the fall of 1962. By making it clear that a Pakistani second front against India would be the end of the U.S. alliance with Karachi, JFK ensured that Galbraith's worst nightmare of a Sino-Pakistani assault on India did not materialize in 1962.

JFK proved to be the ultimate crisis manager in 1962. His deft handling of two global crises simultaneously involving the two great communist adversaries of the United States was a tour de force of policymaking at the highest level. America, India, and the world were lucky to have JFK and Ken in 1962.

ACKNOWLEDGMENTS

Many institutions assisted in the research for this book, including George Washington's Mount Vernon Presidential Library, the Eisenhower National Historic Site at Gettysburg, the John F. Kennedy Presidential Library and Museum in Boston, the National Security Archive at George Washington University, the Miller Center at the University of Virginia, the Centre on Asia and Globalization at the Lee Kuan Yew School of Public Policy in Singapore, the Center for the Study of Intelligence at the Central Intelligence Agency and its Freedom of Information Act Electronic Reading Room, the School for Advanced International Studies at Johns Hopkins University, the Office of the Historian at the Department of State, the Cuban Missile Crisis Document Archive at the National Security Agency, and, most important, the Brookings Institution and especially its library.

And many individuals helped as well with the research; they include Aysha Chowdhry, Tanvi Madan, Michael O'Hanlon, Bradley Porter, Irena Sargsyan, and Strobe Talbott. Special thanks are due to Jim Blight and Janet Lang who reviewed the manuscript and gave me the benefit of their years of scholarship on the Cuban missile crisis.

Place names in Asia have changed in the last half-century, and what name one uses can have political implications. For example,

ACKNOWLEDGMENTS

Peiping is now Beijing and Bombay is Mumbai. The North East Frontier Agency where the biggest battles of the 1962 war were fought is now called Arunachal Pradesh in India and South Tibet in China. Aksai Chin, where the war was fought in the west, is regarded by Indians as part of the Indian State of Jammu and Kashmir called Ladakh, the eastern portion of Kashmir. The Chinese regard it as part of Tibet. The spelling of some names has also evolved; Mao Tse Tung is now more often written as Mao Zedong. In this book I use the more contemporary names for places and people, except when directly quoting from a source that uses an older version.

This book has been reviewed prior to publication by the Central Intelligence Agency to ensure that there has been no inadvertent disclosure of classified information. All statements of fact, opinion, or analysis are my own and do not reflect the official positions or views of the CIA or any other U.S. government agency. Nothing in the contents should be construed as asserting or implying U.S. government authentication of the information or the agency's endorsement of my views.

The research and writing of this book have taken me on a journey back to the Kennedy era. From Boston to New Delhi, my wife, Elizabeth, traveled with me on this journey and made it very special.

CHRONOLOGY

1962

OCTOBER 8   China tells USSR it will attack India

OCTOBER 15   United States discovers Soviet missiles in Cuba

OCTOBER 20   First Chinese attack on India begins

OCTOBER 21   Galbraith returns from London to New Delhi

OCTOBER 22   Kennedy reveals Soviet missiles in address to nation, demands removal, imposes naval quarantine

OCTOBER 24   Soviet ships halt en route to Cuba

OCTOBER 27   First Chinese offensive in India ends

U-2 shot down in Cuba, pilot killed

OCTOBER 28   Khrushchev agrees to remove missiles from Cuba

OCTOBER 29   Nehru asks United States and United Kingdom for immediate arms shipments

NOVEMBER 1   USAF and RAF supply underway to India

NOVEMBER 7   Ayub Khan asks Kennedy for compensation in Kashmir to ensure Pakistan neutrality in Sino-India war

NOVEMBER 12   Kennedy demands removal of IL-28 bombers from Cuba

NOVEMBER 16   Second Chinese attack on India begins

NOVEMBER 19   Nehru asks Kennedy for airpower intervention; Kennedy sends Harriman mission and aircraft carrier battle group to India

NOVEMBER 20   Khrushchev agrees to remove IL-28 bombers from Cuba; Kennedy lifts the quarantine

Chinese cease-fire announcement

NOVEMBER 22   Harriman mission arrives in New Delhi

DECEMBER 1   Chinese withdrawal begins in NEFA

NOTES

PROLOGUE

1 Mohammad Ayub Khan, *Friends Not Masters: A Political Autobiography* (Islamabad: Mr. Books, 2002), p. 139.

2 Dennis Kux, *Disenchanted Allies: The United States and Pakistan, 1947–2000* (Johns Hopkins University Press, 2001), p. 122.

3 Stephen Kinzer, *The Brothers: John Foster Dulles, Allen Dulles, and Their Secret World War* (New York: Times Books, 2013), p. 274.

4 Ibid., p. 277.

5 Khan, *Friends Not Masters*, p. 136.

6 The discussion between the two presidents on Tibet and the CIA covert operation is recorded in Kenneth Conboy and James Morrison, *The CIA's Secret War in Tibet* (University Press of Kansas, 2002), pp. 158–60.

7 Kux, *Disenchanted Allies*, pp. 122–23.

8 The spectacular dinner at Mount Vernon is described by Letitia Baldrige, Jacqueline Kennedy's social secretary, in her book, *In the Kennedy Style: Magical Evenings in the Kennedy White House* (Toronto: Madison Press, 1998), pp. 48–60. Letitia was a former executive at Tiffany's. The presidential library at George Washington's Mount Vernon estate kindly provided me access to their files concerning the event, which include the guest list and many newspaper accounts of the evening. I want

to express my sincere appreciation to the staff of the presidential library for their invaluable help.

9 Quoted in Joe Bageat, "CIA's Secret War in Tibet," *Military History*, February 2004.

10 Chris Pocock, *The U-2 Spyplane toward the Unknown: A New History of the Early Years* (Atglen, Pa.: Schiffer Military History, 2000), p. 143.

INTRODUCTION

1 Theodore Sorenson, *Kennedy: The Classic Biography* (New York: Harper Modern Classics, 2013), p. 662.

2 Ibid., p. 662.

3 Arthur M. Schlesinger Jr., *A Thousand Days: John F. Kennedy in the White House* (Boston: Houghton Mifflin, 1965), pp. 840–41.

4 Francine R. Frankel, *India's Political Economy, 1947–2004* (Oxford University Press, 2005), pp. 214–15.

5 J. P. Dalvi, *Himalayan Blunder* (New Delhi: Orient Paperbacks, 1968), p. 410.

6 John Kenneth Galbraith, *A Life in Our Times: Memoirs* (Boston: Houghton Mifflin, 1981), p. 428.

7 "Modi Meets Xi Jinping, Says Meeting Was Useful," *Hindustan Times*, July 15, 2014.

8 John W. Garver, "India, China, the United States, Tibet, and the Origins of the 1962 War," *India Review* 3, no. 2 (April 2004), pp. 174–75.

9 John Kenneth Knaus, *Orphans of the Cold War: America and the Tibetan Struggle for Survival* (New York: Public Affairs, 1999) tells the story of the CIA's covert operation in Tibet. Knaus was the chief of the CIA's Tibet Task Force.

10 Somnath Mukherjee, "India-China Border Dispute—The Real Issue Is Tibet," *China India Brief*, no. 46, Center on Asia and Globalization, Lee Kuan Yew School of Public Diplomacy, February 24, 2015.

CHAPTER 1

1 I am indebted to the staff of the Eisenhower National Historic Site in Gettysburg, especially supervisory historian Carol Hegeman, for information on the Nehru visit to Eisenhower's home.

2 "Personal Requirement Suggestions: Visit of Prime Minister Nehru of India," Nehru Visit—December 16–20, 1956, Confidential declassified September 13, 1978, at the National Park Service Eisenhower National Historic Site website.

3 Dwight D. Eisenhower, *Waging Peace* (New York: Doubleday, 1965), p. 107.

4 Kenneth Conboy and James Morrison, *The CIA's Secret War in Tibet* (University of Kansas Press, 2002), p. 34.

5 Eisenhower, *Waging Peace*, pp. 108–09.

6 Ibid., p. 109.

7 Ibid., p. 113.

8 Stanley Wolpert, *Nehru: A Tryst with Destiny* (Oxford University Press, 1996), p. 467.

9 David Halberstam, *The Coldest Winter: America and the Korean War* (New York: Hyperion, 2007), p. 359.

10 Ibid., p. 433.

11 Lauren Strainge, "The Experiences of African Americans in Occupied Japan," *World Outlook* 44 (Fall 2013), p. 31.

12 Halberstam, *The Coldest Winter*, p. 53.

13 Ibid., p. 374.

14 Stanley Weintraub, *MacArthur's War: Korea and the Undoing of an American Hero* (Singapore: Free Press, 2000), p. 19.

15 Halberstam, *The Coldest Winter*, pp. 373–77.

16 Weintraub, *MacArthur's War*, pp. 20–21.

17 Halberstam, *The Coldest Winter*, pp. 390–91.

18 Weintraub, *MacArthur's War*, pp. 187–91.

19 Ibid., pp. 229–33.

20 Max Hastings, *The Korean War* (London: Simon and Schuster, 1987), p. 170.

21 Halberstam, *The Coldest War*, p. 326.

22 Sheila Miyoshi Jager, *Brothers at War: The Unending Conflict in Korea* (New York: Norton, 2013), p. 110.

23 John Kenneth Knaus, *Orphans of the Cold War: America and the Tibetan Struggle for Survival* (New York: Public Affairs, 1999), p. 51.

24 K. M. Panikkar, *In Two Chinas: Memoirs of a Diplomat* (London: George Allen, 1955), p. 82.

25 Ibid., p. 110.

26 Halberstam, *The Coldest War*, p. 236.

27 Percy Cradock, *Know Your Enemy: How the Joint Intelligence Committee Saw the World* (London: John Murray, 2002), pp. 96–102.

28 Ibid., p. 100.

29 "Chinese Communist Intervention in Korea," National Intelligence Estimate NIE 2, November 6, 1950 and NIE 2/1, November 24, 1950. Available at the CIA Center for the Study of Intelligence Freedom of Information Act Electronic Reading Room in "Baptism by Fire: CIA Analysis of the Korean War, 1948–1953," released March 24, 2010.

30 Cradock, *Know Your Enemy*, p. 101, and Halberstam, *The Coldest War*, p. 337.

31 Halberstam, *The Coldest War*, p. 337.

32 Panikkar, *In Two Chinas*, pp. 108–12.

33 Knaus, *Orphans of the Cold War*, p. 2.

34 John Rowland, *A History of Sino-Indian Relations: Hostile Co-Existence* (Princeton: Nostrand, 1967), pp. 48–49.

35 Panikkar, *In Two Chinas*, p. 112.

36 B. N. Mullik, *My Years with Nehru: The Chinese Betrayal* (Bombay: Allied Publishers, 1971), pp. 70–71 and 81.

37 Conboy and Morrison, *The CIA's Secret War in Tibet*, pp. 11–15.

38 Ibid., p. 15.

39 Knaus, *Orphans of the Cold War*, pp. 88, 100.

40 Panikkar, *In Two Chinas*, p. 125.

41 Ibid., p. 175.

42 Mullik, *My Years with Nehru*, p. 155.

43 Rowland, *A History of Sino-Indian Relations*, pp. 84–94.

44 Ibid., p. 95.

45 Ibid., p. 74.

46 Directorate of Intelligence Staff Study, "The Sino-Indian Border Dispute, 1963–1946," published in Anuj Dhar, ed., *CIA's Eye on South Asia* (New Delhi: Manas Publications, 2009), p. 114.

47 Arthur Schlesinger Jr., *A Thousand Days: John F. Kennedy in the White House* (Boston: Houghton Mifflin, 1965), p. 241.

48 Stephen Kinzer, *The Brothers: John Foster Dulles, Allen Dulles, and Their Secret World War* (New York: Times Books, 2013), pp. 15–22.

49 Mohammad Ayub Khan, *Friends Not Masters: A Political Biography* (Islamabad: Mr. Books, 2002), p. 154.

50 Kinzer, *The Brothers*, p. 146. See also Stephen Kinzer, *All the Shah's Men* (Hoboken, N.J.: Wiley, 2003).

51 Kinzer, *The Brothers*, p. 132.

52 Conboy and Morrison, *The CIA's Secret War in Tibet*, pp. 42–53 and p. 60.

53 Ibid., pp. 60–65.

54 Rowland, *A History of Sino-Indian Relations*, p. 102.

55 Ibid., p. 105.

56 Mullik, *My Years with Nehru*, pp. 218–19.

57 Harry Rositzke, *The CIA's Secret Operations: Espionage, Counterespionage and Covert Action* (New York: Readers Digest Press, 1977), p. 174.

58 Schlesinger, *A Thousand Days*, p. 241.

59 Chris Pocock, *The U2 Spyplane: Toward the Unknown—A New History of the Early Years* (Atglen, Pa.: Schiffer Military History, 2000), p. 46.

60 Ibid., pp. 100–06.

61 Ibid., pp. 143–44.

62 Ibid., pp. 158–61.

63 Dennis Kux, *Disenchanted Allies: The United States and Pakistan, 1947–2000* (Johns Hopkins University Press, 2001), pp. 102 and 112.

64 Khan, *Friends Not Masters*, p. 59.

65 Grant's epic world tour is best described in Frank A. Burr, "Tour around the World," *The Life and Deeds of General U.S. Grant* (Philadelphia: National Publishing Company, 1885), pp. 887–965.

66 Michael Korda, *Ike: An American Hero* (New York: Harper, 2007), p. 709.

67 Laurent Gayer, *Karachi: Ordered Disorder and the Struggle for the City* (Oxford University Press, 2014), p. 28.

68 Kux, *Disenchanted Allies*, p. 107.

69 Mullik, *My Years with Nehru*, pp. 196–99.

70 Dhar, *CIA's Eye on South Asia*, p. 117.

71 Neville Maxwell, *India's China War* (New Delhi: Natraj, 2013), pp. 145–50.

72 Dennis Kux, *Estranged Democracies: India and the United States, 1941–1991* (Washington: National Defense University Press, 1993), pp. 164–67.

73 Knaus, *Orphans of the Cold War*, p. 210.

74 Mullik, *My Years with Nehru*, pp. 155–56.

75 Maxwell, *India's China War*, p. 157.

76 Kux, *Estranged Democracies*, p. 167.

77 Conboy and Morrison, *The CIA's Secret War in Tibet*, p. 97.

78 Ibid., p. 115.

79 Pocock, *The U2 Spyplane*, pp. 143–44.

80 Ibid., p. 190, and Evan Thomas, *Ike's Bluff: President Eisenhower's Secret Battle to Save the World* (New York: Little, Brown, 2012), p. 371.

81 Thomas, *Ike's Bluff*, pp. 366–67.

82 Ibid., p. 370.

83 Ibid., p. 374.

84 Larry Devlin, *Chief of Station Congo: A Memoir of 1960–67* (New York: Public Affairs, 2007), pp. 78–87.

CHAPTER 2

1 Richard Parker, *John Kenneth Galbraith: His Life, His Politics, His Economics* (New York: Farrar, 2005), pp. 5–14.

2 Ted Sorensen, *Kennedy* (New York: Harper, 2013), p. 370.

3 Parker, *John Kenneth Galbraith*, pp. 324–25, 334.

4 Ibid., p. 279. See also John Kenneth Galbraith, *A Life in Our Times: Memoirs* (Boston: Houghton Mifflin, 1981), p. 334.

5 Parker, *John Kenneth Galbraith*, p. 326.

6 Chris Matthews, *Jack Kennedy: Elusive Hero* (New York: Simon and Shuster, 2011), pp. 116–17.

7 Jacqueline Kennedy, *Historic Conversations on Life with John F. Kennedy* (New York: Hyperion, 2011), p. 238. See also Arthur Schlesinger, *A Thousand Days: John F. Kennedy in the White House* (Boston: Houghton Mifflin, 1965), p. 522.

8 Robert Dallek, *An Unfinished Life: John F. Kennedy, 1917–1963* (Boston: Back Bay Books, 2013), p. 168.

9 Robert Dallek, *Camelot's Court: Inside the Kennedy White House* (New York: Harper Collins, 2013), pp. 2, 41.

10 Dennis Kux, *Disenchanted Allies: the United States and Pakistan, 1947–2000* (Baltimore: Johns Hopkins University Press, 2001), p. 61.

11 John F. Kennedy, "Imperialism—The Enemy of Freedom," July 2, 1957, can be found on the JFK Presidential Library website. See also Theresa Romahn, "Colonialism and the Campaign Trail: On Kennedy's Algerian Speech and His Bid for the 1960 Democratic Nomination," *Journal of Colonialism and Colonial History* 10 (Fall 2009).

12 Alistair Horne, *A Savage War of Peace: Algeria 1954–1962* (New York: Viking, 1977), p. 247.

13 John F. Kennedy, "Remarks of Senator John F. Kennedy, Conference on India and the United States, Washington, May 4, 1959," which can be found on the JFK Presidential Library website.

14 Dallek, *An Unfinished Life*, p. 102.

15 Peter Wyden, *Bay of Pigs: The Untold Story* (New York: Touchstone, 1979), p. 95.

16 Ibid., p. 95.

17 Peter Kornbluh (ed.), *Bay of Pigs Declassified: The Secret CIA Report on the Invasion of Cuba* (New York: New Press, 1998), pp. 41, 53, 55, and 57. This is a declassified version of the CIA's own postmortem on the invasion written by its inspector general, Lyman Kirkpatrick.

18 James G. Blight and Peter Kornbluh (eds.), *Politics of Illusion: The Bay of Pigs Invasion Reexamined* (London: Lynne Rienner, 1998), p. 65.

19 Ibid., p. 65.

20 Wyden, *Bay of Pigs*, pp. 265–70.

21 Dallek, *An Unfinished Life*, pp. 143–44.

22 Christopher Andersen, *These Few Precious Days: The Final Year of Jack and Jackie* (New York: Gallery Books, 2013), p. 114.

23 Blight and Kornbluh, *Politics of Illusion*, p. 2.

24 Wyden, *Bay of Pigs*, p. 268.

25 Ibid., p. 322.

26 Michael Dobbs, *One Minute to Midnight: Kennedy, Khrushchev and Castro on the Brink of Nuclear War* (New York: Knopf, 2008), p. 207.

27 Dallek, *An Unfinished Life*, p. 149.

28 Director of Central Intelligence, "Sino-Indian Relations," National Intelligence Estimate Number 100-2-60, May 17, 1960. Approved for Release June 2004. Part of the China Collection available on the CIA website under the Center for the Study of Intelligence.

29 Ibid., pp. 5–6.

30 Ibid., p. 5.

31 Kenneth Conboy and James Morrison, *The CIA's Secret War in Tibet* (University Press of Kansas, 2002), pp. 138–39.

32 John Kenneth Knaus, *Orphans of the Cold War: America and the Tibetan Struggle for Survival* (New York: Public Affairs, 1999), pp. 154–55.

33 Ibid., pp. 187, 233.

34 Conboy and Morrison, *The CIA's Secret War in Tibet*, pp. 139–44.

35 Knaus, *Orphans of the Cold War*, pp. 238–44.

36 Ibid., p. 188.

37 Ibid., pp. 322–23.

38 Ibid., pp. 245, 264.

39 Evan Thomas, *The Very Best Men: Four Who Dared: The Early Years of the CIA* (New York: Simon and Schuster, 1995), p. 277.

40 Conboy and Morrison, *The CIA's Secret War in Tibet*, p. 155.

41 Knaus, *Orphans of the Cold War*, p. 243.

42 Thomas, *The Very Best Men*, p. 277.

43 John Kenneth Galbraith, *Ambassador's Journal: A Personal Account of the Kennedy Years* (Boston: Houghton Mifflin, 1969), p. 43.

44 Galbraith, *A Life in Our Times*, pp. 394–97.

45 Knaus, *Orphans of the Cold War*, p. 216.

46 Conboy and Morrison, *The CIA's Secret War in Tibet*, p. 156.

47 Knaus, *Orphans of the Cold War*, p. 121.

48 Conboy and Morrison, *The CIA's Secret War in Tibet*, pp. 155–56, 282.

49 Ibid., p. 160.

50 Ibid., p. 158.

51 Office of the Historian, U.S. Department of State, Foreign Relations of the United States, 1961–1963, Vol. XIX, South Asia, Document 29, SNIE 32-61, Prospects for Pakistan, 5 July 1961 (Washington: U.S. Government Printing Office, 1996), paragraphs 15–16.

52 Conboy and Morrison, *The CIA's Secret War in Tibet*, p. 159.

53 Photograph, Shotgun for President of Pakistan Mohammad Ayub Khan, July 1961, Papers of John F. Kennedy, Presidential Papers, John F. Kennedy Presidential Library and Museum.

54 Conboy and Morrison, *The CIA's Secret War in Tibet*, p. 162.

55 Knaus, *Orphans of the Cold War*, p. 250. In his memoirs written years later Galbraith claimed he did shut down the Tibet operation late in 1961 with the help of Bobby Kennedy. That may be an example of a memoir reporting what the author wanted to remember, because the operation was not ended in 1961. See Galbraith, *Ambassador's Journal*, p. 397 for a colorful memory of Ken and Bobby persuading JFK to stop the Tibet mission while Kennedy was in the bathtub and one of Bobby's sons was listening to "these deeply secret matters."

56 Stephen Kinzer, *The Brothers: John Foster Dulles, Allen Dulles and Their Secret World War* (New York: Times Books, 2013), p. 303.

57 Warren Bass, *Support Any Friend: Kennedy's Middle East and the Making of the U.S.-Israel Alliance* (Oxford University Press, 2003), p. 208.

58 Dallek, *An Unfinished Life*, pp. 288, 293.

59 Percy Cradock, *Know Your Enemy: How the Joint Intelligence Committee Saw the World* (London: John Murray, 2002), p. 181.

60 Cynthia Helms, *An Intriguing Life: A Memoir of War, Washington and Marriage to an American Spymaster* (New York: Rowman & Littlefield, 2013), p. 93.

61 Conboy and Morrison, *The CIA's Secret War in Tibet*, p. 167.

62 Dallek, *An Unfinished Life*, pp. 215–17.

63 Knaus, *Orphans of the Cold War*, p. 253.

64 Parker, *John Kenneth Galbraith*, p. 347.

65 Ibid., p. 353.

66 Dallek, *An Unfinished Life*, p. 196

67 Frederick Kempe, *Berlin 1961: Kennedy, Khrushchev and the Most Dangerous Place on Earth* (New York: Berkley Books, 2011) is the best account of the Vienna summit and the Berlin crisis that followed.

68 Galbraith, *An Ambassador's Journal*, p. 54.

69 Ibid., p. 174.

70 Ibid., p. 223.

71 Parker, *John Kenneth Galbraith*, p. 351.

72 Mark Epernay, *The McLandress Dimension* (Boston: Houghton Mifflin, 1963), p. 66. The author is identified as "evidently a distinguished observer of politico-economic trends."

73 Galbraith, *An Ambassador's Journal*, pp. 170–72.

74 Dennis Kux, *India and the United States: Estranged Democracies, 1941–1991* (Washington: National Defense University Press, 1992), pp. 186–87.

75 Schlesinger, *A Thousand Days*, p. 523.

76 Ibid., pp. 523–24.

77 Clint Hill with Lisa McCubbin, *Mrs. Kennedy and Me* (New York: Gallery Books, 2012), p. 100.

78 Stanley Wolpert, *Nehru: A Tryst with Destiny* (Oxford University Press, 1996), p. 480.

79 Sorenson, *Kennedy*, p. 578.

80 Galbraith, *An Ambassador's Journal*, pp. 246–48.

81 Sorenson, *Kennedy*, p. 578.

82 Schlesinger, *A Thousand Days*, pp. 324–25.

83 Galbraith, *An Ambassador's Journal*, p. 248.

84 Wolpert, *Nehru*, p. 480.

85 Jacqueline Kennedy, *Historic Conversations*, p. 280.

86 Ibid., p. 279.

87 Parker, *John Kenneth Galbraith*, p. 367.

88 Ibid., p. 372.

89 Galbraith, *An Ambassador's Journal*, p. 232.

90 Ibid., p. 239.

91 Ibid., p. 246.

92 Neville Maxwell, *India's China War* (New Delhi: Natraj, 2013), p. 391.

93 B. G. Verghese, "The War We Lost—1962 Sino-Indian Conflict," *Tibet Sun*, October 5, 2012, p. 4.

94 Schlesinger, *A Thousand Days*, p. 526.

95 Jacqueline Kennedy, *Historic Conversations*, p. 292.

96 Schlesinger, *A Thousand Days*, pp. 526–27.

97 Galbraith, *An Ambassador's Journal*, p. 249

98 Schlesinger, *A Thousand Days*, p. 529.

CHAPTER 3

1 Christopher Andrews, *These Few Precious Days: The Final Year of Jack and Jackie* (New York: Gallery Books, 2013), p. 163.

2 Ibid., p. 160.

3 John Kenneth Galbraith, *Ambassador's Journal: A Personal Account of the Kennedy Years* (Boston: Houghton Mifflin, 1969), pp. 257–67.

4 Clint Hill with Lisa McCubbin, *Mrs. Kennedy and Me* (New York: Gallery Books, 2012), p. 128.

5 Galbraith, *Ambassador's Journal*, p. 269.

6 Jacqueline Duheme, *Mrs. Kennedy Goes Abroad* (New York: Artisan, 1998), pp. 30–32. Duheme was a French artist who accompanied Jackie on the trip to make intricate miniature paintings of the various stops. Galbraith wrote the introduction to this book, which is a collection of the paintings accompanied by a description of the trip.

7 Gerald Blaino with Lisa McCubbin, *The Kennedy Detail: JFK's Secret Service Agents Break Their Silence* (New York: Gallery Books, 2010), p. 112.

8 Galbraith, *Ambassador's Journal*, p. 277

9 See Alex von Tunzelmann, *Indian Summer: The Secret History of the End of an Empire* (New York: Picador, 2007) for a study of the relationship between Edwina and Nehru.

10 Galbraith, *Ambassador's Journal*, p. 279.

11 Duheme, *Mrs. Kennedy Goes Abroad*, p. 42.

12 Galbraith, *Ambassador's Journal*, pp. 279–80.

13 Duheme, *Mrs. Kennedy Goes Abroad*, p. 44.

14 Ibid., p. 46.

15 Galbraith, *Ambassador's Journal*, p. 277.

16 Hill, *Mrs. Kennedy and Me*, p. 140.

17 Duheme, *Mrs. Kennedy Goes Abroad*, p. 50.

18 Andrews, *These Few Precious Days*, p. 162.

19 Hill, *Mrs. Kennedy and Me*, p. 145.

20 Duheme, *Mrs. Kennedy Goes Abroad*, p. 58.

21 Director of Central Intelligence, "Prospects for Communist China," National Intelligence Estimate number 13-4-62, May 2, 1962. Approved for release June 2004. Part of the China Collection available on the CIA website under the Center for the Study of Intelligence.

22 Ibid., pp. 1, 4.

23 Ibid., pp. 1–2.

24 Ibid., Annex B, p. 15.

25 Ibid., Annex B, p. 16.

26 Ibid., p. 9.

27 Ibid., p. 4.

28 Ibid., p. 8.

29 Ibid., p. 2.

30 Office of the Historian, Department of State, Foreign Relations of the United States, 1961–1963, Vol. XIX, South Asia, Document 127, National Intelligence Estimate, "The Prospects for India," May 31, 1962 (Washington: U.S. Government Printing Office, 1996), paragraphs A, D, and E.

31 John Kenneth Knaus, *Orphans of the Cold War: America and the Tibetan Struggle for Survival* (New York: Public Affairs, 1999), p. 322.

32 Kenneth Conboy and James Morrison, *The CIA's Secret War in Tibet* (University Press of Kansas, 2002), p. 167.

33 Ibid., p. 168.

34 Parakram Rautela interview with Neville Maxwell, *The Times of India*, April 2, 2014, p. 2.

35 Neville Maxwell, *India's China War* (New Delhi: Natraj Publishers, 2013), pp. 248–49.

36 Ibid., p. 225.

37 Ibid., p. 265.

38 Rautela, *The Times of India* interview, p. 2.

39 B. N. Mullik, *The Chinese Betrayal: My Years with Nehru* (Bombay: Allied Publishers, 1971), pp. 324–25.

40 Ibid., pp. 329–30.

41 Ibid., p. 332.

42 Director of Central Intelligence, "Sino-Indian Relations," National Intelligence Estimate Number 100-2-60, May 17, 1960. Approved for release June 2004. Part of the China Collection available on the CIA website under the Center for the Study of Intelligence.

43 Mullik, *The Chinese Betrayal*, p. 333.

44 Ibid.

45 J. P. Dalvi, *Himalayan Blunder* (New Delhi: Orient Paperbacks, 1968), p. 172.

46 Maxwell, *India's China War*, p. 302.

47 Dalvi, *Himalayan Blunder*, pp. 140–42.

48 Dalai Lama, *My Land and My People: Memoirs of His Holiness, the Dalai Lama* (New Delhi: Srishti, 1997), p. 86.

49 Dalvi, *Himalayan Blunder*, p. 47.

50 See the book jacket front cover from the 2013 Indian version of *India's China War.*

51 Allen S. Whiting, *The Calculus of Chinese Deterrence: India and Indochina* (University of Michigan, 1975).

52 Li Zhisvi, *The Private Life of Chairman Mao* (New York: Random House, 1994), p. ix, 76, and 77.

53 Ibid., pp. 77, 516.

54 Ibid., p. 125.

55 John. W. Garver, "China's Decision for War with India in 1962," Georgia Institute of Technology, unpublished paper, 2005, p. 48.

56 Ibid., p. 6.

57 Ibid.

58 Ibid., pp. 13–15.

59 Ibid., p. 17.

60 Ibid., p. 33.

61 Ibid., p. 39.

62 Dalai Lama, *My Land and My People*, p. 153.

63 John W. Garver, *Protracted Conflict: Sino-Indian Rivalry in the Twentieth Century* (University of Washington Press, 2001), p. 61. Italics from original.

64 Ibid., p. 24.

65 Robert Dallek, *An Unfinished Life: John F. Kennedy, 1917–1963* (Boston: Back Bay Books, 2013), p. 415.

66 Harold Macmillan, *At the End of the Day, 1961–1963* (London: Harper and Row, 1973), p. 227.

67 Stanley Wolpert, *Zulfi Bhutto of Pakistan* (Oxford University Press, 1993), p. 60.

68 Shuja Nawaz, *Crossed Swords: Pakistan, Its Army and the Wars Within* (Oxford University Press, 2008), p. 193.

69 Ibid., p. 186.

70 Hill, *Mrs. Kennedy and Me*, p. 187.

71 Kux, *Disenchanted Allies*, p. 126.

72 National Security Agency, "Unusual Number of Soviet Passenger Ships en Route Cuba," July 24, 1962. Available on the Cuban Missile Crisis Documents Archive, National Security Agency Central Security Service website.

73 James Blight and David Welch, *On the Brink: Americans and Soviets Reexamine the Cuban Missile Crisis* (New York: Noonday Press, 1989), pp. 332–33.

74 Ernest R. May and Philip D. Zelikow (eds.), *The Kennedy Tapes: Inside the White House during the Cuban Missile Crisis* (New York: Norton, 2002), pp. li, 3–5.

75 Office of Current Intelligence, Central Intelligence Agency, Current Intelligence Memorandum "Recent Soviet Military Aid to Cuba," August 22, 1962. Laurence Chang and Peter Kornbluh (eds.), *The Cuban Missile Crisis, 1962: A National Security Archive Documents Reader* (New York: New Press, 1992), p. 57.

76 Director of Central Intelligence, Special National Intelligence Estimate Number 85-3-62, "The Military Buildup in Cuba," September 19, 1962. Chang and Kornbluh, *The Cuban Missile Crisis 1962*, pp. 63–65.

77 Max Holland, "The Photo Gap that Delayed Discovery of Missiles," *Studies in Intelligence, Journal of the American Intelligence Professional* 49 (December 2005) and David M. Barrett and Max Holland, *Blind over Cuba: The Photo-Gap and the Missile Crisis* (Texas A&M University Press, 2012).

78 Blight and Welch, *On the Brink*, p. 251.

CHAPTER 4

1 John Kenneth Galbraith, *Ambassador's Journal: A Personal Account of the Kennedy Years* (Boston: Houghton Mifflin, 1969), pp. 405–06.

2 Richard Parker, *John Kenneth Galbraith: His Life, His Politics, His Economics* (New York: Farrar, Straus and Gioux, 2005), p. 395.

3 Neville Maxwell, *India's China War* (New Delhi: Natraj, 2013), p. 346.

4 John W. Garver, "China's Decision for War with India in 1962," Georgia Institute of Technology, unpublished paper, p. 48.

5 Ibid., p. 51.

6 John Rowland, *A History of Sino-Indian Relations: Hostile Co-Existence* (Princeton: Van Nostrand, 1967), p. 165.

7 Maxwell, *India's China War*, p. 385.

8 Parker, *John Kenneth Galbraith*, p. 399.

9 Maxwell, *India's China War*, pp. 387–89.

10 Ibid., p. 392.

11 Steven A. Hoffman, *India and the China Crisis* (University of California Press, 1990), p. 163.

12 Galbraith, *Ambassador's Journal*, p. 373.

13 Ibid., p. 374.

14 Michael Dobbs, *One Minute to Midnight: Kennedy, Khrushchev and Castro on the Brink of Nuclear War* (New York: Knopf, 2008), pp. 26–28, 176, and 352.

15 Ernest May and Philip Zelikow, eds., *The Kennedy Tapes: Inside the White House during the Cuban Missile Crisis* (New York: Norton, 2001), p. xi.

16 See, for example, oral history projects on the missile crisis in James G. Blight and David Welch, *On the Brink: Americans and Soviets Reexamine the Cuban Missile Crisis* (New York: Noonday Press, 1989).

17 John Kenneth Galbraith, *A Life in Our Times: Memoirs* (Boston: Houghton Mifflin, 1981), p. 388.

18 Ibid., pp. 374–75.

19 The Kennedys entertained the Maharaja of Jaipur on October 23 for dinner at the White House, reciprocating his hospitality in hosting Jackie in the spring. The British ambassador was also a guest. The Chinese invasion was undoubtedly discussed, but I have found no account of the conversation. The maharaja had no official responsibility in the Indian government, and it was a social event.

20 Galbraith, *A Life in Our Times*, p. 374.

21 Ibid., p. 376.

22 John W. Garver, *Protracted Conflict: Sino-Indian Rivalry in the Twentieth Century* (University of Washington Press, 2001), p. 96.

23 Maxwell, *India's China War*, pp. 324–25.

24 Kenneth Conboy and James Morrison, *The CIA's Secret War in Tibet* (University Press of Kansas, 2002), p. 171.

25 Galbraith, *A Life in Our Times*, pp. 378–79.

26 Ibid.

27 Conboy and Morrison, *The CIA's Secret War in Tibet*, p. 172.

28 Harold Macmillan, *At the End of the Day, 1961–1963* (London: Harper and Row, 1973), p. 229.

29 B. N. Mullik, *My Years with Nehru: The Chinese Betrayal* (Bombay: Allied Publishers, 1971), pp. 350–51, 406–07.

30 Director of Central Intelligence, Special National Intelligence Estimate Number 13/31-62, "Short Term Outlook and Implications for the Sino-Indian Conflict," November 9, 1962, declassified June 2004. Part of the CIA's declassified China series, paragraphs 8, 9, and 19.

31 SNIE 13/31-62, paragraphs 13 and 14.

32 Galbraith, *A Life in Our Times*, p. 372.

33 Ibid., pp. 384–85, 387.

34 Wolfgang Saxon, "Walter McConaughy, 92, Envoy in Asia Dies," *New York Times*, November 14, 2000.

35 Galbraith, *A Life in Our Times*, p. 385.

36 Ibid.

37 Mohammad Ayub Khan, *Friends Not Masters: A Political Autobiography* (Islamabad: Mr. Books, 2002), p. 135.

38 Ibid., pp. 140–43.

39 Ibid., pp. 142–43.

40 Ibid., p. 143.

41 Ibid., p. 145.

42 Nehru shared his letter to Ayub Khan with Galbraith, who sent it to Washington. State Department Telegram New Delhi 1835, November 15, 1962. John F. Kennedy Presidential Library and Museum, India: Subjects: Nehru correspondence, November 1962: 11–19.

43 Galbraith, *A Life in Our Times*, p. 412.

44 Ibid., p. 402, 412–13.

45 Ibid., p. 414.

46 Hoffman, *India and the China Crisis*, pp. 180–81.

47 Maxwell, *India's China War*, p. 449.

48 Hoffman, *India and the China Crisis*, p. 186.

49 Maxwell, *India's China War*, p. 461.

50 T. B. Henderson Brooks and P. S. Bhagat, Review, Top Secret, pp. 188–90. The review remains classified today, but excerpts can be found at www.indiandefencereview.com, www.indiatoday.com, and www.nevillemaxwell.com.

51 Galbraith, *A Life in our Times*, pp. 421–23.

52 Ibid., p. 434.

53 Galbraith, *Ambassador's Journal*, p. 423.

54 Parker, *John Kenneth Galbraith*, p. 402.

55 Galbraith, *The Triumph; A Novel of Modern Diplomacy* (Boston: Houghton Mifflin, 1993). p. 124.

56 Mullik, *My Years with Nehru*, pp. 434–35.

57 Galbraith, *A Life in our Times*, p. 423.

58 Inder Malhotra, "J.N. TO JFK, 'EYES ONLY,'" *Indian Express*, November 15, 2010.

59 Embassy New Delhi 1891, November 19, 1962 EYES ONLY PRESIDENT, SECRETARY AND SECDEF NIACT, John F. Kennedy Presidential Library and Museum, India: Subjects: Nehru correspondence, November 1962: 11–19.

60 Embassy New Delhi 1889, November 19, 1962 EYES ONLY PRESIDENT, SECRETARY AND SECDEF NIACT, John F. Kennedy Presidential Library and Museum, India: Subjects: Nehru correspondence, November 1962: 11–19.

61 Galbraith, *A Life in our Times*, p. 423.

62 U.S. Department of State Outgoing Telegram for Amembassy New Delhi 2167, November 19, 1962. EYES ONLY FOR AMBASSADOR NIACT. John F. Kennedy Presidential Library and Museum, India: Subjects: Nehru correspondence, November 1962: 11–19.

63 Dennis Kuk, *India and the United States: Estranged Democracies, 1941–1991* (Washington: National Defense University Press), p. 207.

64 Macmillan, *At the End of the Day*, p. 230.

65 Galbraith, *A Life in our Times*, pp. 423–24.

66 Ibid., p. 424.

67 Dennis Kux mistakenly identifies the carrier dispatched to India as the USS *Enterprise*, which in fact was on duty in the Atlantic enforcing the quarantine of Cuba, Kux, *India and the United States*, p. 207. It was the USS *Kitty Hawk*.

68 Galbraith, *A Life in our Times*, pp. 425–26.

69 Ibid., p. 426.

70 Maxwell, *India's China War*, pp. 475–76.

71 Ibid., p. 484.

72 Ibid., p. 488.

73 Katherine Frank, *Indira: The Life of Indira Nehru Gandhi* (London, Harper Collins, 2001), p. 266.

74 Galbraith, *A Life in our Times*, p. 428, and Mullik, *My Years with Nehru*, p. 449.

75 Galbraith, *A Life in our Times*, p. 426.

76 Ibid., p. 427.

77 J. P. Dalvi, *Himalayan Blunder* (New Delhi, Orient Paperbacks, 1968), p. 410.

78 Mullik, *My Years with Nehru*, pp. 448–50.

79 Galbraith, *A Life in our Times*, p. 429.

80 Ibid., p. 437.

CHAPTER 5

1 John F. Kennedy Press Conference, September 12, 1963, Audio Tape Accession Number WH-215, John F. Kennedy Presidential Library and Museum.

2 Office of the Historian, Department of State, Foreign Relations of the United States, 1961–1963, Vol. XIX, South Asia, Document 202, Memorandum for the Record, Subject: Presidential Meeting on Sino-Indian Conflict, November 19, 1962 (Washington: U.S. Government Printing Office, 1996), paragraphs 1–2.

3 Dennis Kux, *India and the United States: Estranged Democracies, 1941–1991* (Washington: National Defense University Press, 1992), p. 209.

4 Harold Macmillan, *At the End of the Day, 1961–1963* (London: Harper and Row, 1973), p. 231.

5 John Kenneth Knaus, *Orphans of the Cold War: America and the Tibetan Struggle for Survival* (New York: Public Affairs, 1999), p. 264.

6 John Kenneth Galbraith, *Ambassador's Journal: A Personal Account of the Kennedy Years* (Boston: Houghton Mifflin, 1969), p. 429.

7 John Kenneth Galbraith, *The Triumph: A Novel of Modern Diplomacy* (Boston: Houghton Mifflin, 1993), is dedicated to Averell Harriman.

8 Macmillan, *At the End of the Day*, p. 235.

9 Kux, *India and the United States*, p. 242. See also Foreign Relations of the United States, 1961–1963, Document 215, Memorandum of Meeting of the Executive Committee of the National Security Council, December 3, 1962, on Harriman's recommendations to Kennedy from his trip.

10 Galbraith, *Ambassador's Journal*, p. 455.

11 Kux, *India and the United States*, pp. 211–17.

12 Macmillan, *At the End of the Day*, p. 235.

13 Mohammad Ayub Khan, *Friends Not Masters: A Political Autobiography* (Islamabad: Mr. Books, 2002), pp. 151–52.

14 Galbraith, *Ambassador's Journal*, p. 446.

15 Ibid., p. 456.

16 Howard Schaffer, *The Limits of Influence: America's Role in Kashmir* (Brookings, 2009), p. 86.

17 Galbraith, *Ambassador's Journal*, p. 480.

18 Letter from J. Nehru to President Kennedy, February 16, 1963, Presidential Papers, John F. Kennedy Presidential Library and Museum.

19 Schaffer, *The Limits of Influence*, p. 87. Schaffer's book is the most complete and insightful history of the Kashmir negotiations engaged in by the Kennedy administration.

20 Dennis Kux, *Disenchanted Allies: The United States and Pakistan, 1947–2000* (Johns Hopkins University Press, 2001), p. 143.

21 Ibid., pp. 144–46.

22 Joe Pascal, "An Appreciation: The Benazir Bhutto I Knew," *U.S. News and World Report*, December 28, 2009.

23 Galbraith, *Ambassador's Journal*, p. 435. See also Evan Thomas, *The Very Best Men: Four Who Dared: The Early Years of the CIA* (New York: Simon and Schuster, 1995), p. 193.

24 John Kenneth Galbraith, *A Life in Our Times: Memoirs* (Boston: Houghton Mifflin, 1981), p. 436.

25 Knaus, *Orphans of the Cold War*, p. 265.

26 Kenneth Conboy and James Morrison, *The CIA's Secret War in Tibet* (University Press of Kansas, 2002), pp. 184, 190–91.

27 Knaus, *Orphans of the Cold War*, p. 273.

28 Conboy and Morrison, *The CIA's Secret War in Tibet*, pp. 187, 192.

29 Knaus, *Orphans of the Cold War*, p. 281, and Conboy and Morrison, *The CIA's Secret War in Tibet*, p. 193.

30 Conboy and Morrison, *The CIA's Secret War in Tibet*, pp. 198–99, 246.

31 Ibid., p. 175, 182–83, and Knaus, *Orphans of the Cold War*, p. 275.

32 Jeffrey Richelson, *Spying on the Bomb: American Nuclear Intelligence from Nazi Germany to Iran and North Korea* (New York: Norton, 2006), pp. 100–01.

33 Director of Central Intelligence, "The Chances of an Imminent Communist Chinese Nuclear Explosion," Special National Intelligence

Estimate 13-4-64, August 26, 1964. Approved for release May 2004. Part of the China Collection available on the CIA website under the Center for the Study of Intelligence, p. 1.

34 Conboy and Morrison, *The CIA's Secret War in Tibet*, p. 205.

35 Ted Sorensen, *Kennedy* (New York: Harper Collins, 2013), p. 752.

36 Chester Bowles, *Promises to Keep: My Years in Public Life, 1941–1969* (New York: Harper and Row, 1971), p. 489.

37 Ibid., p. 457.

38 Ibid., p. 463.

39 Ibid., pp. 437, 457–58.

40 Ibid., pp. 477, 481.

41 Ibid., pp. 482–83.

42 Ibid., pp. 483–84.

43 Ibid., p. 484.

44 Feroz Hassan Khan, *Eating Grass: The Making of the Pakistani Bomb* (Stanford University Press, 2013), p. 42, and John W. Garver, *Protracted Conflict: Sino-Indian Rivalry in the Twentieth Century* (University of Washington Press, 2001), p. 195.

45 Office of the Historian, U.S. Department of State, Foreign Relations of the United States, 1964–1968, Vol. XXV, South Asia, Document 186, Memorandum Prepared in the Office of Current Intelligence, Central Intelligence Agency, September 6, 1965, "Possible Sino-Pakistani Military Arrangement."

46 Farooq Bajwa, *From Kutch to Tashkent: The Indo-Pakistan War of 1965* (London: Hurst, 2013), p. 226.

47 Garver, *Protracted Conflict*, p. 202.

48 Office of the Historian, U.S. Department of State, Foreign Relations of the United States, 1964–1968, Vol. XXV, South Asia, Document 205, Special National Intelligence Estimate, SNIE 13-10-65, September 16, 1965, "Prospects of Chinese Communist Involvement in the Indo-Pakistan War."

49 Bajwa, *From Kutch to Tashkent*, pp. 300–03.

50 Bowles, *Promises to Keep*, p. 504.

51 Ibid., p. 503.

52 Anand Giridharadas, "JFK Faced India China Dilemma," *New York Times*, August 26, 2005.

53 Ibid., p. 574.

54 Michael Pizzi, "Report: India Remains World's Largest Arms Buyer," *Al Jazeera*, March 17, 2014.

55 Garver, *Protracted Conflict*, p. 317.

56 Ibid., p. 317.

57 Gary Bass, *The Blood Telegram: Nixon, Kissinger and a Forgotten Genocide* (New York: Vintage, 2013), pp. 226, 229–35.

58 Richard Sisson and Leo E. Rose, *War and Secession: Pakistan, India and the Creation of Bangladesh* (University of California Press, 1990), p. 253.

59 Strobe Talbott, *Engaging India: Diplomacy, Democracy and the Bomb* (Brookings, 2004), pp. 1–3.

60 "Nuclear Anxiety: Indian's Letter to Clinton on the Nuclear Testing," *New York Times*, May 13, 1998.

61 Quoted in Garver, *Protracted Conflict*, p. 338.

62 Jaswant Singh, *In Service of Emergent India: A Call to Honor* (Indiana University Press, 2007), pp. 42, 129.

63 Defence R&D Organization, Ministry of Defence, Press Release April 19, 2012, Wheeler Island, Odisha, India.

64 Andrew Small, *The China-Pakistan Axis: Asia's New Geopolitics* (Oxford University Press, 2015), pp. 24–37.

65 Khan, *Eating Grass*, p. 57.

66 Jane Perlez, "Xi Jinping Heads to Pakistan, Bearing Billions in Infrastructure Aid," *New York Times*, April 20, 2015, and Saeed Shah and Jeremy Page, "China to Unveil Massive Pakistan Spending," *Wall Street Journal*, April 17, 2015.

67 Toshi Yoshihara, "Undersea Dragons in the Indian Ocean?" China-India Brief #37, Centre on Asia and Globalization, Lee Kuan Yew School of Public Policy, October 14, 2014.

68 Saurav Jha, "New Orientation in Indian Defense Policy," *South Asia Journal* 2 (Fall 2014), p. 59.

69 Vijaira Singh, "India to Build 1800 km Highway along China Border in Arunachal," *Nation*, October 15, 2014.

70 "China Expresses Concern about Indian Border Road Plan," *Mail Online*, October 15, 2014. www.dailymail.co.uk/wires/reuters/article -2793750/China-expresses-concern-India

71 "No One Can Threaten India, Says Rajnath Singh on China's Reaction to Arunachal Border Road Issue," *Deccan Chronicle*, October 16, 2014.

72 "China Rejects India's Consulate Pleas," *Global Times*, April 18, 2014.

73 Ananth Krishan, "Indo-China Trade: Record $31 Billion Deficit in 2013," *The Hindu*, January 10, 2014.

74 Rajan Menon, "The India Myth," *The National Interest* 134 (November/December 2014), pp. 46–57.

75 "China Says Pakistan 'Most Reliable Friend,' Vows to 'Help in All Respects,'" *Dawn*, January 26, 2015.

76 Max Holland, "The Photo Gap that Delayed Discovery of Missiles," *Studies in Intelligence*, Center for the Study of Intelligence, Central Intelligence Agency, 49, no. 4 (April 2007), p. 9.

77 Ernest R. May, *Strange Victory: Hitler's Conquest of France* (New York: Hill and Wang, 2000), p. 463.

78 Kux, *Disenchanted Allies*, p. 136.

BIBLIOGRAPHY

Allison, Graham. 1971. *Essence of Decision: Explaining the Cuban Missile Crisis*. Boston: Little, Brown.

Andersen, Christopher. 2013. *These Few Precious Days: The Final Year with Jack and Jackie*. New York: Gallery Books.

Andersen, Walter, and Shridhar Damle. 1987. *The Brotherhood in Saffron: The Rashtriya Swayamasevak Sangh and Hindu Revivalism*. New Delhi: Vistaar.

Bajwa, Farooq. 2013. *From Kutch to Tashkent: The Indo-Pakistan War of 1965*. London: Hurst.

Baldridge, Letitia. 1998. *In the Kennedy Style: Magical Evenings in the Kennedy White House*. Toronto: Madison.

Barrett, David M., and Max Holland. 2012. *Blind over Cuba: The Photo-Gap and the Missile Crisis*. Dallas: Texas A&M University Press.

Bass, Gary. 2013. *The Blood Telegram: Nixon, Kissinger and a Forgotten Genocide*. New York: Knopf.

Bass, Warren. 2003. *Support Any Friend: Kennedy's Middle East and the Making of the U.S.-Israeli Alliance*. Oxford: Oxford University Press.

Beschloss, Michael. 2007. *Presidential Courage: Brave Leaders and how They Changed America, 1789–1989*. New York: Simon and Schuster.

Blight, James, and Peter Kornbluh (eds.). 1998. *Politics of Illusion: The Bay of Pigs Invasion Reexamined*. Boulder: Lynne Rienner.

Blight, James, and Janet Lang. 2012. *The Armageddon Letters: Kennedy, Khrushchev and Castro in the Cuban Missile Crisis*. New York: Rowman & Littlefield.

Blight, James, Janet Lang, and David Welch. 2009. *Vietnam if Kennedy had Lived: Virtual JFK*. New York: Rowman & Littlefield.

Blight, James, and David Welch. 1990. *On the Brink: Americans and Soviets Reexamine the Cuban Missile Crisis*. New York: Noonday Press.

Bowles, Chester. 1971. *Promises to Keep: My Years in Public Life, 1941–1969*. New York: Harper and Row.

Chang, Jung, and Jon Halliday. 2005. *Mao: The Unknown Story*. New York: Alfred Knopf.

Chang, Laurence, and Peter Kornbluh (eds.). 1992. *The Cuban Missile Crisis, 1962*. New York: New Press.

Chaudhuri, Rudra. 2014. *Forged in Crisis: India and the United States since 1947*. London: Hurst.

Cohen, Stephen P. 2001. *India: Emerging Power*. Washington: Brookings.

Cohen, Stephen P. 2001. *The Indian Army: Its Contribution to the Development of a Nation*. New Delhi: Oxford University Press.

Conboy, Kenneth, and James Morrison. 2001. *The CIA's Secret War in Tibet*. Lawrence: University of Kansas.

Cradock, Sir Percy. 2001. *Know Your Enemy: How the Joint Intelligence Committee Saw the World*. London: John Murray.

Dalai Lama. 2006. *My Land and My People: Memoirs of His Holiness, the Dalai Lama*. New Delhi: Srishti.

Dallek, Robert. 2003. *An Unfinished Life: John F. Kennedy, 1917–1963*. Boston: Back Bay Books.

Dallek, Robert. 2013. *Camelot's Court: Inside the Kennedy White House*. New York: Harper.

Dalvi, J. P. 1968. *Himalayan Blunder: The Angry Truth about India's Most Crushing Military Blunder*. New Delhi: Orient.

Devlin, Larry. 2008. *Chief of Station Congo: Fighting the Cold War in a Hot Zone*. New York: Public Affairs.

Dhar, Anuj. 2009. *CIA's Eye on South Asia*. New Delhi: Manas.

Dobbs, Michael. 2008. *One Minute to Midnight: Kennedy, Khrushchev and Castro on the Brink of Nuclear War*. New York: Knopf.

Duheme, Jacqueline. 1998. *Mrs. Kennedy Goes Abroad*. New York: Artisan.

Dunham, Mikel. 2004. *Buddha's Warriors: The Story of the CIA-Backed Tibetan Freedom Fighters, the Chinese Invasion and the Ultimate Fall of Tibet*. New York: Penguin.

Epernay, Mark. 1963. *The McLandress Dimension*. Boston: Houghton Mifflin.

Frank, Katherine. 2001. *Indira: The Life of Indira Nehru Gandhi*. London: Harper Collins.

Frankel, Francine. 2005. *India's Political Economy, 1947–2004*. Oxford: Oxford University Press.

Frankel, Francine, and Harry Harding (eds.). 2004. *The India-China Relationship: What the United States Needs to Know*. New York: Columbia University Press.

French, Patrick. 2011. *India: A Portrait*. New York: Knopf.

Fursenko, Aleksandr, and Timothy Naftali. 1998. *One Hell of a Gamble: Khrushchev, Castro and Kennedy, 1958–1964*. New York: Norton.

Galbraith, John Kenneth. 1969. *Ambassador's Journal: A Personal Accounting of the Kennedy Years*. Boston: Houghton Mifflin.

Galbraith, John Kenneth. 1981. *A Life in Our Times: Memoirs*. Boston: Houghton Mifflin.

Galbraith, John Kenneth. 1993. *The Triumph: A Novel of Modern Diplomacy*. Boston: Houghton Mifflin.

Garthoff, Douglas F. 2005. *Directors of Central Intelligence as Leaders of the U.S. Intelligence Community, 1946–2005.* Washington: Center for the Study of Intelligence, Central Intelligence Agency.

Garver, John. 1990. "China's Decision for War with India in 1962." Georgia Institute of Technology, unpublished paper.

Garver, John. 2001. *Protracted Contest: Sino-Indian Rivalry in the Twentieth Century.* Seattle: University of Washington Press.

Greenfield, Jeff. 2013. *If Kennedy Lived: The First and Second Terms of President John F. Kennedy: An Alternative History.* New York: Putnam.

Gupta, Ramachandra. 2007. *India after Gandhi: The History of the World's Largest Democracy.* New York: Harper Collins.

Halberstam, David. 2007. *The Coldest Winter: America and the Korean War.* New York: Hyperion.

Hall, Richard. 1996. *Empires of the Monsoon: A History of the Indian Ocean and Its Invaders.* London: Harper Collins.

Haqqani, Husain. 2013. *Magnificent Delusions: Pakistan, the United States and an Epic History of Misunderstanding.* New York: Public Affairs.

Hastings, Max. 1988. *The Korean War.* New York: Simon and Schuster.

Hill, Clint, with Lisa McCubbin. 2012. *Mrs. Kennedy and Me.* New York: Gallery.

Hoffman, Steven A. 1990. *India and the China Crisis.* Berkeley: University of California Press.

Holland, Max. 2007. "The Photo Gap that Delayed Discovery of Missiles." *Studies in Intelligence* 49, no. 4 (April), pp. 15–30.

Jacob, J. F. R. 2011. *An Odyssey in War and Peace.* New Delhi: Roli.

Jager, Sheila Miyoshi. 2013. *Brothers at War: The Unending Conflict in Korea.* New York: Norton.

Kaplan, Robert. 2012. *The Revenge of Geography.* New York: Random House.

Kempe, Frederick. 2011. *Berlin 1961: Kennedy, Khrushchev and the Most Dangerous Place in the World*. New York: Berkley.

Kennedy, Jacqueline. 2011. *Historic Conversations on Life with John F. Kennedy: Interviews with Arthur M. Schlesinger, Jr., 1964*. New York: Hyperion.

Khan, Feroz Hassan. 2012. *Eating Grass: The Making of the Pakistani Bomb*. Stanford: Stanford University Press.

Khan, Mohammad Ayub. 2002. *Friends Not Masters: A Political Biography*. Islamabad: Mr. Books.

Knaus, John Kenneth. 1999. *Orphans of the Cold War: America and the Tibetan Struggle for Survival*. New York: Public Affairs.

Korda, Michael. 2007. *Ike: An American Hero*. New York: Harper.

Kornbluh, Peter (ed.). 1998. *Bay of Pigs Declassified: The Secret CIA Report on the Invasion of Cuba*. New York: New Press.

Kux, Dennis. 1993. *Estranged Democracies: India and the United States, 1941–1991*. Washington: National Defense University.

Kux, Dennis. 2001. *Disenchanted Allies: The United States and Pakistan, 1947–2000*. Baltimore: Johns Hopkins University Press.

Leamer, Laurence. 2001. *The Kennedy Men, 1901–1963*. New York: Harper Collins.

Li, Zhisui. 1994. *The Private Life of Chairman Mao*. New York: Random House.

Madan, Tanvi. 2012. "With an Eye to the East: The China Factor and the U.S.-India Relationship, 1949–1979." Ph.D. dissertation, University of Texas.

Maier, Thomas. 2003. *The Kennedys: America's Emerald Kings*. New York: Basic Books.

Marston, Daniel P., and Chandar S. Sundaram (eds.). 2007. *A Military History of India and South Asia: From the East India Company to the Nuclear Era*. Bloomington: Indiana University Press.

Matthews, Chris. 2011. *Jack Kennedy: Elusive Hero*. New York: Simon and Shuster.

Maxwell, Neville. 2013. *India's China War*. New Delhi: Natraj.

May, Ernest, and Phillip D. Zelikow (eds.). 2012. *The Kennedy Tapes: Inside the White House during the Cuban Missile Crisis*. New York: Norton.

Mitter, Rana. 2013. *Forgotten Ally: China's World War II, 1937–1945*. Boston: Houghton Mifflin Harcourt.

Mohan, C. Raja. 2004. *Crossing the Rubicon: The Shaping of India's New Foreign Policy*. New York: Palgrave.

Mohan, C. Raja. 2012. *Samudra Manthan: Sino-Indian Rivalry in the Indo-Pacific*. Washington: Carnegie.

Mullik, B. N. 1971. *My Years with Nehru: The Chinese Betrayal*. Bombay: Allied Publishers.

Pantsov, Alexander V., with Steven I. Levine. 2012. *Mao: The Real Story*. New York: Simon and Schuster.

Parker, Richard. 2005. *John Kenneth Galbraith: His Life, His Politics, His Economics*. New York: Farrar, Straus and Giroux.

Perkovich, George. 1999. *India's Nuclear Bomb*. London: University of California Press.

Pocock, Chris. 2000. *The U2 Spyplane toward the Unknown: A New History of the Early Years*. Atglen, Pa.: Schiffer Military History.

Richelson, Jeffrey T. 2009. *Spying on the Bomb: American Nuclear Intelligence from Nazi Germany to Iran and North Korea*. New York: Norton.

Robarge, David. 2014. "CIA's Covert Operations in the Congo, 1960–1968: Insights From Newly Declassified Documents." *Studies in Intelligence* 58, no. 3, pp. 1–9.

Rositzke, Harry. 1977. *The CIA's Secret Operations: Espionage, Counterespionage and Covert Action*. New York: Reader's Digest Press.

Rowland, John. 1967. *A History of Sino-Indian Relations: Hostile Co-Existence*. Princeton: Norstrand.

Schaffer, Howard. 2009. *The Limits of Influence: America's Role in Kashmir*. Washington: Brookings.

Schlesinger Jr., Arthur M. 1965. *A Thousand Days: John F. Kennedy in the White House*. Boston: Houghton Mifflin.

Singh, Jaswant. 2007. *In Service of Emerging India: A Call to Honor*. Bloomington: Indiana University Press.

Sisson, Richard, and Leo E. Rose. 1990. *War and Secession: Pakistan, India and the Creation of Bangladesh*. Berkeley: University of California Press.

Small, Andrew. 2015. *The China-Pakistan Axis: Asia's New Geopolitics*. New York: Carnegie.

Smith, Jeff M. 2014. *Cold Peace: China-India Rivalry in the Twenty-First Century*. Toronto: Lexington.

Sorensen, Theodore. 2013. *Kennedy: The Classic Biography*. New York: Harper Modern Classics.

Talbott, Strobe. 2004. *Engaging India: Diplomacy, Democracy and the Bomb*. Washington: Brookings.

Tharoor, Sashi. 2003. *Nehru: The Invention of India*. New York: Arcade.

Thomas, Evan. 1995. *The Very Best Men: Four Who Dared: The Early Years of the CIA*. New York: Simon and Schuster.

Thomas, Evan. 2012. *Ike's Bluff: President Eisenhower's Secret Battle to Save the World*. New York: Little, Brown.

Weintraub, Stanley. 2000. *MacArthur's War: Korea and the Undoing of an American Hero*. Singapore: Free Press.

Wersto, Thomas J. 1983. "Tibet in Sino-Soviet Relations." *Asian Affairs* 10, no. 3, pp. 70–85.

Westad, Odd Arne. 2012. *Restless Empire: China and the World since 1750*. New York: Basic Books.

Whiting, Allen S. 1960. *China Crosses the Yalu: The Decision to Enter the Korean War*. New York: Macmillan.

Whiting, Allen S. 1975. *The Chinese Calculus of Deterrence: India and Indochina*. Ann Arbor: University of Michigan Press.

Wolpert, Stanley. 1996. *Nehru: A Tryst with Destiny*. Oxford: Oxford University Press.

Wyden, Peter. 1979. *Bay of Pigs: The Untold Story*. New York: Touchstone.

INDEX

INDEX

India (cont.)
reports on, 85–86; JBK trip to, 77–82; JFK administration aid to, xii–xiii, 150–52, 162; JFK relations with, 62, 69, 147, 167–68; JFK Senate speech on (May 1959), 49–50, 112–13; JFK's planned visit to, 160; Johnson's visit to (1961), 69; joint U.S.-UK military aid to after Sino-Indian war, 152; Korean War and, 16–21; largest arms buyer in world, 168; LBJ military aid to, 162, 167; LBJ's lost opportunity in Indo-American relations, 161–63, 178; Mountain Strike Corps, 173; Nixon and, 47; as nuclear power, 5, 168–72, 175; Obama visits to, 175–76; on Pakistan-China agreement on Kashmir border, 154–55; Pakistan conflict (1965), 129, 164–68; Pakistan conflict (1971), 160, 169–70; Pakistan conflict (1999), 148, 171–72, 175; Soviet relations with, 101–02, 163, 168; Tibet and, 5, 38, 61, 86, 100, 157–60, 174, 179; in UN Congo peacekeeping mission, 67; underestimation of China, 113–14, 129; U.S. Embassy in New Delhi, 109–10, 161; warning to U.S. and allies about Korean situation, 11, 16, 17–18; weakness of army, 88–89, 91, 111. See also Nehru,

Jawaharlal; Sino-Indian war (1962)
Indian Communist Party, 60, 89–90
Indian Intelligence Bureau, 37
Indian Ocean, 173
Indian People's Party (BJP), 170
India's China War (Maxwell), 87, 95
Indo-Soviet Treaty of Peace, Friendship and Co-operation (1962), 101–02
Intelligence operations: diplomacy to enable covert actions, 178–79; how to evaluate usefulness of, 177–78; president's need to handpick intelligence leadership, 177; unanticipated consequences often result from, 179–80. See also specific countries and conflicts
Intercontinental ballistic missiles (ICBMs), 40
Iran, 30–31, 83
Islamabad, 36
Israel: arms to India, 168; secret nuclear reactor of, 64

Jaipur, maharajah of, 81
John F. Kennedy Presidential Library and Museum, 5, 135
Johnson, Lyndon (LBJ), 69–70, 159–67, 178
Johnson Line, 22, 112
John XXIII (Pope), 79
Joint Chiefs of Staff (JCS), 53, 54

National Intelligence Estimates
(NIEs) (cont.)
war, 122–23; on Sino-Soviet
relations, 84; on Soviet military
aid to Cuba, 106–07
National Security Action
Memorandum No. 209
(December 10, 1962), 151
National security adviser's office,
55–56
National Security Agency (NSA),
105
NATO (North Atlantic Treaty
Organization), 28, 48, 50, 73
Naval fleet (U.S.) in Bay of
Benghal, 139–40
NEFA. *See* North East Frontier
Authority
Nehru, Braj Kumar, 70, 137, 138
Nehru, Jawaharlal: on Aksai Chin,
37–38; ambitions attributed
to, 97–98; background of, 8;
Bowles as ambassador and, 161;
on Chinese seat on UN Security
Council, 9–10, 16, 69; on
Cuban missile crisis, 117; Dalai
Lama and, 9, 10, 38, 99, 101,
180; death of, 163; Eisenhower's
relationship with, 8–10, 37, 39;
Forward Policy and, 87–88;
Galbraith as ambassador and,
67, 69, 120, 125; Galbraith's
early meetings with (1956 &
1959), 45; Goa and, 73–75;
JBK and, 77, 79, 80, 82; JFK
meeting with (1951), 46;
JFK meeting with (1961), 70;

JFK relationship with, 5, 70–72,
75, 120, 181; Johnson meeting
with (1961), 69; Kashmir and,
36, 104, 153–54; Khan and,
126, 128; Mao and, 97, 142;
Mullik and, 61; nuclear weapons
opposed by, 168; popularity of,
56, 85; reaction to aid U.S.-UK
aid package, 152; Tibet and,
99–100, 158; viewed as "soft"
on communism, 17, 27; visits
to U.S., 4, 7–8; on weapons
purchase from Soviets, 102;
Zhou and, 38, 141. *See also*
Sino-Indian War
Nepal, 58, 59, 85
Neutrality in cold war, 17, 27, 47,
126, 130
New York Herald Tribune on
Nehru's intentions re Sino-
Indian war, 113
New York Times on Galbraith, 44
NIEs. *See* National Intelligence
Estimates
Nitze, Paul, 150
Nixon, Richard, 20, 47–48, 94,
102, 169
North Atlantic Treaty
Organization (NATO), 28, 48,
50, 73
North East Frontier Authority
(NEFA): Chinese withdrawal
from, after Sino-Indian war,
140–42; road construction,
174; in Sino-Indian war, 91–92,
110, 112, 118, 122, 130,
132–33, 137

Soviet Union (cont.)
 Korean War and, 12; Sino-
 Indian War and, 112, 120; U-2
 plane shot down by, xii, 40–42.
 See also Cuban missile crisis;
 Khrushchev, Nikita
Special Frontier Force (SFF), 5, 158
Special National Intelligence
 Estimates (SNIEs). *See* National
 Intelligence Estimates (NIEs)
Stalin, Joseph, 12, 19, 149
Stevenson, Adlai, 75
Stockholm International Peace
 Research Institute, 168
Stone, Edward D., 109, 172–73

Taj Mahal, 77, 81
Talbot, Phillips, xi, 148, 150
Talbott, Strobe, 171, 175
Taylor, Maxwell, xi, 72
Thapar, P. N., 87, 88
Tibet, 21–27, 55–65; Chinese
 invasion of and troops in,
 11–12, 56, 94, 123, 179–80;
 CIA covert support for rebellion
 in, xii–xiv, 3–4, 31–32, 39, 51,
 57–63, 75, 86, 150, 157–60,
 178–80; Indian support for U.S.
 clandestine operations in, 150,
 157–60; JFK Senate speech
 (1959) and, 50; Nehru's appeals
 to JFK for U.S. military
 assistance in, 138; resistance
 to Chinese occupation, 3,
 85, 86, 100, 158, 180; road
 construction in, 85, 91, 98;
 Sino-Indian war and, 149; as

sticking point between India
 and China, 5, 38, 174. *See also*
 Dalai Lama
Times of India on JBK visit to
 India, 83
Trade between India and China,
 174
Training of Indian military pilots,
 160
Training of Tibetan troops
 in U.S., xii, 3, 31–32, 57–58,
 61, 158–59
Truman, Harry, 12, 15, 161
Tuchman, Barbara, 181
Turkey, U.S. withdrawing missiles
 from, 2

U-2 operations: Arctic mission off
 course, entering Soviet territory,
 116; Cuba, spy plane shot down
 over, 116; Dulles's backing of,
 33–34; initial missions, 34;
 Pakistan as base for, xii; Royal
 Air Force (RAF) involvement
 in, 34–35; Soviet Union, spy
 plane (Gary Powers) shot
 down over, xii, 40–42, 105;
 termination and restart of
 Cuba flyovers, 107, 177; Tibet
 flyovers, 40
Uban, Sujan Singh, 119, 158
United Kingdom (UK). *See* Britain
United Nations: Communist
 China's admission to, 104;
 Congo peacekeeping mission,
 67; fighting force in Korean
 War, 12; General Assembly